D0952436

STARTUP

A FIELD GUIDE TO SCALING UP YOUR BUSINESS

MATT BLUMBERG

WITH

HANNY HINDI

WILEY

Cover design: C. Wallace
Cover illustration: Business group © iStockphoto.com/
Pavel Losevsky; Office Interior by C. Wallace

Published by John Wiley & Sons, Inc., Hoboken, New Jersey.
Published simultaneously in Canada.

ISBN 9781118548363 (Hardcover); ISBN 9781118683279 (ePDF);
ISBN 9781118683156 (ePub)

Printed in the United States of America
10 9 8 7 6 5 4 3 2 1

To our board and team at Return Path, who have patiently helped me go through almost 14 years of on-the-job training in the matter; and to Mariquita, Casey, Wilson and Elyse, who have patiently lived with someone who is both a startup CEO and co-CEO of our family.

"It is not the critic who counts: not the man who points out how the strong man stumbles or where the doer of deeds could have done better. The credit belongs to the man who is actually in the arena, whose face is marred by dust and sweat and blood, who strives valiantly, who errs and comes up short again and again, because there is no effort without error or shortcoming but who knows the great enthusiasms, the great devotions, who spends himself for a worthy cause; who, at the best, knows, in the end, the triumph of high achievement and who, at the worst, if he fails, at least he fails while daring greatly, so that his place shall never be with those cold and timid souls who knew neither victory nor defeat."

Theodore Roosevelt, "Citizenship in a Republic,"
speech at the Sorbonne, Paris, April 23, 1910

CONTENTS

FOREWORD

The public face of a startup CEO can seem pretty glamorous—dramatic product announcements, exciting travel and speaking appearances, leading a team as it grows and takes steps to fulfill its mission.

What you don't see is what a CEO does on a regular basis, day after day after day. Nobody imagines Google CEO Larry Page working out the mechanics of the option pool or the global sales team's reporting structure and *The Social Network* certainly didn't include a montage of Mark Zuckerberg interviewing potential executives about the finer points of operating leverage. These, nonetheless, are the types of things that CEOs spend the vast majority of their time doing (as more than a couple of once-eager entrepreneurs have learned, to their dismay). One startup CEO I know who has made those realities central to his public persona is Return Path's CEO, Matt Blumberg.

I've had the pleasure of working with Matt for many years. He was on my board of directors at FeedBurner before the Google acquisition in 2007 and he's been a valuable colleague and adviser ever since.

For nearly a decade, Matt has documented every element of the startup CEO experience. The product launches and mergers and acquisitions are all there—but so are the vacation policies, the meeting routines, the forecasting models, and the best practices for recruiting talent. They're not as glamorous as the Next Big Thing but they're the key to every startup's success.

When he launched Return Path in 1999, Matt started with this simple idea: an "Email Change of Address" database that would do for the digital world what the Post Office's "Change of Address" service does for snail mail. He and his team expanded their focus to a much wider set of email-related problems: building distribution lists, conducting online customer surveys, and so on. As markets shifted, Matt narrowed the company's focus to "email deliverability." As that business grew ever more successful, Return Path has set its larger sights on "email intelligence," solving domain-related problems like spoofing, phishing and competitive tracking.

As a four-time CEO (currently at Twitter), I can say this with a relative degree of certainty: most companies don't survive that many changes in direction over that many years. Return Path, by contrast, has survived and thrived: they have 400 employees around the world and they're closing in on $100 million in revenue. How did they do it? By focusing on all the unglamorous bits and building a company resilient enough to weather major pivots, the occasional divestiture and (most recently) a global economic crisis.

Matt's experience proves that the hard work of building a company is far more important than the excitement of coming up with The Idea. Until this book, I have yet to see anybody lay out all the details of this extremely difficult and unique job. He started the process on his blog, *Only Once*, and he brings it to fruition in this wonderful book. Read it and you will get a master class in building companies from someone who's honed that skill for more than a decade.

DICK COSTOLO
CEO of Twitter
April 2013

ACKNOWLEDGMENTS

The list of people to thank for their role in the development of this book is long but it has to start with my long-time board member and friend Brad Feld. Brad and I started our respective blogs, *Feld Thoughts* (www.feld.com) and *Only Once* (www.onlyonceblog.com) on the same day—May 10, 2004—sitting next to each other in our shared office space in Superior, Colorado and trying to figure out how to use Typepad templates. Brad has been a great friend and valuable business partner for more than a decade now. When Brad started writing books with John Wiley & Sons as his publisher, we had a conversation about my someday writing a book inspired by the content of my blog. I was one of the many contributors to his first book, *Do More Faster: Techstars Lessons to Accelerate Your Startup;* then when he asked me to read a draft of his second book, *Venture Deals: Be Smarter Than Your Lawyer or Your Venture Capitalist*, I returned the manuscript with a markup that became a series of about 40 or 50 sidebars called "The Entrepreneur's Perspective." Brad got good feedback on those contributions from many of his readers and introduced me to his publishing team at Wiley about this book and the rest is history. Brad offered a number of valuable insights on this book as well as helping me navigate the publishing process along the way.

I would like to acknowledge the rest of our board as well for their contributions to my education as a CEO over the years as well as their specific contributions to this book. Fred Wilson, Greg Sands, Scott Weiss, Scott Petry, and Jeff Epstein all play a role as current directors in my day-to-day life as CEO. Other Return Path board members that I've worked with over the years, including Ben Perez, Bob Knapp, Jonathan Shapiro, Eric Kirby, Phil Summe, Chris Wand, Chris Hoerenz, and James Marciano, played that role in the more formative days of the company. The CEOs of the organizations on whose boards I've sat as a director or chairman, Dick Costolo, Jim

Follett, Larry Kimmel, and Linda Woolley have also significantly informed my experience as CEO by giving me a closer-than-average look at how other CEOs operate.

This book would also not exist without my team at Return Path, who challenge, inspire and teach me things every day. When I say team, I mean all of our nearly 400 employees worldwide, I want to specifically acknowledge my long-time executive team of George Bilbrey, Jack Sinclair, Anita Absey, Angela Baldonero, and Andy Sautins; newer executive team members Josh Baer, Dave Wilby and Matt Spielman; long-time team members Andrea Ponchione, Ken Takahashi and Tami Forman; and former senior team members Karl Florida, Mary Lynn McGrath, John Ventura, Tim Dolan, Jennifer Wilson, Dave Paulus, Ninon Brown Traugott, Stephanie Miller, Vince Sabio, Michael Mayor, Marty Donner, Craig Swerdloff, Rob and Jeff Mattes, Chuck Drake, and Rebecca Flavin. Extra thanks to George for lots of specific help on the book, especially on Part One.

This book would also not be possible without a few other people who have helped teach me my job along the way. Marc Maltz from Triad Consulting has been one of my secret weapons as my executive coach. Members of my CEO Forum have been unbelievably helpful: Cella Irvine, Jonathan Shapiro, Adam Slutsky, Alan Masarek, and David Kidder (David's latest book, *Startup Playbook*, was researched and written as this book got under way—there are lots of synergies between the two, though they're quite different). The other senior leaders I've worked with at prior jobs, Andrew Jarecki, Bill Ford, Neal Pomroy, Eleanor Leger, and Mike Sargent, all helped me get where I am in business and influenced the way I manage and lead Return Path.

I want to thank the team at Wiley, Bill Falloon and Meg Freeborn, for their thoughtful feedback and editorial support. Brad's prior books, his new books, *Startup Communities, Startup Life, Startup Boards, Startup Metrics*, and this book are all part of the Startup Revolution series (www.startuprev.com). This book would also not be possible without the efforts of Hanny Hindi, who was the book's project manager, the curator of content I'd already written on my blog and my occasional ghost writer and editor. There's no chance I could have cranked out this many words on my own while running a company! Special thanks as well to Clare Tischer from TechStars who volunteered to do a hardcore copy edit for us, just because she liked the topic and wanted to help make the end product great when I didn't think I could possibly edit my own work effectively one more time.

I want to end by thanking my family for their insights and feedback about this book and their patience while I was doing double duty to write it and still do my day job. I owe the ultimate debt of gratitude to my parents,

Bob and Joyce, for teaching me most of the life lessons I learned—all of which shape how I manage and lead—and to my dad, a fellow CEO, for a few additional content-specific lessons related to this book's topic. My kids, Casey, Wilson and Elyse, probably had no idea I was doing this work and until the illustrated version comes out or another decade passes, they probably still won't be aware of it. The pitter-patter of their feet running to the front door and cheerfully greeting me after work is something that always brings a smile to my face. Finally, I'm not sure I'd be nearly as successful of a CEO or grounded a person as I have been without Mariquita, the love of my life and my best and most reliable sounding board throughout the life of the business.

ABOUT THE AUTHOR

Matt Blumberg founded Return Path in 1999 because he believed the world needed email to work better and because he wanted to build a model workplace for the knowledge economy. Matt is passionate about enhancing the online relationship between email subscribers and marketers so that both sides of the equation benefit. It is with great pride that he has watched this initial creation grow to a company of more than 400 employees with the market-leading brand, innovative products and the email industry's most renowned experts. Return Path has also been rated among "The Best Places to Work" by Crain's New York Business and *Fortune* magazine.

Before Return Path, Matt ran marketing, product management and the Internet group for MovieFone, Inc. (later acquired by AOL). Prior to that, he served as an associate with private equity firm General Atlantic Partners and was a consultant with Mercer Management Consulting. He holds a BA from Princeton University.

INTRODUCTION

Startup CEO is not a book about how to start a company or find early-stage financing. While these topics are essential to entrepreneurship, they're well covered elsewhere. This book is also not about sales, marketing, engineering, finance, or other disciplines inside the company. It's not the story of my company, Return Path, though there are a lot of examples from Return Path in it. It's not my blog, *Only Once* (www.onlyonceblog.com), though my blog posts inspired bits and pieces of the material in this book and I still continue to write for it and for *Startup Revolution*. (The Web icon in the margin indicates that supporting material can be found at www.startuprev.com.)

I set out here to write the book I wish someone had given me on my first day of work as CEO of Return Path almost 14 years ago. There is no instruction manual, no field guide, to being a CEO. If you become the CEO of General Electric or General Motors, you have been groomed for the job for decades. If you're starting your own company—and have never done it before—you don't have the luxury of that level of grooming. I believed I had as good experience as I possibly could have when I started Return Path at the age of 29. Management consulting. Venture capital. General manager of an Internet startup within a larger company, working for a CEO. Then I got into the job and realized that I didn't have a clue what I was doing.

There is a real craft to being a CEO and leading a full organization and there's no substitute for actually being in the job, especially early in one's career. I've written a blog called *Only Once* for over nine years now that covers a few different topics but is primarily devoted to posts about entrepreneurship, leadership and management. My long-time friend and board member Fred Wilson inspired the name of the blog with a post entitled "You're Only a First-Time CEO Once." In that post, he says:

The hardest job in management is the "first time CEO." I have absolutely no data on this, but I suspect that at least 75% of first time CEO's fail at some level. Many get fired. Many go down with the ship when it sinks. Some quit. Many sell their businesses before they've realized their full potential because they just can't figure out how to do the job right.

But in venture capitalism, among the most pure forms of capitalism there is, failure isn't all bad. Because, as I said yesterday, "you are only a first time CEO once." Most talented business people come up the learning curve quickly. And the next time, they don't make the same mistakes. They move faster. They listen better. They spend less. They hire better. The list goes on and on.

So, what does this mean for VCs? It means back serial entrepreneurs who have done it before. But if you can't do that, and are backing a first time CEO, recognize the risks of that. Mentor, coach, and pay a lot more attention.

What does this mean for entrepreneurs and managers? It means that the first time you run a business, you should admit what you are up against. Don't let ego get in the way. Ask for help from your board and get coaching and mentoring. And recognize that you may fail at some level. And don't let the fear of failure get in the way. Because failure isn't fatal. It may well be a required rite of passage.

As a CEO, I feel like I've made every mistake in the book at least once. I'm sure I've made a couple more than once. So this book is my hope to pay forward the lessons of my 14 years of experience as a first-time CEO to other entrepreneurs, whether actual or aspiring. If I can help just one of them not get fired, not go down with the ship, not quit and figure out how to do the job, then I will call this book a success.

Let me issue three caveats before I begin. The first is that this book is based on my experience and the experience of a handful of other CEOs whom I know well. For the most part, that means American CEOs running U.S.-based companies, in and around the Internet sector, that got started between 1990 and 2010 and with fewer than 500 employees. I hope the book proves to be timeless and that it spans cultural and industry boundaries but there will be some inherent limitations based on my own experience. I've tried to broaden that in asking a number of people to contribute sidebars, section openers and section conclusions in this book but that group of contributors is still largely made up of people generally like me.

The second caveat is that I don't have a single clever tagline or overarching premise that's going to answer all questions and challenges associated with the job. Being a CEO is an incredibly complex job at a company of any size and writing a book called *Be Authentic* or something like that wouldn't do it justice. That's why this book is designed more as a practical field guide than a lofty book on philosophy.

The third caveat is that I don't have all of the answers and I haven't figured everything out. The trouble is that no one else has, either. I have, however, figured out many of the questions to ask as well as the answers that come from my own experience. Running a company is situational. You can be a great CEO and miss the occasional curve ball that comes your way. This is my best shot at documenting what I've learned over the years in the job.

Being a CEO is also somewhat personal in nature. because the fact that something works for me doesn't mean it will work for someone else. Each and every leader has a different style, different values and beliefs and a different approach to the world. My intent here isn't to produce value judgments of "this is the only way to do XYZ task" so much as it is to document most of the primary jobs of a CEO in a company from the startup stage (fewer than 25 employees), through the revenue stage (fewer than 150 employees) and into the growth stage (fewer than 500 employees) and give some examples from my own experience of one or two ways of approaching each task.

Coming up with a framework for this book was challenging. I drew once again from one of Fred's blog posts, entitled "What a CEO Does," where he quotes another experienced colleague of his from the venture business in saying that

> A CEO does only three things. Sets the overall vision and strategy of the company and communicates it to all stakeholders. Recruits, hires, and retains the very best talent for the company. Makes sure there is always enough cash in the bank.

I like the simplicity of that framework and I've adapted it somewhat into the outline of this book. Part One of the book focuses on the ideal way to *communicate* your vision: "Storytelling." Part Two is entitled "Building the Company's Human Capital." Then the outline got a bit beyond Fred's framework. While I generally agree that those three things are critical, it's impossible not to add a few other important topics to the list. First, I think you have to broaden the third topic. It's not just about making sure there's enough cash in the bank. It's about execution in general, so Part Three of this book is called "Execution"—both about having the money in the bank and about using it wisely through disciplined execution. Part Four covers a very unique aspect of the CEO's job: "Building and Leading a Board of Directors." Part Five is more about the *how* of doing the job as opposed to the *what:* "Managing Yourself So You Can Manage Others."

This framework encompasses nearly every challenge a startup CEO has to face but it leaves out one crucial area: management and leadership.

As a manager and a leader, I had a number of positive influence points over the course of my career and a number of negative influence points. I vowed to learn from those, both the good and the bad and bring them with me to my job as CEO. In particular, some incredibly poor management practices I'd seen over the years motivated me to create a different kind of workplace.

Sometime after a few years running the business, I took a different approach. I didn't pause when making tough decisions to consider what others would do if they were in my place. I started developing my own reflexes, my own instincts and my own way of talking through things.

I can't remember what the turning point was in finding my voice as a CEO. It might have come out of some specific critical incident. It might have come from working with my coach. It might have just emerged slowly, without a turning point, as I spent more time maturing in the role. From the rearview mirror, I wish I had done more, earlier, to help me find my voice. Mostly, I wish I'd been deliberate about finding it; that certainly would have hastened the discovery!

Throughout this book, I'll introduce some of the management and leadership principles I've developed as a CEO in a feature called "Management Moment." Think about what you agree with, where you're different and what's missing that's important to you. I promise that both you and your organization will benefit from your strength and confidence as a leader.

PART ONE

STORYTELLING

Fred Wilson is right: "setting a company's vision" is one of the three full-time jobs every startup CEO takes on when they found a company. That vision—the new product, the disruptive service, the "Blue Ocean" monopoly—is liable to be a private moment. The first step toward making that vision a reality is to translate it into a *story*.

Stories, like startups, paint a picture of what the future could be. They engage our hearts and minds. They inspire people to act—to give you money, to buy your product, to join your team. Stories have a main character (the customer or user) and a supporting cast (investors, employees, partners, competitors). They have a beginning (the problem), middle (the product), and an end (the solution). Stories take a jumble of facts (profit-and-loss statements, customer surveys, market realities) and give them meaning.

Part One of this book explains how to tell startup stories. Begin with a problem your customer faces and the solution you and your team propose to build. Continue through the trials of market obstacles and changes of plan. Bring it to life in the transformation of your story into the reality of your business.

CHAPTER ONE

DREAM THE POSSIBLE DREAM

You don't need to come up with the idea for a story yourself to be an effective startup CEO, but you do need a sense of which stories could come true—and which ones most likely won't. When you find that story, you have to tell it, shape it as you go and make sure it comes to life as a real business.

ENTREPRENEURSHIP AND CREATIVITY

I hear from people all the time who say that they *can't* be entrepreneurs because they aren't creative. I used to say it about myself. As a case in point, I didn't have the original idea to build an email change-of-address service. My original co-founder, James Marciano, did. Nor did I come up with the idea for an email deliverability business. My colleague George Bilbrey did. Nor did the idea for an inbox organizer consumer application occur to me. That was my colleague Josh Baer's idea. All of these ideas are part of the Return Path story and I've led the organization that either brought these ideas to life or shaped and turbo-charged them to scale.

It takes a lot of creativity, a significant amount of business acumen and great communication and execution skills to get from an idea to a business—or from a small business to a big one.

Many great companies begin with a wildly new invention, but sometimes the best ideas are borrowed from others or combined from sets of existing things. There's nothing wrong with that! After Steve Jobs died, Malcolm Gladwell wrote an article claiming that he'd built the world's largest company by doing exactly that: tweaking other people's ideas, from the graphical user interface (from Xerox PARC) to the digital music player (do you remember the Diamond Rio?). This might not seem all too glamorous, but, Gladwell points out, it is essential to real growth:

> In 1779, Samuel Crompton, a retiring genius from Lancashire, invented the spinning mule, which made possible the mechanization of cotton manufacture. Yet England's real advantage was that it had Henry Stones, of Horwich, who added metal rollers to the mule; and James Hargreaves, of Tottington, who figured out how to smooth the acceleration and deceleration of the spinning wheel; and William Kelly, of Glasgow, who worked out how to add water power to the draw stroke; and John Kennedy, of Manchester, who adapted the wheel to turn out fine counts; and, finally, Richard Roberts, also of Manchester, a master of precision machine tooling—and the tweaker's tweaker. He created the "automatic" spinning mule: an exacting, high-speed, reliable rethinking of Crompton's original creation. Such men, the economists argue, provided the "micro inventions necessary to make macro inventions highly productive and remunerative."

Inventors create solutions without precedent—often to problems nobody had noticed before. The stories they tell and bring to life require an enormous imaginative leap, like the one Samuel Crompton made when he envisioned an automatic process for spinning cotton. Business builders flesh those stories out. Most often, the biggest detail they include is the main character: the customer.

Where Crompton focused on the technical challenges of the original spinning wheel, Stones imagined workers diligently smoothing out the fabric coming out of the spinning mule, and added rollers. Hargreaves imagined them struggling to deal with a jerky mechanism that accelerated and decelerated too rapidly and smoothed the transitions. Kelly imagined the muscle power required to run the current models and added water power. Keep the *whole* story in mind: customer, problem, product, solution.

"A FASTER HORSE"

One of the first things my co-founders and I did when we started Return Path was to stand outside of our offices with clipboards and Starbucks gift cards. We asked people walking by to take a survey in order to get a free coffee. It was our first bit of customer research and the foundation of our first strategic plan. I still have the clipboard in a drawer somewhere and smile every time I come across it.

We haven't done anything exactly like this in years and we won't do it again. Our company has grown beyond that stage but that doesn't mean strategic planning is a one-time exercise. You should do it throughout the life of your company, even when things are going well. It would be excessive to undertake this exercise with every major product release, but you should do it at least every three years. This planning exercise should always begin with your most important stakeholders: your customers.

The purpose of any business plan is to find new and better ways of serving your customers. You can do that in one of two ways:

1. Come up with a new set of assumptions about what your customers need and want and test those assumptions with customers.
2. *Ask* your customers what they need and want.

Either way, there's a pretty straightforward rule of thumb when taking ideas and turning them into a company: listen to your prospective customers! Of course there are thoughtful objections to this approach—including one from the most successful entrepreneur of all time. Here's Steve Jobs, from Walter Isaacson's 2012 biography:

> Some people say, "Give the customers what they want." But that's not my approach. Our job is to figure out what they're going to want before they do. I think Henry Ford once said, "If I'd asked customers what they wanted, they would have told me, 'A faster horse!'" People don't know what they want until you show it to them. That's why I never rely on market research. Our task is to read things that are not yet on the page.

There's always a tension between listening *to* customers and innovating *for* them. Great companies have to do both and know when to do which. That said, as my colleague Hanny Hindi has pointed out, Ford's quote about "a faster horse" isn't really a definitive debunking of market research. Look at it again. Ford's customers didn't say that they wanted a "safer" horse or a "more comfortable" horse. They said that they wanted a *faster* horse. They were perfectly clear about what they wanted: *speed.*

Jobs is right: "Our task is to read things that are not yet on the page." Very often, those things are clearly written in between the lines. If you don't speak with your customers, you'll miss those subtle—but crucial—insights. When we started Return Path with the idea in mind to create a centralized service for capturing people's change of email address online, no prospective customer said, "I want a system called ECOA that looks like the post office's NCOA system." They did say, "I don't know what to do when I get a bounce. I just delete the email address from my database."

With those caveats in mind, customer interviews are invaluable. In addition to questions specific to your company and business, be sure to cover the following broad areas if you're an existing company diving into new areas and refreshing your business direction:

- What are the major problems your customers are facing today?
- What new products and services could you provide to address those problems?
- Are they looking for an upgrade to a current solution or something completely new?
- What would it be worth for them to solve this problem (i.e., how much would they be willing to pay to solve it)?

A former mentor of mine used to say that people buy things either out of fear or out of greed and that there is a fear/greed continuum where you can actually plot out the behavior of particular buyers. Find out which button your product presses and make sure you orient your questions, development, and sales and marketing around that.

VETTING IDEAS

Aren't all great companies founded on that one great idea? "Great ideas" are exciting, inspiring and often life changing. The Model-T. The telephone. The personal computer. Some entrepreneurs will say that you can create a system for generating ideas like these. Thomas Edison's 1,093 patents suggest that they might be right—but I think it's a bit like lightning striking.

What I think you *can* create is a system for *vetting* ideas. We all have a limited amount of time on this planet—figuring out what problem area you want to operate in is an incredibly important first step in starting a business or even expanding one. In its broadest strokes, this kind of idea vetting system is simple. You can build it in Excel in a few minutes (or you can download my template at www.startuprev.com). On the *y*-axis, list all of your ideas. On the *x*-axis, list the (weighted) criteria you will use to judge those ideas. These are the criteria we have used at Return Path:

- *Customer pain (30%).* Does the market need your idea?
- *Market opportunity (10%).* How many people need your idea? Today (Size)? Tomorrow (Growth)?
- *Can we win? (20%).* Are there already competitors in your chosen space (Competitive Positioning)? If so, will you beat them (Feasibility)?
- *Strategic fit (10%).* Is this a problem you can solve? Do you have the right expertise, networks, and so on?
- *Economics (30%).* Can you afford to solve this problem?

Score each idea between 1 and 5. (Don't try to be more specific: this isn't about calculating specific market sizes or investment opportunities.) Multiply by your weighting criteria. Consider the scores. You might be surprised which one wins.

One thing should be clear from the weighting: a huge "market opportunity" isn't a good enough reason to ignore all of the other factors. You may have a billion-dollar idea, but if you don't have a team that can execute on it ("Can We Win?") or the funding you need ("Economics"), it won't matter. You don't have to go with the highest-scoring idea. But you need to have a good reason for choosing another one. "This could be huge!" isn't good enough.

As Simple as the Wheel

There are lots of ways to evaluate startup ideas. One of the most popular for technology entrepreneurs is to identify what Jerry Colonna, a CEO coach in New York City and former venture capitalist at Flatiron Partners, first called the "the analog analogue." The concept is that figuring out how a digital idea mirrors an offline idea is a better way of handicapping future success than understanding pure technology analogs.

At Return Path, nearly every business we've been in has a clear analog analogue. Our email change-of-address business was analogous to the postal change of address. Email list rental was analogous to post list rental. Email market research was analogous to telephone market research. And so on.

Every one of those ideas has been the result of real brainstorming processes and complex, nuanced thinking.

Innovation doesn't have to be complex. One of my favorite examples of this is luggage: for decades, we all carried around suitcases and garment bags and totes that gave us pinched nerves and bad backs as they hung from our shoulders or strained our grips. We sprinted through airports in extreme discomfort, and we assumed that there was no better way.

Then someone decided to put wheels on luggage. Wheels, for goodness' sake. Not electric cars. Not the Human Genome Project. Not cold fusion. Wheels! Those wheels changed the luggage industry and the way we travel for the better.

What's the "wheel" that your industry needs? Don't search for an analog analogue if there's something simpler staring you in the face that can explode your market.

Management Moment

Be Passionate about the Substance of Your Business

When Terry Semel was CEO of Yahoo! in the early 2000s, one of his employees described Terry's method of communication: "sitting in between Terry and the Internet is a secretary and a printer." He had his emails printed out, wrote his responses longhand, and then had the secretary type them in. He didn't use the Internet. Seriously.

Can you imagine Twitter CEO Dick Costolo not tweeting? Or the CEO of General Motors driving a Mercedes? Or the CEO of American Airlines being afraid of flying? I'm not saying that an overweight middle-aged white guy can't be the CEO of a company that makes beauty products for hip, young Latina women, but it sure is tough to have a high degree of credibility within your organization if you are that personally disconnected from what your company does.

CHAPTER TWO

DEFINING AND TESTING THE STORY

The adoption of lean methodologies has been a huge advance for startups. For decades, countless startups failed after spending too much time on insular product development and too little time "in-market" discovering what their customers want and need. The new model pushes startups into the marketplace much more quickly. In fact, it might push them into the marketplace *too* quickly without maintaining some real discipline.

Contrary to popular wisdom, I still think that it's valuable to formalize your initial assumptions and hypotheses—and to write them down so you can take them out for a test drive before you spend lots of time and money trying to bring them to life. In this chapter, I'll explain how to more crisply define and test your story out before you start telling it to the world. I wish this school of thought had existed in 1999 and 2000 when we started Return Path. We probably would have saved ourselves a couple of years of our lives and several million dollars in burn if it had.

START OUT BY ADMITTING YOU'RE WRONG

Here is how a major enterprise might tell the story of their upcoming product release: "Our customers, who number *x*, have *y* problem, and they will pay *z* dollars for our solution. This is our plan for rolling that solution out and these are our cost and revenue projections for the next 18 months."

Here, by contrast, is how a startup should tell *its* story: "We believe that *x* potential customers face *y* problem. Our proposed solution to *y* problem is solution *z* at a cost of *q* dollars—but we're also going to test the effectiveness of solutions *a*, *b*, *c*. Here is our plan for testing that hypothesis."

A mature enterprise might tell its story in an 80-page document with multiple appendices, while a startup might tell its story on a single page or in fewer than a dozen slides. However, as significant as those differences in format are, the real difference is in the nature of the assumptions. To put it bluntly: traditional business plans assume that their assumptions are correct, and startup business plans assume that their assumptions are probably wrong.

As an entrepreneur, the story you start with is probably wrong. But until you start testing your underlying hypotheses, you don't know *how* you're wrong. Unlike enterprise managers, you don't have the luxury of decades of data from comparable initiatives or huge pools of resources from which you can draw. You're creating a new product or market, rather than placing a new product into a mature market. If you spend months in planning and development before sending your product into the market, the result could easily be a swing and a miss. Of course, if you go out to market a lot more quickly, the result could *still* be a swing and a miss, but you won't have burned through all your resources before your first at-bat.

That is the insight behind the agile and lean methodologies championed by Silicon Valley thought leaders like Eric Ries and Steven Gary Blank: the failure of early startup initiatives is predictable, so that failure should be built into the process rather than treated as a crisis when it happens. My only concern is that the past few years have led to an overcorrection. It's true: the first story you tell about your startup will probably be wrong. The problem is that many entrepreneurs have taken that as license to start with any old guess that occurs to them. Luckily, there's a middle ground: a process of formalizing and communicating hypotheses that doesn't take months of work and lead to hundreds of spreadsheets—and one that allows considerable flexibility in execution.

The "Lean" Classics

"Lean startups" focus on finding product-to-market fit through a process of rapid product development and quick iterations based on customer feedback. It's the opposite of porting MBA techniques to the startup world—and much more effective. Here is our short list of smart, interesting books about starting a business:

- *The Lean Startup: How Today's Entrepreneurs Use Continuous Innovation to Create Radically Successful Businesses* by Eric Ries

- *The Four Steps to the Epiphany: Successful Strategies for Products that Win* by Steven Gary Blank
- *Running Lean: Iterate from Plan A to a Plan that Works* by Ash Maurya
- *The Entrepreneur's Guide to Customer Development: A Cheat Sheet to The Four Steps to the Epiphany* by Brant Cooper and Patrick Vlaskovits
- *How to Start a Business* by Jason Nazar and Rochelle Bailis (eBook)

A LEAN BUSINESS PLAN TEMPLATE

The goal of a lean business planning process should be to produce three outputs. First is a single slide that you'll use to define your business model and your underlying hypotheses. Second is a short presentation for partners and investors. Third is your mission, vision, and values statement. Here, I'm going to focus on the first output: the internal slide.

My favorite template for startup business plans is the "Lean Canvas" that Ash Maurya presents in his book *Running Lean*. If you're really at the pure startup stage, it's worth reading the whole book, but one notable line from the book is, "your job isn't just building the best solution, but owning the entire business model and making all the pieces fit . . . the bigger risk for most startups is building something nobody wants."

Maurya's Lean Canvas business plan is shown in Figure 1.1 and it's a simple road map to, as he says in the book, "systematically de-risk" each element of your business model. While the Lean Canvas uses some of the same criteria that I noted that I use above for vetting ideas, it's the place where you start to document the specifics of those criteria so you can go out and test the things that *must be true* in order for your business model to work.

Following is a section-by-section guide to test *what must be true* in each of the nine boxes of Maurya's Lean Canvas.

Problem

What problem are you trying to solve, and for whom? In Steve Blank's "Customer Development" model, defining your audience and your

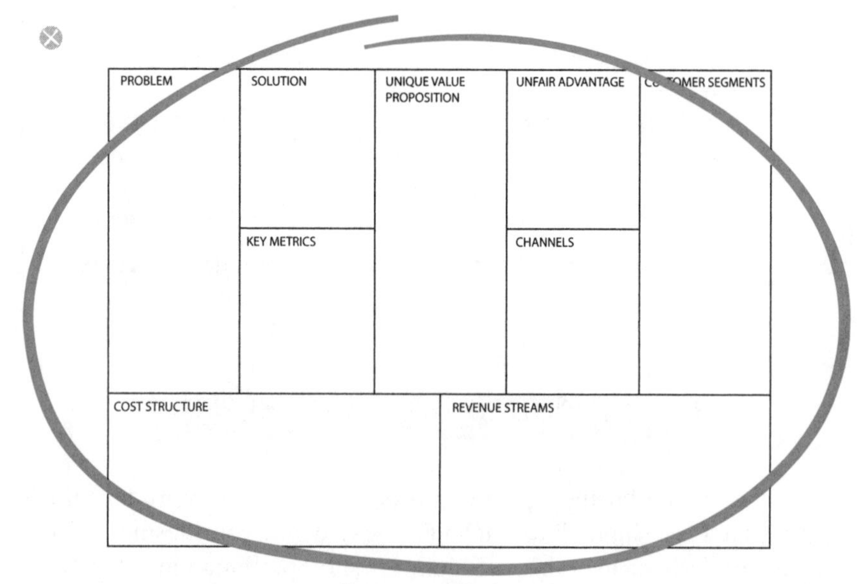

FIGURE 2.1 Maurya's Lean Canvas Business Plan

product come concurrently as you build a minimum viable product (MVP). Your solution needs to address a specific problem or pain point that affects a well-defined audience. You don't want to develop "a solution in search of a problem" (see sidebar). The assumption you're trying to test in this box on the Lean Canvas is that *this type of person* has *this exact problem*.

Solution

You can only describe your solution *after* defining your audience and their problems. This might seem a little backwards, but it insures against the danger of putting solutions ahead of problems and declaring that "everybody" will need what you have to offer, rather than forcing yourself to decide exactly who will buy what you're selling, and for how much. The assumption you're trying to test in this box on the Lean Canvas is that *this exact solution* is what solves the problem for the audience specified in the prior box.

A Solution in Search of a Problem

Remember Pointcast? In the mid-1990s, this service that pulled headlines into screensavers (and clogged corporate networks) seemed to be on every corporate workstation. Then the fad passed. Pointcast had a solution—but to what exactly?

Tech startups often have a very cool solution that *could* solve many potential problems for many potential customers. After an obsessive and insular process of product development, none of those potential customers materialize. The solution never finds its problem.

The key to getting past this hurdle is to force yourself to tell a very clear story about your product—one that begins with your customer rather than your idea. "*This* person has *this* problem and would be willing to pay *this* amount to solve it." You may end up with two or three of these statements, and that's okay. The next task is to test them in the market and see which story comes true.

Key Metrics

How are you going to test your hypotheses? What would need to happen to prove them right or to disprove them? Remember: revenue is a lagging metric of success. You need to define metrics further up the sales funnel—lead generation, sign-ups, and so on—or your data will come in too late. What you're trying to outline in this box on the Lean Canvas is the short list of metrics you will need to track up front to tell if your solution is taking root with your target audience.

Unique Value Proposition and Unfair Advantage

The idea is only one part of the story. Your story needs to encompass much more, including your team. What is the unique value of your solution? Marginal improvements usually aren't enough to base a startup on. What's the radical improvement that you're offering? And what advantage does your team offer?

Who else is competing in this space? How similar do their solutions look to what you're offering? What is your competitive advantage or your solution's unique value proposition? If you're offering only a marginal improvement over a well-established competitor, it's going to be much harder to get traction in the marketplace. Either innovate in a field without much competition—like the email deliverability business Return Path started working on 10 years ago when no one was focused on that value proposition—or offer such a large improvement over the competition that it essentially changes the nature of the game.

The assumption you're trying to test in this box on the Lean Canvas is a very honest assessment of your place within the competitive ecosystem in which you plan to operate.

Channels

In my view, this is probably the most important box on the Lean Canvas to test, because it's where the rubber meets the road—the go-to-market plan. How are you going to sell to your customers? (Or, as Ash Maurya asks in *Running Lean*, "what are your paths to customers?") Are you going to engage in direct sales via e-commerce? Act as a technology provider and leverage another organization's sales force? Or are you running a business-to-consumer (B2C) business with a freemium model that depends on organic user growth? Whatever the answer (or hypothesis), state it here. The assumption you're trying to test in this box on the Lean Canvas is fundamentally how you will reach customers and derive revenue.

Customer Segments

When articulating the audience (or audiences) for your solution, be as specific as possible. While a strategic plan should certainly be aspirational, it can't be unrealistic. For whom is your solution a "need to have" rather than a "nice to have"? Is that audience large enough to build a business around? The critical item to get right here is the problem you're solving, and you can be quite vivid in your description of your archetypal customer and use case.

Customer segmentation not only helps you define your target audience, it also starts you on the road to quantifying your total addressable market (TAM), which is a critical element of your Lean Canvas to test. How many of your target customers are out there? How much do you think they'll pay for your solution? That's the beginning of your TAM. But if your TAM is $1 billion and there are four companies going after it, you are unlikely to see $1 billion in revenue any time soon.

Pay careful attention to indirect competitors or substitute products. These will eat away at the TAM, even if you don't think of them as a competitor. For example, if you were starting an airline running between New York and Washington, D.C., you'd look at Amtrak as a substitute product even though it's not an airline.

Cost Structure and Revenue Streams

The financial part of the Lean Canvas isn't about creating a profit-and-loss statement (P&L). It isn't about convincing someone to invest in your business. It's helping you articulate what the basic numbers will or should look like on your path from idea to functional prototype, or MVP.

On the revenue side, pull from your customer segmentation or TAM data. To prove out that you have a viable solution, how many customers do you expect to pay what price for your product? On the cost side, how many people will be working on the solution at what price, for how many weeks or months? What are your hosting or other technology costs to get to MVP?

With your hypotheses laid out, it's time to go test them. Hit them hard. Again, there's much more detail in Ash Maurya's *Running Lean*, but his test methodologies revolve around problem interviews (is there really a problem?) and solution interviews (if I build it, will you pay for it?).

This all may seem like an extraordinary investment for the sake of a single page, but consider what it gives you: a clear statement of your current hypotheses in a format that's easily testable. It brings everybody who is part of your founding team into alignment around the same goal: proving, or disproving, your business hypotheses, and responding to the results.

Management Moment

Exploit Big Opportunities

For an American history buff like me, the example of a Big Opportunity is the Louisiana Purchase. Thomas Jefferson, an opponent of executive reach and the centralization of federal power, got an amazing opportunity from a French emperor with other things on his mind: for 50 million francs, the United States could almost double its territory and secure free access to the Mississippi River and the port of New Orleans. Jefferson didn't hesitate for a moment.

Exploiting big opportunities means understanding your company's true drivers of success; being on the lookout for signs that it's time to invest more heavily in them; being nimble enough to make those investments when the time is right; and developing the intellectual or infrastructural underpinnings to make those investments matter.

It also means making tough, far-reaching decisions that are outside the mainline of your business's day-to-day operations. This often produces some internal strife, and it's your job to address it. At the time, many people complained that the Louisiana Purchase was unconstitutional. On another day, Jefferson might have agreed. But he was the leader, and he couldn't let an opportunity like that go. Today, nobody disputes the decision.

CHAPTER THREE

TELLING THE STORY TO YOUR INVESTORS

Once you've iterated a few times on your Lean Canvas and tested assumptions, you're likely off and running and building your product. Now, as CEO, you can turn your focus to telling the story of your company—the customer, problem, and solution—to your key stakeholders.

In short, you need some kind of a business plan.

THE BUSINESS PLAN IS DEAD—LONG LIVE THE BUSINESS PLAN

The phrase "business plan" conjures images of massive tomes filled with charts and graphs of every variety. Startup business stories come in short bursts rather than dozens of chapters. There are two main constituencies to whom you need to be telling the story at this stage.

First, you need to convince investors to fund the effort. Then you have to articulate how you want your employees to fulfill the problem-solution set you're building so you can start building a company alongside your product. While those stories are similar, they aren't identical. For example, your team is primarily interested in what their work lives are going to look like over the next 18 months, while your investors will want to focus on what the likely return from their investment will be.

These two versions of the story need to be told in two different ways, depending on the audience: 10 to 12 slides for investors and a blueprint document for *how* you'll execute on that plan—your mission, vision, and values—for the team.

The business plan isn't dead. It's just gotten a lot shorter.

THE INVESTOR PRESENTATION

As I wrote in one of my sidebars in *Venture Deals*, "There are only a few key things most VCs look at to understand and get excited about a deal." They are:

- The elevator pitch
- The size of the opportunity
- Your competitive advantage
- Current status and roadmap from today
- The strength of your team
- Summary financials

Some of these details—the problem you're solving, your competitive advantage (or "unfair advantage"), and your summary financials—overlap considerably with details in the "Lean Canvas" I described in the previous chapter, though some are different.

The Elevator Pitch

Start by clearly articulating what problem you're solving and for whom. By now, you should have enough clarity around your big ideas to be able to state them quickly and succinctly. Can't do it? Go back over your notes. Were there a few stumbling points? Spots where either you had difficulty stating your ideas or where the people you were speaking about pushed back? Most likely, a lack of clarity around those specific ideas is holding you back. Take a few steps back, and reconsider them. When you come back to your elevator pitch later, it should be much easier to write.

Your elevator pitch needs to be short and punchy. It needs to fit on one slide. It needs to be something that, unless you're in an incredibly technical niche, is understandable by average people who aren't on your team. Try explaining the problem and solution you're working on to someone outside your business world, like a friend or a relative, in order to refine it.

The Size of the Opportunity

Next, you need to pull some elements from the work you did on your Lean Canvas into one slide. Who specifically is your target audience, and how big is your total addressable market (TAM) and your realistic take of the TAM, based on your initial pricing and competitive landscape? These items will vary considerably depending on your business. The average order for mops and Tilex is going to be considerably lower than what BNP Paribas would pay for a new system to clear its trades. That's why the market opportunity needs to include *both* market size and transaction size. Are you selling a $10 product to 20 million potential customers, or a $10 million solution to 20 potential customers? How many of those potential customers do you have to reach for this plan to work? Where else are they spending money today on similar solutions, or how much is their problem costing them?

Your Competitive Advantage

For this section, you can draw largely from your work on unique value proposition and unfair advantage on the Lean Canvas. Investors tend to get very excited about underdog startups that can show a path to disrupting larger incumbents in proven markets. This is your time to shine on that front.

Current Status and Road Map from Today

When we started Return Path in 1999, most startups didn't have a "current status" slide in their investor presentations. You raised money first and built product later because, for the most part, *you had to*. Today, it is so inexpensive to get prototype products to market that you can do an enormous amount of work on your Lean Canvas—testing hypotheses, validating your market—that investors other than your immediate friends and family *expect* you to have completed before you approach them to raise capital.

This section of the investor presentation then becomes critical. Where are you today, and, more importantly, what have you learned along the way? Again, since we all know that most initial business ideas are wrong somehow, bring potential investors along for the ride. Where did you start out, what did you test, what did you learn, how did you iterate? This is not a sign of weakness—it's a sign of strength!

Once you describe your current status, you need to articulate the road map from today. You know where you want to be in three years. How are you going to get there from where you are right now? This is one section of the investor presentation that needs to start getting into some details. How will you judge your success over the next year? What milestones and key metrics are you looking to hit? What other hypotheses need to be tested? What roles will you need to hire? What investments will you need to make? When will you launch?

The Strength of Your Team

At the dawn of a startup, your first investors are not investing for cash flow, since the business is likely not profitable. They aren't even investing at a valuation that is a multiple of revenue, since there is usually no significant revenue. They are investing in your idea and your market opportunity as well as your theory about how to prosecute that opportunity, in the early work and learning you've done. They're investing in your story. In short, they're investing in the strength of your team.

Unless your team is 100 percent made up of people with zero business experience and zero direct experience as a potential customer of the product you're building, you should take this opportunity to show off your talent. Why should the investor give you his or her money? You need to communicate why you'll be a good steward of that investment based on the experience you have as a collective team. The only thing you need to make sure you do in this section is to be 100 percent scrupulously honest. Today, it takes only a couple of clicks of the mouse to check facts on LinkedIn or Google. If you were an actual founder of a company before, say so. But if you worked at a startup as an intern during its founding period, don't pretend you were a founder!

Summary Financials

This needs to be the most detailed section of your investor presentation, even more so than your road map from today. Even though, as with all forward-looking plans around a startup, the numbers will be wrong over time (and the further out you get, the more wrong they will be!), it's critical to demonstrate to your prospective investors, and to yourselves, that you understand all of the financial drivers of your business at a detailed level. It's also important to show that you know how to build a financial model and that you understand how to manage a business around cash. Finally, it's important to have a good financial model so you know how much cash you're looking to raise!

On the revenue side, you can draw heavily from your TAM work and from the revenue hypotheses you tested on the Lean Canvas. How many customers will you add or lose each month, and how much will they spend with you?

On the cost side, model out the four main expense items: cost of goods, salaries/benefits, marketing, and capital expenditures (CapEx).

Cost of goods is usually defined as the "raw materials" that go into producing your product, or expenses that are variable with revenue. If you're running a software company, these tend to be things like hosting and bandwidth, credit card processing fees, and sales commissions.

Determining your spending on salaries and benefits starts with a headcount plan. What bodies do you need in what seats, and when, in order to execute your plan? How much will you be spending on health care and payroll taxes? Look at every functional area that's appropriate for your area of business, and map out the resources you have today (if any) against where you are today. If you are missing a functional area and don't know how to plan it, ask for help from an adviser.

Marketing and CapEx will differ dramatically based on the kind of business you're running. But you need to think carefully about all the elements of each, as well as the planning that has to go into making the expenses come to life. If you need to renovate your office or expand to a new location in order to accommodate new hires, you need to give your office manager significant lead time to make arrangements. Don't let the excitement of hiring a new sales team turn into a scramble to find desks and monitors.

Don't let your resource planning stop there. Look at every single line item on an income statement. If you're just starting out, a basic accounting software package can be your guide, as can Google or Wikipedia. From rent to travel expenses, to consultants, to the software your people will be using, your planning needs to include every dime.

Revisiting the Big Classics

When you're developing your business and investor presentation, every year and every situation is different. There is probably a shelf of books for every specific challenge you're facing and it's worth making your way through them when you're trying to get a handle on the specific challenges your company is facing. This is also the time to revisit the big classics: the books that you instinctively reach for every time you're stuck; the ones that defined the way you think about every major problem; the ones that inspired you to take on the challenge of starting a company in the first place.

Market research, stakeholder interviews, and a careful review of the literature on your immediate challenges will help you make many of the small decisions that every strategic plan must encompass. The big classics will remind you to take a step back and situate your plan in a much larger context. My favorites are:

Profitable Growth Is Everyone's Business by Ram Charan
The Innovator's Dilemma, *The Innovator's Solution*, and *Seeing What's Next* by Clay Christensen
Good to Great and *Built to Last* by Jim Collins
Purple Cow and others by Seth Godin
The Advantage by Patrick Lencioni
The Goal and *It's Not Luck* by Eliyahu M. Goldratt
Blue Ocean Strategy by Chan Kim and Renee Mauborgne
Crossing the Chasm, *Inside the Tornado*, and *Escape Velocity* by Geoffrey Moore
The Underdog Advantage by David Morey and Scott Miller
Competitive Strategy and *Competitive Advantage* by Michael Porter
Positioning: The Battle for Your Mind by Al Ries and Jack Trout
Hardball by George Stalk and Rob Lachenauer (also check out "Curveball," Stalk's 2006 follow-up article in the *Harvard Business Review*)

INVESTOR PRESENTATIONS FOR LARGER STARTUPS

Unless you invent not only cold fusion but a model that funds your business without requiring outside capital, you'll go through the process described in this chapter a number of times as you scale up your business. This may seem like a hassle, but it's actually a good thing for you as the entrepreneur in the end. If you have to absorb $20 million in losses before building a profitable business, better to raise the money in chunks at escalating valuations so you minimize dilution. More to the point, it's required, since investors will always want to see you derisk their investment piece by piece over time.

As you get larger and larger, the preceding steps are still relevant as an outline, but the work you do to flesh out the outline has to get more and more detailed. New sections or slides have to be added. Who are some reference customers? How are they using and liking the product? If you lost a couple of customers (or are in a consumer business where you lose lots of customers), why did you lose them? How did actual financials compare to your plan? How specifically will you use the dollars invested in the business? Are your early investors going to put more money in this round?

Virtually every company in the world has investors and shareholders. Learning how to tell your company's story to them is an incredibly important part of running a company. Even if you're a product-oriented CEO, or the company's best engineer, if your title is CEO, you are doing this work yourself. Although a good CFO will participate in this process, especially as you get larger, raising money is the process of selling someone else on your vision of the business and of a world made better by it. This is awfully hard to delegate to someone else.

CHAPTER FOUR

TELLING THE STORY TO YOUR TEAM

If you've spent enough time conceiving, writing, and revising your story and telling it to investors, you're ready to move on to the next phase: telling it to your team. What is the goal you and your team are moving toward (your mission)? What will the world look like once you've achieved that goal (your vision)? What are you willing to do—and what are you *not* willing to do—to realize that vision (your values)? Most startup CEOs will have answers to those questions before Day 1. Like every other part of the startup story, your answers will only improve as you learn more about your customers and your marketplace, and respond accordingly.

DEFINING YOUR MISSION, VISION, AND VALUES

As a startup CEO, you'll never stop adjusting your goals and behaviors to market realities. At a certain stage, you should have a clear idea of who your customers are and how your company serves them. In fact, it should be clear enough to state in a handful of short sentences. As David J. Collis and Michael G. Rukstad wrote in the *Harvard Business Review* article "Can You Say What Your Strategy Is?," most executives can't do this. "It's a dirty little secret: Most executives cannot articulate the objective, scope, and advantage of their business in a simple statement. If they can't, neither can anyone else." Hopefully, this statement doesn't apply to the senior people at your company, but what if it does? And if it's not applicable to senior people, could it be true for others in your company?

Even if you're a crazy micromanager, the minute you have more than a handful of people, you will be delegating a vast percentage of the company's work and decisions. It is vitally important that your team has clear, codified guideposts for doing things that work and making those decisions. Once you've defined your business strategy and defined what kind of company and culture you want to build, that's where a good set of mission, vision and values statements comes into play.

Over the years at Return Path, we've done a few rounds of defining and redefining who we are as a company and where we are going. This includes what our mission is, what our strategy is, our source of competitive advantage, and what our values are. We haven't used a consistent framework for this—though we've always used *some* framework. In the end, it's less important how you do this work than that you take the time to create a simple governing document for your organization.

Simulmedia CEO Dave Morgan on Defining Successful Companies

Every startup CEO you speak with will emphasize the importance of vision and strategy to a startup's success. As a three-time entrepreneur, Dave Morgan has proven the importance of those repeatedly, first at 24/7 Real Media, then at Tacoda Systems and now at Simulmedia.

My father, a former district attorney in rural western Pennsylvania, always sent his witnesses off for cross-examination with the admonition, "Think your answers through to the very last word before you open your mouth to speak the first." There's an important lesson in that statement for entrepreneurs: it is critical to think through and articulate the last word of your company's vision and strategy before you start executing on the first.

The world of most startups, particularly the world of tech startups, is a dynamic place full of ever-changing products, market conditions and consumer behaviors. In that world, you don't have the luxuries of predictability, defined rules, and procedures, or the ability to plan and prepare with the level of detail that major enterprises are accustomed to. Your world is one of chaos and uncertainty. You plan in advance as best you can and improvise as obstacles and opportunities present themselves—recognizing that they almost never present themselves as anticipated.

In this world of constant improvisation, entrepreneurs and their teams have no better friend than a clear, concise, and well-understood vision and strategy for their company. You and your team can't survive and thrive in the unpredictable world of startups without a well-thought-out point of view on the future of your market and what it is that you are trying to accomplish in that market. Additionally, you need to know how you intend to achieve it.

This vision and strategy doesn't have to be perfect. It doesn't have to be all encompassing and fixed for time immemorial. It doesn't have to anticipate all potentialities. However, it needs to be bold enough to excite and motivate. It needs to be focused enough to serve as your magnetic north. It needs to be clear enough to help you prioritize your people, time and money. It needs to be far-sighted enough that it doesn't need to be rewritten every quarter.

Setting the vision and strategy for your company can be one of the hardest and most intellectually and emotionally challenging phases of a startup, but it's also one of the most gratifying and unifying. More important, it can also help you build a much better business by forcing you to confront assumptions that might otherwise slip by unchallenged.

My father learned that forcing his witnesses to think through their cross-examination answers in their entirety resulted in very different—and much better—answers than they were initially inclined to give. So, too, for entrepreneurs. Those who work diligently at setting their company's vision and strategy from the beginning not only have more focus, a better framework for decision making and a more unified team; they also end up launching their businesses in different—and much better—ways than they had initially planned.

Dave Morgan, CEO, Simulmedia

THE TOP-DOWN APPROACH

In the early years of a startup, the only way to define your mission, vision, and values is by way of a top-down process. There's a simple reason for this: at this stage, your company consists almost entirely of co-founders and executives. There is no crowd of employees to crowd-source from. Either the CEO or a few members of the senior team have to sit down and craft these basic statements, being careful to separate the *what* (mission and strategy) from the *how* (values).

When Return Path turned nine years old, we were ready to take another approach. The company had gone through a major reorganization (we had sold or spun off a several business units and refocused on a new, tightly defined core). We had grown from a small team to over a hundred employees in offices around the world. We could have run another top-down process, but we felt like that was the wrong approach for us as a talent-centric business. It was time to redefine our company from the bottom up.

THE BOTTOM-UP APPROACH

When we ran the process of defining our mission, vision and values at Return Path, we thought we had a pretty clear sense of our values, as well as where we were going as a business. To test that hypothesis, we decided to solicit opinions from the entire company.

The framework we selected for the process was from the *Harvard Business Review* article by Collis and Rukstad I mentioned at the beginning of this chapter. (You can read the article at http://hbr.org/2008/04/can-you-say-what-your-strategy-is/ar/.) We divided the company up into about a dozen teams of 10 people each. The team assignments were random, and each team was led by a senior person in the organization (*not* someone on the executive team). Each team received a copy of the Collis/Rukstad article and we had an all-hands meeting where we talked about what we were doing and what we were trying to achieve. Then we sent each team a template to fill out and gave everyone a month to come back with their answers.

Then we held our breath. We weren't quite sure what was going to come back. On the day all the completed templates were returned, we reviewed them at a team meeting. Although they obviously differed a bit here and there, we were pleased that the 12 teams had come up with fairly similar views of the company's mission, values and strategy. This was less surprising about some aspects than others. For example, I wasn't surprised that there was a high degree of convergence in the way people thought about the organization's values since we had a strong values-driven culture that people were living every day, even if those values hadn't been well articulated in the past. But it was a little surprising that we could effectively crowdsource a strategy statement and key performance metrics at a time when the business was at a fork in the road.

Given this degree of alignment, our task as an executive team became less about picking concepts and more about picking words. We worked together to come up with a solid draft that took the best of what was submitted to us. We worked with a copywriter to make the statements flow well. Then we shared the results with the company and opened the floor for comments. About 40 employees took the time to redline the document and send it back. Again, we looked through the comments and selected the best of them. We went back to the copywriter, finished up, and published the results to the company.

THE HYBRID APPROACH

Four years later, we felt that it was time to review these statements. Our business had grown from 120 to 350 people, and from $15 to almost $60 million in revenue. We went from having two offices to having 12 offices on four continents. We had released a bunch of new products that broadened the scope of our business. Our strategy and mission had broadened slowly over the years, without redefinition. Our values hadn't changed dramatically, but living with the statements we'd written for four years taught us that the statements themselves were clunky. It seemed like time for a refresh.

The first thing we decided to do was to pick a different framework. The Collis/Rukstad formula was a little heavy for us. We decided to borrow from Patrick Lencioni's fantastic book, *The Advantage: Why Organizational Health Trumps Everything Else in Business*, and answer five simple questions for ourselves:

- Why do we exist?
- How do we behave?
- What do we do?
- How will we succeed?
- What is most important, right now?

We might have crowdsourced the process again, even with 350 people, if we had felt that we were at a real turning point in the life of the business. Because we viewed this exercise as more of a refresh, we did a hybrid of top-down and bottom-up approaches. This time, we started by working through drafts of the governing document as an executive team. We were able to get to a solid working draft in about three hours.

From there, we presented the results at an all-hands meeting and walked the company through the current statements, the logic of needing a refresh, the change in framework, and the working draft. Following that, we circulated the working draft to the company and the executive team did a blitz of roundtable meetings that were attended by nearly all of our employees within about a week. People came to the meetings extremely engaged and with detailed feedback, which we compiled and fed back into the revision of the working draft. We circulated that document to the entire company and invited a final round of comments and received a handful of redlines. Voila! A new set of mission, vision and values statements emerged, about 30 days after starting the process.

The second part of the Lencioni framework is something I'll come back to in Chapter 19 when I talk about translating the Mission and Vision into an Operating Plan.

Return Path's Mission, Vision, and Values

Our "Statements of Purpose" as a 13-year-old company were quite different than they were at the beginning of the company's life but, especially in the case of our company's values, evolved smoothly over time. Below are the statements as our "hybrid approach" produced them, along with the questions they answer from Patrick Lencioni's framework in *The Advantage*.

Our Mission and Vision

Why do we exist? We are building an extraordinary company that helps people and businesses communicate more reliably, effectively and securely.

How do we behave? We put people first, do the right thing and succeed together.

What do we do? We analyze email data and build solutions that generate insights for senders, mailbox providers and users to ensure that inboxes contain only messages that users want.

How will we succeed? We will succeed by building unique solutions to email's most challenging problems. We will cultivate a team of passionate email experts and trusted industry relationships. We will aggregate and analyze data that drive our customers' business results and our end users' experiences.

What is most important, right now? In 2013, we will deliver a scalable, repeatable sales model.

Our Values—The Detail behind "How Do We Behave?"

- People First
    - *Job 1.* We are responsible for championing and extending our unique culture as a competitive advantage.
    - *People power.* We trust and believe in our people as the foundation of success with our clients and shareholders.
    - *Think like an owner.* We are a community of A players who are all owners in the business. We provide freedom and flexibility in exchange for consistently high performance.
    - *Seriously fun.* We are serious about our job and lighthearted about our day. We are obsessively kind to and respectful of one another and appreciate each other's quirks.
- Do the Right Thing
    - *No secrets.* We are transparent and direct so that people know where the company stands and where they stand, so that they can make great decisions.
    - *Spirit of the law.* We do the right thing, even if it means going beyond what's written on paper.
    - *Raise the bar.* We lead our industry to set standards that inboxes should only contain messages that are relevant, trusted, and safe.
    - *Think global, act local.* We commit our time and energy to support our local communities.
- Succeed Together
    - *Results focused.* We focus on building a great business and a great company in an open, accessible environment.
    - *Aim high and be bold.* We learn from others, then we write our own rules to be a pioneer in our industry and create a model workplace. We take risks and challenge complacency, mediocrity, and decisions that don't make sense.
    - *Two ears, one mouth.* We ask, listen, learn, and collect data. We engage in constructive debate to reach conclusions and move forward together.
    - *Collaboration is king.* We solve problems together and help each other out along the way. We keep our commitments and communicate diligently when we can't.
    - *Learning loops.* We are a learning organization. We aren't embarrassed by our mistakes—we communicate and learn from them so we can grow in our jobs.
    - *Not just about us.* We know we're successful when our clients are successful and our users are happy.

DESIGN A LOFTY MISSION STATEMENT

In *The Advantage* (p. 82), Patrick Lencioni describes the main criteria of a good mission statement:

> An organization's purpose—why it exists—has to be completely idealistic. Many leadership teams struggle with this, afraid that what they come up with will seem too grand or aspirational. Of course, that's the whole point. Employees in every organization, and at every level, need to know that at the heart of what they do lies something grand and aspirational. They're well aware that ultimately it will boil down to tangible, tactical activities. All organizations exist to make people's lives better . . . to aspire to anything less would be foolish . . . the point will be somewhere just shy of "to make the world a better place."

My friend Jonathan Shapiro runs an e-commerce company called PetCareRX that sells pet medication and basics like flea and tick treatments. How lame would it be if his organization's statement of purpose was "to rid the world of fleas and ticks"? Or, even worse, "to be the leading e-commerce company focused on the pet vertical"? Instead, Jonathan and his team crafted this statement of purpose: "Adding Love to the World by Enhancing the Lives of Pets & Pet Parents." Adding love to the world is awesome. Images of a cute puppy licking the face of a laughing child come to mind. Who doesn't want that?

Live the Organization's Values

You cannot, in a million years, expect the people in your company to live by your organization's values and policies if you don't do those things yourself. Do you think Jim Bakker's and Jimmy Swaggart's employees found it easy to accept their bosses' sermons about the sins of adultery after their own public confessions? In an example that hits closer to home, I worked at a company years ago that was incredibly frugal and had a super tight expense policy with strict enforcement. For example, employees couldn't spend more than $150/

night on a hotel when traveling for business in major cities. (One employee stayed at a place that cost $180/night once, and the CFO made him refund the extra $30.) But when our CEO traveled for business, he routinely stayed at the Four Seasons, even if he was on a trip with other employees who had to stay elsewhere. When he was questioned about not following the rules, he changed the policy to exempt himself from it. You think that made it easy for the rest of the team to embrace frugality?

Moz CEO and Founder Rand Fishkin on Living Your Company's Values

As founder and CEO of Moz (formerly SEOmoz), Rand Fishkin has not only done a great job of codifying his companies values; he's done an amazing job of making them a part of the entire Moz culture.

When we started Moz in 2004, we had no clearly defined culture, no specific mission or vision, no stated values, and our primary goal was just to make enough money to pay the rent. We managed to make ends meet, and the company culture grew organically, but there was clearly something missing. In 2007, we began a process to establish core values, and out of that came TAGFEE (an acronym representing Transparency, Authenticity, Generosity, Fun, Empathy, and Exceptionalism). Looking back, it's incredible to me the difference that having a formalized set of values has made.

For us, TAGFEE works like a set of architectural blueprints over every action and decision we take in the business. It affects how we build products, how we resolve conflicts, how we choose who we work with, and, most importantly, how we interact with one another. It's embedded into our hiring process: there's actually a set of questions we call the "TAGFEE screen." No matter how well a candidate does on other aspects of the interview, we won't hire unless they're a culture and values fit. It's part of how we rate and review performance across teams, but also on the formal, individual reviews we do every 6 months.

It's my personal belief that core values are critical to the long-term success of any startup, but thanks to the work of folks like Jim Collins (who wrote *Good to Great* and *Built to Last*), there's a lot of research suggesting a high correlation between companies that scale successfully and those that embrace core values into their culture.

There are a few guidelines I'd suggest following when establishing and implementing values:

1. *Core values come from within.* Your values must be part of the founder's identity. That doesn't mean they should be an exact reflection of who you are in day-to-day life. In fact, I'd suggest choosing values you must strive for: the four to six principles that represent the part of yourself that you're always striving to become.
2. *Bake values into your interviews and your performance reviews.* If you don't, you're just paying lip service and your team will quickly realize that your core values aren't taken seriously.
3. *Encourage critical analysis of big decisions from a values perspective.* Your core values should be the foundation of how arguments are shaped and judged, not an afterthought.
4. *Accept that values will sometimes come into conflict with one another.* This is healthy, but extraordinarily painful if you don't have a system for prioritization. For example, at Moz, transparency and empathy are often at odds. In a scenario where both cannot be achieved, we rank empathy highest.
5. *Let employees go if they don't live up to your core values, even if they're phenomenal performers.* If you don't, you're showing the rest of your team that values come second (or third, or fourth) to other things—and those "other things" become your true, if unspoken, core values. Much of the dreaded "politics" of corporate culture stems from this failure. When you spot a problem, communicate extensively with the employee and make an effort to fix it. If that doesn't work, you have to act.

Some entrepreneurs I talk to have a sense that core values are merely an extra layer of "HR stuff," or that stating values "sets you up for failure" by making it more difficult to "pivot" and move at the speed of startups. I wholly reject those ideas. If your mission and vision is merely to make lots of money by exploiting a temporary opportunity, ignore this advice. But, if you believe that organizations exist to accomplish what individuals alone could not, and you intend to build something that lasts, I encourage you to establish and embrace core values.

CHAPTER FIVE

REVISING THE STORY

Rough drafts are written to be discarded. Every writing manual is in agreement on this point, and the same is true for startup rough drafts. The moment you move from the planning phase to the shark-infested waters of the marketplace, you'll appreciate the truth of Steve Blank's maxim: "No business plan survives first contact with customers." Startups live or die by how they respond to this harsh reality. Deny the facts, and you'll fail. Sense and respond—even when responding means a radical pivot—and you'll survive and thrive.

WORKSHOPPING

The writer's workshop is perhaps the most mortifying and humbling experience in higher education. You've put your heart and soul into a story, and now you have to read it out loud to a critical audience. Your hope is that they will be dumbstruck by your brilliance; the reality is that they'll immediately start poking holes in your work.

Testing your business plan in front of a live audience—of customers, partners, team members, industry experts—is no different. You can start the process of writing a business plan by filling out the "Lean Canvas" template yourself. There's no shame in throwing out a rough draft to get the conversation started, but then you need to present it your key stakeholders—customers, team members, investors, industry contacts—and ask for their input. Doing so is frequently humbling, but it's always absolutely necessary.

Try It On for Size

I've always been a big fan of taking a decision or a change in direction I'm contemplating and trying it on for size. You never know how a pair of pants is really going to fit until you slip it on in a dressing room, and you often don't know how a decision will feel until you try it out.

Sometimes, I'm simply trying to see how words sound when they come out of my mouth. As Homer Simpson periodically muses, "Did I think that, or did I say that out loud?" There's no substitute for articulating a new phrase, or theory, out in the open and seeing if it sounds the way *you* expect.

Other times, I'm trying to see how different messages or stories play with different audiences. Finally, there are times when my objective in trying something on for size is to understand the specific downstream effects of a decision. Throwing something out into the open and taking copious notes as people give you their "blink" concerns and reactions are invaluable.

The one thing I'm careful about when I'm trying something on for size with employees is to let them know that's what I'm doing, either before or after I do it. The times I haven't done this, people have taken my Homer Simpson moments as directives, and that can't be a good thing.

KNOWING WHEN IT'S TIME TO MAKE A CHANGE

The interviews you conduct—and the input you get directly from the marketplace—are only as valuable as your willingness to act on them. Are customers responding well to part of your solution while ignoring another? Are the people you interview clear about what they *would* buy if only you would offer it? Are you willing to respond to this feedback? Or are you confident that it's just a matter of time before customers see the light and buy your product?

Startups have no choice but to quickly change gears in response to company performance and market conditions. As much work as it takes to build a strategic plan, you have to be willing to rewrite it completely if circumstances demand it. Don't cry "uncle" prematurely, but don't deny reality forever.

Knowing when to insist on your vision and when to cede to the marketplace is as much an art as it is a science. The best you can do is to watch out for some important signs and use your judgment to determine whether the situation is temporary—or potentially terminal.

- *Data disprove your original thesis.* Every startup is a leap into the unknown: you have a business thesis and you want to test it in the marketplace. In the best-case scenario, you'll eventually hit on the right idea. Usually, your original thesis is wrong, in whole or in part, and you have to make adjustments along the way. We experienced this at Return Path a few years ago: when we expanded to a number of email-related business lines, our assumption was that the same buyer would want to buy two or three of the five services we offered. In the end, it was usually one and very occasionally two. Even in the cases where companies *did* buy multiple services from us, we were dealing with different buyers and budgets within those companies. That meant different sales forces and a lack of efficiencies. It was time to focus.
- *Poor results.* There is no better indicator of whether your business is working than bottom-line results. Creating new marketplaces takes patience, and your investors won't (or, rather, shouldn't) expect immediate returns. But if you're constantly in the "startup" phase and never making your way into "scaling" or "growth"—if you're never closing major deals, if you're perpetually spending more than you make, if you're endlessly diluting equity in round after round of fundraising—it's probably time for a change.
- *Internal noise.* Even if your thesis is working and your company is performing well, the foundation your success is built on might be too flimsy. It's too hard to get things done; your management team is constantly putting out fires; everything is at the edge of chaos at all times. Lots of entrepreneurs will tell you that this is simply the reality of founding a business. I disagree. It's easy to get addicted to startup chaos. Your goal should be to minimize it.

There's an infinite variety of ways that you might pivot in response to one or many of these signs, but it ultimately comes down to a choice between two options: changing the *company* or changing the *business*.

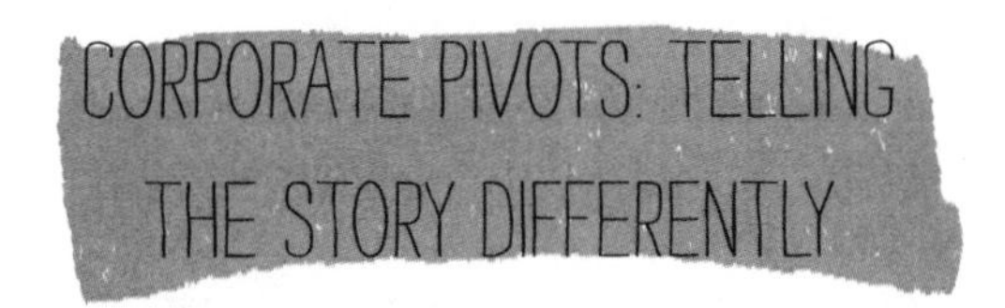

"In matters of grave importance, style, not substance, is the crucial thing." This is one of Oscar Wilde's most famous statements—or, rather, overstatements.

As exaggerated as it is, it's worth considering. Most startup CEOs focus on *what* they do rather than *how* they operate—the "substance" of their businesses rather than the "style" of their companies. As a result, they're liable to think that all pivots are related to what their companies do rather than how their companies operate. "Corporate" pivots (changes in "style") are as important and potentially transformative as "business" pivots (changes in "substance").

Usually, startups pivot because their product-market fit is off or because their strategy isn't working. Occasionally, though, opportunities present themselves and you have to act. They may be the result of broad macroeconomic shifts like the one we experienced in 2008 and 2009, or they could be specific to your industry. Whatever the occasion, you'll have to act quickly. Pivots *should* be the result of long-term strategic planning—but sometimes, they can't be.

Consolidating

The most common opportunity you'll encounter is *an opportunity to consolidate*. Startups often create new marketplaces or industries, or enter ones that are immature. Ideally, you'll want your startup to be a market leader in the industry that you're creating. (By the way: that's the Blue Ocean Strategy in a nutshell.) If you're the first to market, you'll be a market leader by default—if only temporarily. Eventually, competitors will come along.

Competition can't be eliminated—usually. There are two occasions when it can: during a macroeconomic downturn or during a moment of crisis at a competing startup. If you're doing a great job as CEO and your business is fundamentally sound, a recession or two shouldn't put you out of business. The same might not be true of your competitors, and they may welcome an exit. Read the tea leaves and choose the right moment to make an offer.

At Return Path, we acquired direct competitors at two different points in our history. One was following the Internet bubble, when we and a Colorado-based company called Veripost were both relatively new startups (less than two years old) struggling to gain adoption in a new product category at a time when all of the most likely potential buyers were going out of business. That acquisition greatly accelerated revenue generation by eliminating the competitive element to the sales process. It literally kept us alive at a time when I'm not sure we otherwise would have survived.

The second competitor we acquired was a much smaller direct competitor called Habeas, back in 2008. The company was running out of cash and didn't have financing in sight, and we were just about to hit the great recession of 2008 (financial markets had already started getting jittery in 2007). The result of this acquisition was primarily financial gain. As a completely direct competitor with substantial business operations, we were extremely disciplined about eliminating redundant costs and platforms. We ended up keeping something like 75 percent of the company's revenue and only 10 percent of its cost structure.

Given how difficult it is to successfully run a startup, your competitors may not need a broad economic shift to bring them to the brink. If they have something you need—either technology or people—make an offer. If they don't, prepare your sales team to poach their clients.

Note: You and your competitors aren't competing only for customers or market mind share. You're also competing for talent. Chances are that you are interviewing a lot of the same people—or interviewing outgoing employees as other startups tighten their belts. All other things aside, those interviews are great sources of competitive intelligence. Use them to determine how your competitors are doing, and whether they would be amenable to an offer.

Diversifying

Every entrepreneur starts their business on the assumption that they've got a billion dollar idea. Most come to the sad realization that the idea won't cover their costs. In between, there are companies that have a good idea—but one that just isn't broad enough. To build a large business, they need to do more. They need to *diversify*.

Diversifying doesn't mean entering a radically different marketplace or ramping up on an entirely new technical challenge. It means finding new ways to innovate and solve problems *within* your marketplace.

One way to diversify is with an opportunistic acquisition. Unlike the ones I discussed above, these aren't about consolidating a single marketplace but expanding your revenue streams by incorporating a company that offers similar but not identical products to your customers offering the opportunity for new revenue streams.

The other way to diversify is by adding a new line of business to your company—one that leverages existing talent, even if it requires an infusion of new hires. Whether you do one or the other depends on whether it's cheaper to "buy" or "build" the new business unit. We reviewed this question in detail in the previous chapter; the same principles hold here.

We diversified Return Path's business over the years as well, acquiring a couple of new companies and technologies at different points along the way.

Some of those acquisitions went incredibly well: our email intelligence grew out of our acquisition of Assurance Systems in 2003; our professional services practice grew out of the acquisition we made of GasPedal Consulting that same year; and the acquisition of Bonded Sender from IronPort got us into the certification business. For very small companies, diversifying can be particularly tricky, but if you have a partial solution and adding some new technology or products give you a whole solution, it may make a lot of sense.

Focusing

As much success as we've had with *some* of our acquisitions, our experience at Return Path has proven that the road to hell is paved with failed diversification strategies. The AOL/Time Warner merger is probably the most famous example: "convergence" never materialized and both companies came close to failing. Even with that counterexample staring us in the face, we tried the convergence route at Return Path—and it almost brought down our company.

When Return Path first made the transition from startup to scaling, the story we told was all about diversification and convergence. "Email is a crucial and complex part of every business. Companies that buy one email solution—deliverability, customer research, marketing lists—will jump at the opportunity to buy others." That was the theory, at least, but very little of the operating and sales leverage we'd expected across the different products materialized, leaving us a collection of small businesses being run by a single management team off of one small balance sheet. We'd built a company that was too complex. Our board member Scott Weiss started calling us "the world's smallest conglomerate," and he wasn't smiling when he said it. He was right.

We'd quickly grown from $2 million to $30 million in revenue, but our business was a nightmare to run. We had to eliminate some of the complexity in the business, which came from adding lines of business that ended up having a lot less in common with each other than we thought. One of the most significant days in the history of the company was the day in 2007 that we decided to focus on one line of business and divest the others, setting the stage for much more rapid and sustainable growth. By the time we'd finished divesting all the businesses we deemed "noncore," we'd shrunk the company from $30 million in revenue down to about $11 million. But, in the ensuing five years, our growth has been even stronger. As of this writing, we're at $70 million.

Realizing that your original idea isn't going to be the next Google or Facebook is always a sobering experience, but sometimes it's accompanied by a bit of good news: a business line that you once considered ancillary to your business *may in fact be* the next big thing. (According to Steve Blank in *The Four Steps to the Epiphany*, this is just about the *only* way startups actually manage to break through.) Accept what the marketplace is telling you, and focus on the winner.

Depending on how mature your once-primary business unit is, this might be a good time to secure an infusion of cash with a well-executed divestiture. If the idea never got off the ground, you'll simply need to pivot your team in a new direction. The case we're discussing here is simply a reallocation of resources toward an existing business line.

Bionic CEO David Kidder on Pivoting Your Business Direction

As a three-time entrepreneur and the author of The Startup Playbook, *Bionic CEO David Kidder knows as much about pivoting a business as anyone.*

Startups are like heat-seeking missiles: the target of the missile is defined by the company's vision and purpose; the rocket is steered and propelled by mission and work; and the guidance systems are instructed by values and beliefs. In most cases, "pivoting" isn't about changing the missile's target—the company's vision and purpose—but changing *how* the rocket is steered toward the target. That process will always be treacherous—sometimes fatal, but it doesn't have to be.

The first and most important step is recognizing that success lies not in products but in people. Your teams must understand with incredible clarity your company's vision, mission, and values. Second, while they must have a complete commitment to the core vision, they should also understand that the work often has to change in order to navigate the a changing landscape on the way to the target. If correctly established in your company's culture, changing the mission—or pivoting—does not and should not destabilize a team committed to a startup's vision. The job of a startup CEO is to set this vision, to gain the trust and commitment of the team, and to create an environment that allows the team to shape the mission and achieve the vision—in other words, hit the target.

Another aspect of defining and surviving pivots is creating an emotionally resilient team. This is best developed by setting expectations of change up front, from the very first day. Very often we steer blindly, even with the best road maps and the best-laid plans. The changes in direction required to navigate over and around obstacles must be recognized and accepted by everyone. One of my favorite explanations of the rationale behind pivoting comes from Amazon founder Jeff Bezos (as related to 37signals founder Jason Fried):

> People who were right a lot of the time are people who often changed their minds. I don't think consistency is a particularly positive trait. It's perfectly healthy—encouraged, even—to have an idea tomorrow that contradicted your idea today.
>
> The smartest people are constantly revising their understanding, reconsidering a problem they thought they'd already solved. They're open to new points of view, new information, new ideas, contradictions, and challenges to their own way of thinking.
>
> What trait signified someone who was wrong a lot of the time? Someone obsessed with details that only support one point of view.

To be frank, pivoting can often feel like failing, especially if you have not prepared your team for this possibility. But it's simply irresponsible *not* to pivot around and away from the many fatal obstructions that lie between your team and your collective target—your vision. It's your duty as a startup CEO.

David Kidder, CEO, Bionic

BUSINESS PIVOTS: TELLING A DIFFERENT STORY

Business pivots are what most entrepreneurs have in mind when they think about changing their company's direction. They are much riskier and more complex than changing your position in the marketplace or tweaking your internal model, but they're unavoidable (especially if you're listening to the marketplace rather than trying to force yourself on it). A pivot isn't a leap; it's a change of direction about a fixed point—your core capabilities.

In late 2009, I spoke at the New York City Lean Startup Meetup. My topic was "The Pivot," but the best summary of my position actually came from a member of the audience, who boiled it down to three words: "Pivot, don't Jump!"

When you discover that your prior conception of "product-market fit" is off, the temptation is to leap in a completely different direction. Resist! Every pivot a startup makes should be at the request or urging of your clients (a request they might voice by *not* answering your sales calls) and in a direction in line with your core capabilities.

We've pivoted many times at Return Path. But we've never "jumped." While we have a talented team that could probably execute lots of different businesses very well, it's hard to see us being successful in areas that are far afield from our core competency: email.

Over the years, for example, people have often suggested that we should get into SMS deliverability. "Isn't that going to be a hot topic?" We don't know. We don't spend our lives immersed in text messaging or with mobile carriers. "What about getting in the measurement of social media messaging? Isn't that related?" Maybe, but it's not in our wheelhouse. Expanding from email deliverability software and analytics into services, into data, into whitelisting, into audience measurement—those were pivots, not jumps.

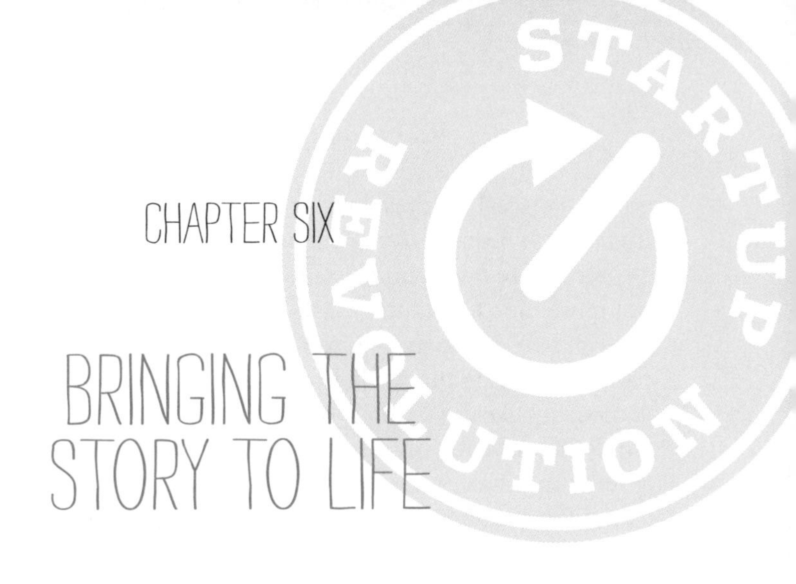

CHAPTER SIX

BRINGING THE STORY TO LIFE

Every parent who reads to his or her children has heard the question: "Did it really happen?" More often than not—and whether we let our kids in on the secret or not—the answer is "no." In the realm of make believe, we wouldn't have it any other way. (Where would we be without hobbits and Hogwarts?) But in the world of startups, our goal is to make all our stories come true.

The "Lean Canvas" slide is meant to state your hypotheses for internal consumption and get your entire team aligned around the goal of testing them. Your investor deck should secure the required funding. Your mission, vision, and values declare what you will do—and what you won't do—to achieve your goal. The intermediate step between those statements and the nitty-gritty details of team building and execution is the process of building your organization. It's much less well defined than the process for building a good business strategy or doing customer development work to find product-market fit. But that doesn't mean it's any less important.

It's what turns your idea into a company.

BUILDING YOUR COMPANY PURPOSEFULLY

One of the most important keys to building a company is to *be intentional about everything*. Things will happen around you that are always harder to change after the fact than to steer up front. Do you come off as a micromanager or, worse, a Monday-morning quarterback? Or do you let things go that you feel aren't right for the direction of your company long term? It's better to be proactive about everything.

Deep into my second decade with Return Path, I've devoted as much if not more time to building the company as I have to building our business lines and products, and I don't regret it at all. In the early years of our company, I did some things that now seem crazy for a brand new, 25-person company—like designing a sabbatical policy that wouldn't kick in until an employee's seventh anniversary. In the long run, this effort was not wasted (even if they were a little wasted in the short run). There are two ways that a focus on building the company—even from the earliest days—pays long-term dividends:

1. *It helps lay the groundwork for scaling.* When you get to that amazing "hockey stick" moment and rapidly scale your business, it's important to do so over a very solid foundation. If you wait until that moment to start "building" your company, it will often be too late—and the growth might kill your company.
2. *The company won't necessarily die if the product or business runs into trouble.* At Return Path, our original "email change-of-address" business basically proved to be a loser by 2002. We pivoted, and, because the *company* was carefully built, we survived.

I'm not saying that there's a right path or a wrong path here when you compare business building with company building. In the end, a good CEO and management team must be concerned about getting both elements right if they want to build an enduring, stand-alone company.

THE CRITICAL ELEMENTS OF COMPANY BUILDING

Here are some of the critical elements of company building. Some are things most people would label *culture*, but they're specific enough to call out here.

- *Geography.* Do you want your team to be primarily in one office? Exclusively in one office? Or do you want to be wherever the talent is? Do you want to build an offshore development capability to optimize development dollars, and do you have the know-how on your team to manage people in India or China? At Return Path, we decided early on that we'd be in multiple locations to take advantage of the best people, since Internet talent was scarce in 1999. If I had to do it all over again, I'd have insisted on one center of gravity for as long as possible. Being virtual and in multiple locations has some real advantages (talent pool, proximity to customers in B2B environment), but we also pay a penalty for it in terms of communications and travel overhead.

- *Type of office.* Do you want an office, or do you want to be virtual for a while? Do you want to be in the city or in the suburbs? Do you want everyone in one big open room or are you okay with offices and cubes? There's really no substitute for proximity in terms of informal or serendipitous conversations. We started Return Path in one big, open room, but that wasn't practical for a number of reasons. Nonetheless, we wanted to have an office on Day 1, and this was the only way we could manage it early on.
- *Systems.* Are you a Mac shop or a Windows shop? Microsoft Office or Google Apps? Exchange or Gmail? Do you have a preferred collaboration tool like Basecamp or Confluence? Are you going to put all development in the cloud from Day 1? (We're a more traditional Wintel/Office shop, but that's a function of having gotten into business in 1999. If we were starting from scratch today, we'd do things differently.)
- *Driving force.* Are you a sales-driven company? A product-driven company? A technology-driven company? A people-driven company? We've always opted for a balanced approach. We aren't sales dominated or product dominated or tech dominated. We are business dominated. That works well for us.
- *Staffing and compensation.* Are you going to pay people top dollar? How do you think about cash versus equity? Do you want to have a senior heavy staff or a bunch of interns? We hired more senior people early on to get experience in the door and drive things forward, but it was expensive. We paid very little at the beginning—everyone made $75k—until we'd raised institutional money. Then we went closer to market comp for cash as well as equity.
- *Policies about time off.* Strict vacation policy? Or open? Do you care about sick days or not? Do you allow people to come and go as they please? Are you pissed off when you walk around and no one is in the office before 8 or after 5? How will you handle maternity leave or requests for paternity leave? While most companies get more formal as they grow, we've gone in the opposite direction.

- *Policies about expenses.* How frugal are you going to be? Are you covering people's cell phones and data plans? Gym memberships? We're frugal in a number of areas—offices, travel, and so on—but generous on things that mean a lot to individuals, like cell phones or gym memberships.
- *Communication patterns.* Are you meeting-centric? Email-centric? Are you even going to have phones? Or will you rely on people's cell phones? Because we've always had multiple locations, we're very email- and IM-centric at Return Path. (More recently, Skype and Cisco videophones have become a big part of our corporate communications.) Historically, we've had phones everywhere, though a number of our employees (especially engineers) hardly ever use them. Recently, we acquired an engineering office that never had phones on every desk—so we're experimenting with that.
- *Personal acknowledgments.* Are you going to celebrate birthdays with parties in the office? Will you track them yourself? What about marking people's employment anniversaries? Is there any kind of standard around holiday presents? We don't have birthday parties at Return Path, but we do celebrate each other in our own unique way.

I will discuss many of these items in more detail later, and surely there are other dimensions of company building that I've left out here, but they all have one thing in common—they are not related to your specific offering. These are issues that every company needs to face. Do so intentionally, and they will fuel productivity and growth. Ignore them, and they'll just "happen"—poorly.

ARTICULATING PURPOSE: THE MORAL OF THE STORY

Companies can and should make the world a better place in multiple, different ways. Certainly, many companies' core businesses do that—just look at all the breakthroughs in medicine and social services over the years brought to market by private enterprises. There are days where I wish Return Path was in the business of curing a disease or feeding the hungry. How awesome would it be to have a business with such powerful intrinsic motivation baked into its mission? Motivating people would be a snap!

But, alas, most companies in the world are like mine; they're not inherently "save the world" in nature. And yet, it's still critical to motivate your team by articulating the purpose of their job and the company's existence. At Return Path, I do this by placing our story within the wider context of all the customers we serve.

For example, one of Return Path's products is Email Certification, which helps marketers, publishers, banks, and other companies make sure their email doesn't get caught in a spam filter by mistake. Doesn't sound particularly impactful for society, does it? But then I did some math on our Certification business. In a given year, we certify about 1 trillion emails. Without our certification, 25 percent of those emails would probably be filtered by mistake. In other words, people around the world probably got 250 billion emails last year that they wouldn't otherwise have received because we exist.

Then I looked at some of our clients: Match.com and eHarmony, UNICEF and the American Cancer Society, and Scholarships.com and the College Board. How many more people get married every year or have babies because Return Path exists? How many more people got food or medicine from nonprofits because Return Path exists? How many more people could afford to go to college because Return Path exists? For most businesses out there, you can connect the work you do in a fairly straight line to creating good in the world, even if the line has to go through a few intermediate data points to get to its destination.

YOU CAN BE A FORCE FOR HELPING OTHERS—EVEN IF INDIRECTLY

Maybe you're not in the business of curing a disease. That doesn't mean your company can't help others who are. Whether you organize community service projects, give money away, or find another way of giving back to the community or world, you can galvanize your team around a mission or an ethos of service that makes your company stand for more than just your products. For many companies, adding this element to your mission and values is great as a recruiting and even a marketing tool, not to mention just a plain old good thing to do.

We've changed our approach to this over the years to try to maximize our impact and also make service a company-building exercise as well. In the early years, we allowed employees to take a limited amount of paid time off for community service work each year (once we established open vacation, this became less relevant). We also responded to requests from individual employees to help sponsor service events that they were involved with. Occasionally, we'd organize a local community project for employees to work at together: we sent a couple of teams down to New Orleans with Habitat for Humanity after Hurricane Katrina, and to the Rockaways for a day to help after Superstorm Sandy.

Other organizations donate money or services to charitable organizations they believe in, or provide matching gift programs for employees' donations. All of these approaches are great, as long as you publicize them internally and make sure people understand the impact the company is having.

Now, we are experimenting with a new program called DreamFund that we launched last year. Our aim is to replace a long list of scattershot efforts with a more focused one. We have basically stopped doing all of the other efforts I noted above, and instead are inviting teams of people across the company to apply for a one-time, $10,000 grant a few times per year to do a project that benefits one of the communities in which we operate. The projects can't just be funneling the money to an organization; the money has to accompany action. So far, teams have included hands-on work to help refurbish and renovate some rooms in a facility for abused children, a walk to raise money for cancer, and a literacy project.

You may not be curing cancer at your company. But are you helping someone who is?

Management Moment

Understand the Importance of Symbolism

Understanding the value of symbolism and when to use it is a key part of being a CEO. Sometimes the symbolic is just that: it's something designed to send a signal to others and not much more. Because there's not a lot of substance to it, it's easy to treat symbolic moves as wastes of time.

But if you're the kind of CEO who is inclined to dismiss the symbolic in favor of the substantive, consider these examples:

In November 2008, the CEOs of GM, Ford, and Chrysler asked the federal government for a bailout. At the time, there were 24 nonstop flights every day between Detroit and Washington, D.C. Nonetheless, the three CEOs flew to Washington on three separate corporate jets for their bailout requests. They didn't even jet pool.

Scott Thompson became Yahoo!'s CEO in January 2012, after a promising run as CEO of PayPal. One of his primary selling points, which he often noted publicly, was that, as an engineer, he was really well suited to help restore Yahoo! to a place of glory in Silicon Valley. Then it turned out that he had falsified his resume to say that he had an undergraduate engineering degree, when in fact he was an accounting major who had taken one computer science class.

When Hillary Clinton became Secretary of State in 2009, New York Governor David Paterson considered appointing Caroline Kennedy to fill Clinton's vacant U.S. Senate seat. Then it was revealed that Kennedy had failed to vote in nearly every election since 1988.

GM and Chrysler got their bailout funds, but the three CEOs were humiliated in front of Congress. Scott Thompson was CEO of Yahoo! for less than five months. The junior senator from New York is now Kirsten Gillibrand.

Symbolism matters.

Return Path Co-Founder George Bilbrey on How a CEO's Role in Vision and Strategy Changes Over Time

As co-founder and product visionary, George Bilbrey has been essential to Return Path's success. He's watched our company's strategy evolve over the past 13 years, giving him a unique perspective on how a CEO's role in vision and strategy changes with time.

As your company grows, the strategic challenges it faces change. The CEO needs to change his or her strategic focus to meet the changing challenges. That's certainly been our experience at Return Path. As we grew, we moved from an early period of figuring out exactly who our client was and what problem we were going solve for them, to our "awkward" teenage years, ending in a more mature period where the key problem is winnowing through a large number of opportunities.

The Early Days: Finding Product-to-Market Fit (Up to 25 Employees)

The challenge: Your company is just getting started. You and your (small) team have a rough idea of your target customer, the problem you're going to solve for them, and how you're going to solve that problem. Your primary job is to test that idea, iterate based on results, and find the *product-to-market fit* for your team. You need to build a minimum viable version of your sales/marketing activities, service activities, and, of course, your product.

Constraints on the CEO: You're likely going to have a lot of generalists on the team at this stage, without much specialized talent. The CEO has to be a "Jack of All Trades."

CEO's strategic role: Your job is to drive product-to-market fit. Depending on you skill set, you may be on early sales calls or building an early prototype. You're building prototype versions of sales/marketing and service processes to see if you can acquire and service clients. And you need to pull together a team of generalists to make that happen.

We've Got Something Here: Time to Scale (25–100 Employees)

The challenge: Congratulations! You've found product-to-market fit. Now it's time to move beyond fit with the early evangelist customers who love the thing you've built. It's time to move to more mainstream customers. To do that, you'll need to continue to work on your value proposition. This may mean making your product or service easier to consume, solving the problems of mainstream customers more directly, and allowing the target customer to do their job better. You need to make sure that the "wrapper" around your product—service, sales, billing—work to improve the value proposition. You are going to need to scale all functions.

Constraints on CEO: There isn't enough of you (or the founding team) to go around. Scaling and building more mature operational processes is your new focus, but not all the founders will be strong at that.

CEO's strategic role: You need to move from doing the work to providing the vision to the folks who are doing the work. You need to hire a competent Level 2 team to help you execute. You need to provide a vision of how the various parts "fit" together. And make sure that the new, "scalable" solution represents an irresistible value proposition. As the team grows, devolve more and more of the vision to the team. Ask them challenging questions and let them come up with the answers.

What's Next? More Resources = More Choices (>100 Employees)

The challenge: Scaling continues to be a problem. However, you now have a stable "base" from which to operate. You'll be looking at a lot of different strategic investments: Do I expand internationally? Do I expand into adjacent markets and solution areas?

Constraints on the CEO: Scaling means that the CEO might start to take his or her eyes off the longer-term vision of where the company is going.

CEO's strategic role: Developing a repeatable capability in the company to innovate beyond the core. You will need to develop a shared way of thinking about where to invest and where not to invest across the leadership team. You will need to develop a portfolio investment framework that your team gets.

George Bilbrey, Co-founder, Return Path

PART TWO

BUILDING THE COMPANY'S HUMAN CAPITAL

Building the company's talent base and reinforcing its organizational behaviors is a key activity for CEOs of just about any kind of company. It consumes as much as 50 percent of your time, but nothing will create more leverage for your business. As Peter Drucker famously wrote, "Culture eats strategy for breakfast." Throw in execution for lunch and a board of directors for dinner, and you get the idea: nothing is more important than your team.

Part Two of this book will go into some of the key elements of running the people side of your company—from team building and culture to the full cycle of employment (recruiting, hiring, onboarding, feedback and performance management, compensation, promoting, rewarding, and firing), to a discussion of the very real and growing challenge of managing remote employees.

CHAPTER SEVEN

FIELDING A GREAT TEAM

Once you graduate from being a gang of cofounders to being a real company, it's time to start the most important job you'll ever do: hiring. Your company will grow only if you create the best and brightest team you can. And after you hire your team, you immediately have to think about scaling it.

Hiring isn't just your most important job—it's also your hardest.

FROM PROTOZOA TO PANCREAS

Our board member Greg Sands once compared the phenomenon of companies growing out of the startup stage to cell development in small organisms. Amoeba or paramecia consist of one cell, and that cell has to do everything: eat, move, sense its surroundings, and respond accordingly. When the cell divides, the new cells still need to do everything—they're just attached to other cells. But as organisms grow more complex, individual cells need to specialize. And when things get *really* complex, you need a liver, a spleen, a stomach, and a pancreas.

By and large, startups work the same way. In the early stages, you have to hire generalists who are both willing and able to take on dozens of tasks at once. Your developers will have to speak with potential customers; your accountants will have to give advice on product direction; and the born salesman on your team will need to put the phone down a few hours a day and set up a new employee's computer.

This is the exciting, four-people-and-an-idea stage popularly associated with startups—but it doesn't last very long. For a lot of your employees, growing out of this phase will be a welcome development: programmers don't want to be in accounting meetings, and salespeople don't want to sit in a dark, quiet room with the engineers. People have talents and skills they want to develop, and a healthy degree of specialization allows them to do that.

Not *everybody* will be happy: one developer left Return Path when we started bursting at the seams with 25 people. (He felt that things were getting "too corporate." Seriously.) Most of your team members should be prepared for this moment and ready to take on their new roles.

THE BEST AND THE BRIGHTEST

Building your team is critical, and you probably have to do almost all of the heavy lifting yourself in the early days: you don't yet have a recruiter or an HR department, and no one can sell the vision of your company better than you can. Since you probably can't pay a ton of money for talent, selling your vision—and the value of stock options—is a key part of team building. Every chapter in this section will touch on ways that you can build, develop, and lead an effective team. If I had to distill hundreds of best practices to a single piece of advice, it would be this: *build the best team you possibly can as early as you possibly can.*

This may seem completely obvious, but surrounding yourself with the best and the brightest can be daunting—or even threatening—to some CEOs. You have no choice: this is something you *have* to do to grow your business, and something you have to *keep* doing to continue growing.

This is how to do it:

- *Pay attention to cultural fit.* Finding the best possible employees for your team means finding the best possible employees *for your team.* The second part of that sentence is too often neglected. The world's greatest Perl developer isn't going to add much value to your company if he can't work with your team.
- *Find outstanding specialists.* As the CEO, you're probably the best generalist at your company. Very soon, you're going to be surrounded by specialists who are older, wiser, more experienced, and more expensive than you are. That's an important part of building a great team. Unless you happen to be the best coder in the world *and* the best salesperson *and* the best accountant, you want to start fielding a great team early.
- *Complement your weaknesses.* If you hire people who complement your strengths, you'll never grow. Do the opposite: shore up your weaknesses with people who excel where your talents are lacking. Of course, that means you'll have to *admit* your weaknesses and embrace

team members who are strong in those areas. (I'm not a world-class product visionary; my co-founder George Bilbrey is.)

- *Don't hire up* ***too*** *much.* You want the best people you can find, but that doesn't necessarily mean the biggest corporate guns you can afford. These types of employees are highly likely to fail at a startup. They're used to clearly defined roles and plenty of resources. Startups have neither. At one of the places I worked earlier in my career, another technology company, the new head of marketing, with impeccable experience at Fortune 500 companies, showed up for his first day of work and asked everyone where the typing pool was. That was the first sign of trouble. You might be tempted to break this rule for salespeople. Don't. A Rolodex doesn't matter if salespeople aren't willing to sell a vision on whiteboard—rather than relying on PDF marketing documents produced to support a beta-tested release.
- *Check references carefully:* Don't get suckered in by resumes. Plenty of successful big-company people don't actually know how to build a business—or really do any work. To validate their claims, you need to dig deep and find some back-channel references.
- *Let your team have input on your team.* Hiring is the most important part of your job, but you can't do it alone. When you're hiring specialists, you need someone who knows more about that area—an engineer, an accountant, a lawyer—to vet their expertise. And nothing better assures a tight cultural fit than an enthusiastic thumbs up from the rest of your team.

Now for the really intimidating part: you're still the CEO. Even after hiring very experienced and talented people into specialized roles, you still have to manage every functional area on your team—even those experts who are older, wiser, more experienced, and more expensive than you are.

Foundry Group VC Brad Feld on Hiring and Managing within Your Area of Expertise

If I have a hiring Achilles' heel, it's marketing. Before starting Return Path, I was VP of marketing and product management at MovieFone and we have struggled with our head of marketing position over the years. Having worked with dozens of CEOs in his career, Brad Feld has seen this same pattern at work many times.

I've always observed that CEOs have two contrary positions with regard to execs that they are hiring. The first is "hire people who know more than me," and the other is "I know how to do this." When these two thoughts collide, it often results in underhiring in the areas where the CEO thinks, "I know how to do this": CEOs who come from sales tend to underhire the VP of sales; CEOs who come from marketing underhire the VP of marketing, and technical CEOs underhire the VP of engineering.

Furthermore, once they've hired this person, they tend to overmanage or undermine them. The CEO who is awesome at marketing either doesn't get out of the way and let the VP of marketing do his job, or the CEO completely disengages, leaving the VP of marketing to "prove that he's got the goods." Or, worst of all, the CEO vacillates between these two extremes, sometimes over managing, sometimes disengaging—but never setting a consistent tone or rhythm for engagement.

When this is a risk, the best thing the CEO can do is rely on his management team to vet and hire the person in the relevant position. The team needs someone who has strong competence, will stand up to the CEO, but will also fit culturally with the rest of the team. If there's a pattern of this person not working out, the senior team needs to be enlisted—optimally by the CEO—to own the hire and help the person succeed.

Of course, there's another option: do it yourself! Hire a junior person to handle administrative tasks and prove your expertise in sales, marketing, engineering—what have you. This isn't always possible, but it's a better option than hamstringing an executive you don't respect.

Brad Feld, Managing Director, Foundry Group

WHAT ABOUT HR?

I'm a big believer in hiring a rock star head of HR early in the company's life. I don't mean someone to handle the transactional aspects of HR—payroll, benefits, that sort of thing. You need a strategic partner to help you craft your organization and be a co-steward of your culture.

It's hard to say exactly when you should make this hire. In theory, the earlier the better. I tried adding this role when we were at 20 people and expecting to reach 100 within a year. If we'd actually grown that quickly, I probably could have used the role at that time, but we stumbled, and then we had to repurpose our HR head into another role. For most companies, hiring a great head of HR is doable at about 50 people; by 100, you're probably too late.

You can't think of this hire as a purely transactional relationship—a salary of "x" for a value of "2x" or "3x" or "4x." That might work for junior salespeople and account managers, but your HR head is going to be your alter ego on culture, a strategic partner as important as your cofounders, investors, or board members.

Who Are Your CPO and COO?

Every senior management team needs a CPO and a COO. No, I'm not talking about privacy and operations. I'm talking about paranoia and optimism. On my leadership team at Return Path, many of us are paranoid, many of us are optimistic, and many of us can play both roles. But I'm fortunate to have two business partners who are the chiefs—George Bilbrey is our chief paranoia officer and Anita Absey is our chief optimism officer. Those monikers fit their respective roles (product and sales) as well as their personalities.

My view is simple: both traits are critical to have around the management table, and they're best when they're in some kind of equilibrium. Optimism keeps you running forward in a straight line. The belief that you can successfully execute on your plan, with a spring in your step and a smile on your face, is very motivating. Paranoia keeps you looking around corners. It may also keep you awake at night, but it's the driving force for seeing potential threats to the business that aren't necessarily obvious and keeping you on your toes.

Too much of either trait would be a disaster for a team's psyche, but both are critical points of view that need a loud voice in any management discussion. It's a little bit like making sure your management team knows its actual and target location along the fear/greed continuum.

WHAT ABOUT SALES AND MARKETING?

One of the most frequent questions I get from fellow entrepreneurs is when they should hire heads of marketing (if they're business-to-consumer [B2C]) or sales (if they're business-to-business [B2B]).

This isn't a technicality, like deciding when to advance from a freelance CPA to an in-house CFO. It's a loaded question: what these CEOs are really asking is, "When do I have to turn outside and start focusing on my customers?"

The answer to this question is probably "yesterday." In the world of customer development, sales and marketing aren't afterthoughts; they should be baked in from Day 1.

When you hire a head of revenue depends entirely on how reliant your business is on external relationship building (in the case of a B2B media or service business) or online marketing testing and planning (in the case of an e-commerce business). Here are three factors to consider:

1. *If your company requires significant customer participation before your initial product is launched, you need to invest in sales months ahead of anticipated revenue.* This was the case for us at Return Path. We hired our first head of sales five months before our anticipated launch because we needed to have 10 to 12 beta customers on board in order to have a successful launch.
2. *If you are a natural born salesperson yourself, you can afford to wait.* However, you can't handle all sales calls yourself. When you find yourself failing to call back high-value prospects within a single business day, it's definitely time to bring someone in. This is especially true if you're in a buzz business where you have prospects calling *you* to ask if they can try out your product.
3. *If you need a head of sales right now, it's too late.* Finding a sales head can take a few months. Determine when you will need someone, and start your recruiting efforts two to three months earlier. It's good to spend a lot of time in the early stages of your company's life selling. But it's not good to spend *all* of your time selling.

Teams of Rivals

Leading a successful management team isn't just about managing individuals; it's about making sure the team functions well *as a team*. Teams in business need to explore all options and consider multiple opinions before making a decision. A management team that finds itself 100 percent in agreement 100 percent of the time is in trouble. A management team that can have disagreements and use that tension productively to drive decisions is much better off. Building such a team requires the CEO to seek out executives who view the world differently, who have the courage to speak their minds in the face of strong opposition, and who have the ability to see different points of view.

My two favorite models for this are from the political world: the very successful presidential administrations of Abraham Lincoln and George Washington.

Derided by his political opponents as a "second-rate Illinois lawyer," Lincoln, who arrived somewhat rapidly and unexpectedly on the national scene at a time of supreme crisis, not only rose to the occasion; he became one of the greatest political leaders of all time. Lincoln clearly had his faults (he waited too long to fire his incompetent generals) but one of his greatest strengths was his ability to co-opt most of his political rivals and get them to join his cabinet, effectively neutering them politically while building a "unity government." This is why Doris Kearns Goodwin's biography of Lincoln is called *Team of Rivals*.

This stands in subtle but important contrast to George Washington, who filled his cabinet with men who were rivals to each other (Hamilton, Jefferson) but who never overtly challenged Washington himself.

Does the "Team of Rivals" concept, in either its Lincoln or Washington forms, have a place in your business? I'd say rarely in the Lincoln sense, but quite often in the Washington sense.

Lincoln, in order to be effective, didn't have much of a choice. Bringing Seward, Chase, and Bates on board was the only way to bring regional and philosophical representation to his cabinet at a time of national crisis. There certainly could be times when corporate leadership calls for a representative executive team or board, for example, in a massive merger with uncertain integration or in a scary turnaround. Other than extreme circumstances like that, the Lincoln model is probably a recipe for weak, undermined leadership—and heartache for the boss.

Managed closely, the Washington model can be quite effective for a company. One could argue that Washington didn't manage the seething Hamilton and frothy Jefferson closely enough but the reality is that the debates between the two of them in the founding days of our government forged better national unity and just plain better results than Washington would have achieved with a cabinet made up of like-minded individuals.

As a CEO, hearing divergent opinion is critical, and it's critical to have team members who feel comfortable challenging your perspective. Your job is ***not*** to create compromises that appease all factions, but to hear multiple, well-articulated points of view as inputs to a decision you have to make. You and your company will end up with far, far better results.

SCALING YOUR TEAM OVER TIME

When Return Path reached 100 employees, our board basically told me that management teams never scale intact as you grow the business. "Someone always breaks." I'm sure that was largely true in their experience. Of course, my team and I took this as a challenge. Ever since then, my senior management team and I have become obsessed with scaling ourselves. Here's what we've done so far.

1. *We appreciate the importance of excellent management.* Management is a completely different skill set from everything else you've learned in your career. Before you can excel at it, you have to recognize the challenge. Here's how you get there:
   a. Management is important.
   b. Management is a unique skill set.
   c. You might not be great at it.

   If you're an overachiever who likes to excel in everything (I haven't met a startup CEO who isn't), then you are setting the stage for the next item on the list.
2. *We consistently work at improving our management skills.* We have a strong culture of 360-degree feedback, development plans, and post-mortems on major incidents—both as individuals and as a senior team. Over the years, most of us have engaged on and off with an executive coach. (My coach, Marc Maltz from Triad Consulting, contributed to Part Five of this book.) At our quarterly off-site meeting, we hold each other accountable for individual performance against our development plans. Learning from the inside is only part of the process.
3. *We learn from the successes and failures of others.* My team devotes significant time to researching our competitors and partners to understand how peers at other companies—preferably ones either like us or larger—operate. We methodically pick our benchmarking candidates, ask for their time and get on their calendars. We share knowledge and best practices back with them. We pay this forward to smaller companies when they ask us for help. And we incorporate the relevant learnings back into our day-to-day work.
4. *We build the strongest possible second-level management bench we can.* Every executive team needs a broad base of leadership and management that complements its own skills. The danger is that you'll

accumulate mediocre managers over the years by promoting your top performers into roles that are higher profile and higher comp—though ones for which they're completely unprepared and unsuited. Don't simply rely on external hires to mitigate this risk. Develop your team to be effective managers. Make no mistake about it—this is a huge investment of time and money. (See Chapter 12 for more on development.) But it's well worth the expense. The alternative is a culture without the possibility of advancement—with predictable effects on your team's motivation.

5. *We are hawkish about hiring from the outside.* That said, sometimes expanding companies require more executives and managers than they can produce internally, even if everyone on the team is scaling well. There are significant perils with hiring from the outside. The *biggest* risk is allowing ineffective managers to stick around and cause difficulties. Your culture is important. Your people are important. New managers at any level instantly become stewards of both. If they are failing as managers, then they need to leave. Now.

Vibrant Media CEO Cella Irvine on Scaling an Executive Team

Cella Irvine, CEO of Vibrant Media and former CEO of About.com, has built two successful executive teams. She knows what it takes to find the right people, and about the tough decisions a CEO needs to make to keep the right team over time.

There is no better predictor of company success than relationships: the relationship of the CEO to the senior executive team, of the senior executives to one another, and of the senior executives to the business. Build a successful team, and you'll build a successful business. Build a dysfunctional team, and you'll wish you'd become a math teacher.

Highly functional team relationships share three common characteristics:

- *Support.* The leadership team supports one another, and seeks support from one another. They keep Machiavelli where he belongs—in the school library.
- *Trust.* Team members consistently demonstrate their willingness to trust one another, and show their ability to be trustworthy.

- *Value.* Each member of the team adds value to the business because they consistently manage their area at the level required for company success, and add to the company's strategic thinking.

If you're building your company's first team, hire the team that is capable of doing what needs to be done in the next 24 months. Many people will advise you to hire ahead; do that, and you'll have a team that is less willing or able to get you to the 12-month mark. Hire only those people whom you're genuinely excited to bring on board. If you have any doubts, pass. Use contractors or consultants if necessary.

Every six months, evaluate for the next 12 months. Take your most forthright advisor or board member, and set aside three hours to talk through your plans and your team. Identify staffing gaps—areas where you didn't need someone four months back but will in five months' time. Start recruiting 160 days before you need that person on board. Find the talent gaps, in which capable team members have some but not all of the capabilities needed to succeed in the next 12 months. For them, invest in development; coaching looks expensive, but compared to having to replace a potentially highly capable leader, it's pennies. And, thankfully, you'll see colleagues who are thriving.

This kind of team doesn't spontaneously generate; it's nurtured into existence. With enough time spent together you'll evolve into a unit, rely on one another, and come to care for one another.

However, that closeness is both a blessing and a curse because the team that's right for the launch of your company will rarely be the right team two years later. Many people will evolve with the company. Inevitably there will be team members who haven't evolved with the company, or are no longer on board with your vision, or who, perhaps because they prefer the startup phase of a company, have started to create friction.

Almost certainly, you will need to let go of or, worse, demote someone who was an essential part of your company's early success. First-time CEOs are often slow to make changes in their teams. Don't be. The risk of keeping the wrong person on board is far greater than the risk of change, which brings us to the First Golden Rule of CEO-dom: Leave enough distance, always, between you and your direct reports. You need to evaluate them, give them negative feedback and, if necessary, fire them. Doing those things effectively requires some level of distance.

Your senior team may be your company's most valuable asset. Give it the care and attention it needs. Having a great team will make you a better CEO.

Cella Irvine, CEO, Vibrant Media

Management Moment

Avoid a Culture of Consensus

Achieving consensus is critical from time to time on important cultural decisions. As important as collaboration is, it can't be your dominant modus operandi as CEO or your company will quickly devolve into a culture of consensus.

You have to make decisions and use a more authoritative style from time to time, or every answer will be a watered-down compromise. You can't abuse that style, but you do have to make decisions. Don't just average out what everyone else thinks—or, worse, not move things forward because someone disagrees.

Too much compromise or too much rule by fiat is unhealthy for an organization because either paralysis or gridlock will ensue. Find the right balance.

CHAPTER EIGHT

THE CEO AS FUNCTIONAL SUPERVISOR

When it comes to talent, your primary role as CEO is to be the leader of the team as a team. You have to set an example, define the culture and create alignment across the organization, from executives to marketing interns. You also have to be a "functional supervisor" of every department at your company. Each presents a unique challenge.

RULES FOR GENERAL MANAGERS

The CEO's role in leading any particular function varies greatly with the CEO's experience. What follows are instructions that apply generally to all kinds of CEOs as the general managers of their companies.

- *Supervising sales.* One of your most important roles is to be a sales leader. This isn't an issue for many business-to-consumer (B2C) companies, but it's essential at business-to-business (B2B) companies. You have to know many of the customers yourself and you'll be personally involved in closing a number of key deals and maintaining customer relationships. Even if you don't have major enterprise deals, knowing your customers and visiting them from time to time is an important part of being "in-market." For my part, I always tell our sales reps that I will go on any client call, at any time, as many times as I'm needed.
- *Supervising business development.* Great salespeople can close deals, with or without the CEO, but strategic business partnerships are more nuanced. They are about executive connections and a shared

vision—things that CEOs should be able to communicate particularly well.

- *Supervising marketing.* A CEO doesn't have to do much to support sales in a B2C company. That doesn't mean they've got extra time on their calendar: in a B2C company, marketing is the main driver of revenue, and supervising marketing is the CEOs most important job. Keep an eye on every detail of marketing, from high-level messaging and positioning to key search engine optimization (SEO) and search engine marketing (SEM) metrics. Once your company has a chief marketing officer (CMO), you'll have a new challenge. For more than a decade, CMOs have had the shortest tenure in the C-suite (the current average is about 20 months). This is a difficult role, especially as online advertising and quantitative advertising continue to revolutionize marketing.
- *Supervising finance.* There are two financial tasks that a CEO (rather than a chief financial officer) needs to take the lead on. The first is guaranteeing the accuracy and timeliness of all financial reporting. You won't produce these yourself, but you have to vouch for them. You also have to set the tone for paying vendors. At one of my prior companies, management viewed every invoice as the starting point for a negotiation and never paid a bill on time. That's one approach. At Return Path, we negotiate prices hard in advance and pay our bills on time. Whatever approach you choose, communicate it and stick to it.
- *Supervising legal.* A solid legal team will protect you from liability risks by forcing you to do things "by the book." What they won't do is protect you from "over-lawyering," which is expensive and restrictive. The CEO's job is to make it clear that the lawyers report to the businesspeople, and not the other way around. They're called "counselors" for a reason. Another CEO I know used to say to his lawyer, "Your job is to keep me out of jail, and that's about it." I'm not sure that's the right approach either, but it certainly kept that CEO's legal bills down.
- *Supervising product.* You don't have to be a technical CEO. But you do have to be attuned to product-market fit. That's the root of your business direction and your go-to-market approach. And while you may not be able to comment on database infrastructure, you have to pay close attention to the end-to-end customer experience. This often gets lost in the shuffle in companies with large product teams.
- *Supervising operations.* Depending on your company, the CEO's role in operations varies greatly. If you're not in an operationally intensive

vertical like manufacturing, you can be hands off: have ops report to someone else, and just manage the metrics. If your company *is* operationally intensive, ops will be a key competitive differentiator. Pay attention to every detail.

- *Supervising human resources.* CEOs are often tempted to make HR a junior position that reports to Finance. But as I wrote in the previous chapter, your HR head is one of your most important strategic partners. Even if you're not a touchy-feely people person, you can't overdelegate cultural stewardship. Recruiting and onboarding are essential CEO tasks that pay huge dividends. At Return Path, our most senior HR person has always reported to me. I will never run an organization any other way.

If you are a product inventor who wrote the company's first code base, you're going to have a different relationship with your engineering and product team than a CEO whose last job was as a head of marketing. Whatever your specific background, you have to supervise every department in your company.

Return Path CTO Andy Sautins on Being a Nontechnical CEO of a Technology Company

Over the course of my career, I've been everything from a management consultant to a marketing lead—but I've never been an engineer or a developer. I did write a lot of code once, but it was Basic (and BasicA) on a TRS-80, and the year was 1982. This presents unique challenges when leading a company as technical as Return Path, but that challenge has been made far easier with the support of my long-time CTO Andy Sautins.

Nontechnical CEOs need to balance driving the goals of the business with sympathy for the problems faced by the technical team. As a technical person, I understand the need to get product out the door, but it can be extremely frustrating to hear someone nontechnical say "Can't you just...?" Can't you just add a feature by tomorrow? Can't you just scale to handle 100× the load? These may seem simple to a nontechnical person but are actually quite challenging.

There are also times when the technical team may feel that work is necessary that just doesn't make sense to you. For example, your team could come to you and say they need to "refactor some code" to make it more maintainable. You want to trust your engineers, but your gut tells you that "refactoring" isn't as important as getting a new feature out the door.

How do you balance listening to your technical team with challenging them when you feel that they're getting lost in the details? I've found two things to be particularly effective:

1. *Leverage your network of CEOs.* It's important for you to have a wide view of what is done in other organizations. While these organizations may be different, they face many of the same challenges that you do. If a given technical challenge just doesn't sit right, use your peers to find the right answer. For example, if your technical team says it will take four months to implement a feature that you feel shouldn't take longer than two months, test your intuition against your peer companies. Is this something they've faced in the past? How long did it take them to implement similar features?
2. *Have your technical team talk with other teams that have aggressive goals.* Involving peer companies not only helps you sanity-check your perspective, but can also bring new ideas you and your technical team haven't considered before.

Embrace the fact that you are a nontechnical CEO working with a technical team. Work with your technical team to understand each other's strengths and weaknesses. While it's important for you to understand the challenges your technical team is facing, it's also important to keep the other areas of your business—such as sales, marketing, and finance—moving forward. With both sides understanding and respecting what the other brings to the table, you have a much better chance of implementing your vision.

Andy Sautins, CTO, Return Path

Management Moment

Don't Be the Grand Lemming

Some people say that successful leadership is figuring out where everyone is going and then getting in front of them and saying "follow me." While it's certainly true that jumping out in front of a well-organized, rapidly moving parade and becoming the Grand Marshal is one path to successful leadership, CEOs have to be careful about selecting the right parade to jump in front of.

The fact that lots of people are going in a specific direction doesn't mean it's the right direction: lots of smart people thought home delivery of a stick of gum made sense and was worth investing in, but CNET has called Webvan "the largest dot-com flop in history." And, even if the parade is a good one, the organization you run might not be best equipped to take advantage of it: Gerry Levin and Steve Case fell in love with convergence story, but in the end the company ended up breaking up into its original components a decade later. There's nothing good about ending up as the Grand Lemming instead of the Grand Marshal. It just means you go over the cliff before the rest of the troops.

CHAPTER NINE

CRAFTING YOUR COMPANY'S CULTURE

Return Path has a very distinct culture, and I'm not going to prescribe it as *the* culture you should build for your own company. Any number of cultures can lead to success. The essential point is to realize that *every* company has a culture, whether it's a deliberate enactment of the company's values or an accidental accretion of behaviors and vibes. Don't let the latter creep up on you. Whatever you do, be deliberate!

INTRODUCING FIG WASP 879

I always draw on great business books to become a better CEO, but it was in a book on evolutionary biology, *Climbing Mount Improbable* by Richard Dawkins, that I found a rich metaphor that is applicable to business in many ways.

There are over 900 kinds of fig trees in the world. Who knew? I was dimly aware there was such a thing as a fig tree, although quite frankly I'm most familiar with the fig in its Newton format.

Some species reproduce wildly inefficiently—like wild grasses, whose pollen is spread through the air; with a lot of luck, one in a billion (with a "b") lands in the right place at the right time and propagates. At the opposite end of the spectrum stands the fig tree. Not only do fig trees reproduce by relying on the collaboration of fig wasps to transport their pollen from one to the next, but there are over 900 different kinds of fig wasps—one per tree species. Only the right kind of fig wasp can successfully help pollinate a given fig tree (fig wasp 879 is a distinct species: somewhere between *Acophila mikii* and *Wiebesia vidua*.) The two have evolved together over thousands of millennia, and while we humans might take the uninformed view that a fig tree is a fig tree, fig wasps have clearly figured out how to differentiate one species from another, all in the name of propagation.

So what the heck does this have to do with business? Plenty, but I want to focus on the lessons about business culture first.

I assume that not only would most of us not be able to discern one tree or wasp type from another, but that we also wouldn't be able to discern any of the 900+ types of trees or wasps from thousands or hundreds of thousands or millions of types of trees or bugs in general! Here's the thing: I know hundreds of Internet companies. I know dozens of *email* companies. And I can tell you within five minutes of walking around the place or meeting an executive which ones I'd be able to work for, and which ones I wouldn't. The older and bigger the company, the more distinct and deeply rooted its culture becomes. The lesson: cultivate your company's culture with same level of care and attention to detail that you would your family—regardless of your role or level in the company!

Return Path SVP of People Angela Baldonero on Saying No to Status Quo

Every startup lives or dies by its team. Products are important, but people come first. Below, Angela Baldonero, my long-time business partner as our Senior Vice President of People , talks about some of the things she believes define a great "people-first" company.

This is an exciting time to start a company, and it's an even more exciting time to build an incredible culture and workplace where people can create, connect, and contribute.

It's relatively easy to create a standard, if better-than-average, company, with fun perks and all the systems and programs that you're *supposed to* implement as you grow. As you hire more people in more locations and set them to work on increasingly complex problems, you will want to create some level of structure to maintain efficiency and avoid duplication of effort. In order to create something extraordinary, CEOs must resist the average, common-sense policies, systems, and procedures.

A new world of work is being born around us. In this new world, most traditional HR practices are ineffective and irrelevant. Instead, there are four key areas you should focus on:

1. *Say no to useless brilliance.* We've all worked with that brilliant person whom an organization thinks it cannot live without. Unfortunately, that brilliant person can't communicate or work on a team. So, most organizations put them in a box in an attempt to minimize the damage they inflict. It never works: the boxes pile up, and so do the silos. And no matter how well constructed the box is, that brilliant person can demotivate 20 co-workers—without contributing much in their silo. It's not worth it.
2. *Say no to policy paralysis.* Policies and rules are created to guard against people doing stupid things to control time and resources. Examples: paid time off, sick time, expense policies, specified work hours, social media guidelines, dress codes, and—my favorite—"the code of ethics." The reality is that 99 percent of your people will make great decisions every day as long as they have clear direction. Misses can be resolved quickly with a clarifying conversation. Instead of locking things down, set them free: say no to creating a policy for every situation you might encounter. Instead, experiment with trusting people to use their judgment.
3. *Say no to values dilution.* This is the toughest category and the one that requires the most courage. Saying no to things that conflict with your organization's values is essential to ensuring that your culture lives and thrives. For example, if you value transparency, then you need to commit to sharing the good, the bad, and the ugly openly (and often). Making endless exceptions will quickly lead to meaningless values posted on the wall.
4. *Say no to executive dysfunction.* We've all seen the all-important and all-knowing executive team—the team that has all the answers but somehow isn't able to execute. I've seen too many executive teams where personal relationships and politics are the real behind-the-scenes drivers. Business is done after hours, over cocktails, and not in broad daylight. Personal agendas trump team goals. People smile and nod politely in meetings, then leave and tell you what they "really think." Don't allow this. Be fiercely committed to the health of the executive team. Check in with each other on individual and team development, and be rigorous about giving each other feedback and holding each other accountable. Be brutally honest with one another and exhaustive about looking in the mirror. Say no to executive dysfunction, personal

agendas, and being too busy to live your values. It will be the best team you've ever worked with.

As your company grows and scales, you have a critical choice to make. The temptation is to lock things down—to create guidelines that will ensure that bad decisions are averted. Don't get caught up in the "What if someone screws up or makes a bad decision?" discussion. Turn the conversation around and focus on your best people. What if everything you do is focused on your top performers? The people you trust? The people who make great decisions? The people who can think critically and creatively and can handle a bit of ambiguity?'

Set your people free to focus on important, high-impact work and solve challenging business problems. That's how companies will win now.

Angela Baldonero, SVP of People, Return Path

SIX LEGS AND A PAIR OF WINGS

I opened this section by claiming that I wouldn't insist on one type of culture over another. You can be fig wasp 328, 236, or 812. Just choose the one that matches your tree.

It's time to qualify that statement somewhat. There are certain values that every company should have—just like every fig wasp has six legs and a pair of wings. If you want your company to be a world-class organization, there are two things you absolutely need: respect for your people and an environment of trust. You can succeed financially without those things to some degree, especially if your business is taking off due to market forces and timing. But why would you want to merely succeed when you could be great?

LET PEOPLE BE PEOPLE

I strongly believe that work-life balance is critical. (For complementary viewpoints, see Danny Meyer's contribution to Part Five on self-management, and *Startup Life* by Brad Feld and Amy Batchelor.) I've worked in a grind-it-out 100-hour-per-week environment. Quite frankly, it sucks. One week

I actually filled in 121 on my hourly time sheet as a consultant. If you've never calculated the denominator, it's only 168. Even being well paid as a first-year analyst out of college, the hourly rate was dreadful. Thinking about that 121 gives me the shivers today—and it certainly puts those 40, 50, 60, even 70-hour work weeks in perspective. All of those still let you have a life. An average week of 40 hours probably doesn't make sense for a high-growth company of relatively well-paid knowledge workers. At 121, you barely get to shower and sleep.

While you may get a lot done working like a dog, you don't get a lot more done hour for hour relative to productive people do in a 50-hour-per-week environment. Certainly not twice as much. People who say they thrive on that kind of pressure are simply lying—or, to be fair, not lying but rationalizing the amount of time they spend at work. Your productivity simply diminishes after some number of hours. As a CEO, even a hard-charging one, I think it's better to focus on creating a productive environment than an environment of sustained long hours.

Work has ebbs and flows just like life has ebbs and flows. As long as the work generally gets done well and when you need it, you have to assume that sometimes people will work long hours in bursts, and sometimes people will work fewer hours. Work-life balance is not measured in days or even weeks, but over the long term. To that end, I've always believed in "letting people be people" as a means of trading off freedom and flexibility for high levels of performance and accountability. At Return Path, we have always tried to create an environment where people can be people by:

- Giving generous maternity leave and paternity leave, at least relative to norms in the United States.
- Having a flexible "work from home" policy.
- Allowing even more flexible work conditions for anyone, and especially new parents: three or four days per week if we can make it work (with salaries reduced pro rata).
- Letting people take a six-week paid sabbatical after seven years, then every five years after that.
- Having an "open vacation" policy where people can take as much vacation as they want, as long as they get their jobs done.

The result of this philosophy is that we have an incredibly productive environment where people have fun, lead their lives, and still get their jobs done well and on time. The details of your own policies can vary, as long as they reflect an essential respect for your team members' lives.

BUILD AN ENVIRONMENT OF TRUST

Trust is the bedrock of relationships. Relationships are the bedrock of an organization. Anything you can do to foster trust strengthens your organization. At the end of the day, transparency, authenticity, and caring create an environment of trust.

What are some examples of that?

- Go over the actual board slides after every board meeting, letting everyone in the company know what was discussed.
- Communicate bad news early and often. People are less freaked out, and the rumor mill won't take over.
- Manage like a hawk. It's important to get rid of poor performers or cultural misfits early, even if it's painful. You can never fire someone too soon.
- Follow all the rules yourself. For example, have relatively modest offices and constantly demonstrate that no task or chore is beneath you—filling the Coke machine, changing the water bottle, cleaning up after a group lunch, packing a box, carrying something heavy.
- When a team has to work a weekend, we're there, too—in person or virtually—even if it's just to show our appreciation.
- When something really goes wrong, you as CEO need to take all the blame.
- When something really goes right, you as CEO need to give all the credit away.

This needs to apply to all your managers, not just the CEO. Your job? Manage everyone to these standards.

Return Path Board Member and IronPort Systems Founder and CEO Scott Weiss on Being a Strong Yet Approachable Leader

Some CEOs run command-and-control startups with strict hierarchies and very little in the way of CEO sociability. Return Path isn't like that. I work hard to be approachable, but, as one leader put it, "the buck stops here." Scott Weiss, founder and CEO of IronPort (acquired by Cisco in 2007) offers his advice about how CEOs can strike that balance.

The best leaders I know are not only smart and decisive; they create an environment where everyone feels comfortable challenging them. This is really hard because it is often assumed that the CEO is the smartest person in the room. However, if he acts that way, he'll never get the feedback necessary to make great decisions. So how does one balance being a strong and approachable leader? Here are a number of practical things that I've found helpful:

- *Be self-aware.* All leaders need feedback. Having an understanding of how others perceive you—through a solid 360-review process—is the crucial first step toward being real. Learn and accept your foibles and faults. Poke fun and work on them out in the open. "I'll try to keep this short, I know I can be long-winded. . ." etc.
- *Talk about failures.* At IronPort, we used to go through exhaustive post-mortems—on everything from customer losses to engineering slips to misplaced strategies—and nothing helps make a leader more approachable than admitting their struggles, screw-ups, and behind-the-scenes thinking on hard calls. If leaders make this a priority, the whole company will be more open to learning from failure.
- *Make it clear that no chore is beneath you.* Naturally and quietly demonstrate this, on a regular basis: clean up after a conference room lunch, carry the heavy crap to a trade show, replace the water cooler, wipe up a spill. When everyone pitches in a little, you can strip out 5 percent in overhead.
- *Learn everybody's name, and something about them.* Up to 500 people with no excuses. This was really hard for me because I have always had a terrible memory. Get creative: when I inherited 900 employees at Cisco, we printed out flashcards from the badge database.
- *Show up to socialize.* Have a beer bust on Friday afternoons. Take a team to lunch. Drop in on a late-night networked video game war. (As a newbie, I was slaughtered pretty quickly.) You must go out of your way to socialize with your team, especially if you're naturally an introvert.
- *Embrace "professional intimacy."* I love this phrase: it describes a leader's willingness to get personal and talk about life at home or their own career struggles. ("My wife once threw my blackberry in the toilet.") Nothing builds more trust than being open and vulnerable with the people you lead.
- *Nix multitask listening.* It's one thing to ask someone what they are working on, and another to really tune in, give them your full attention and ask follow up questions. I constantly see executives checking their watches or

smartphones, or looking over a shoulder to see who else is in the room. That's just phony crap.

- *Loosen up!* This is really about speaking to others as though you really trust them with your thoughts versus reverting to canned responses or the "company line." Leaders that can explore the poles of an issue with employees—in their own words and off the cuff—will gain real trust. This is especially true during all hands company meetings.
- *Improve your speaking skills*. As a CEO, if you are a nervous public speaker, you need to practice. Find a coach; do some videotaping; try Toastmasters. The goal is to have a marathoner's heartbeat when speaking to a crowd so as to be as natural and comfortable as possible.
- *Finally, embrace different views*. Encourage employees to challenge your approach and decisions. Let everyone know that you aren't perfect and that you don't always have the best answer. Sometimes, they have better answers! You are obviously the decision maker but embracing different views will improve openness."

Scott Weiss, Return Path Board Member and IronPort Systems Founder and CEO

Management Moment

Admit Mistakes

At a presidential debate with John Kerry in 2004, George W. Bush stunned viewers by refusing to admit that he had ever made any big mistakes in life other than trading Sammy Sosa when he owned the Texas Rangers. This was well after it had been settled that the decision to go to war with Iraq was based on faulty intelligence information about the imminent danger posed by weapons of mass destruction!

Today's highly polarized political environment discourages politicians from admitting mistakes, and it will take an exceptionally courageous leader to do so. Publicly admitting a mistake as CEO, along with a careful distillation of lessons learned, can go a long way toward strengthening the bond between leader and team, regardless of the size of the company. It encourages risk taking and learning, two skills you want everyone in your organization to have.

CHAPTER TEN

THE HIRING CHALLENGE

Getting a job at Return Path is harder than getting into a good college. We have 400 employees, but we got there by identifying 30,000 potential hires, vetting them, negotiating a deal with the ones we liked, implementing a rigorous, 90-day onboarding process, and capping it off with a 90-day review to make sure that they'll make it over the long haul. All the while, our competitors were trying to do the exact same thing—as were hundreds of other companies drawing from the same pool of talent. It's no wonder that hiring is one of the many full-time jobs you take on when you become a startup CEO.

UNIQUE CHALLENGES FOR STARTUPS

Retaining good people has always been at the top of my list, even in the dark days. But hiring presents some real challenges. Many of these aren't unique to startups—it's always tough to find A players—but there are three things I've observed that are uniquely tough about hiring in an entrepreneurial environment:

- *Defining the job properly*. Most job postings at growth companies are for newly created positions, and even jobs that are open for replacements have usually changed since the original job was created. A clear, crisp job definition is an essential first step in the recruiting process. But more than just spending the time to write out bullet points for key responsibilities, hiring managers in startups need to do two important things. First, they should recognize that today's job definition may evolve over time, and make a determination about what level of generalist versus specialist makes the most sense for the position. Second, vet the job description with anyone inside the company with whom the new employee will interact, in order to get everyone on the same page with the roles, responsibilities, and the inevitable changes to existing roles and processes caused by the addition of someone new into the mix.

- *Finding the time to do it right.* Most managers in small companies are at least a little overworked. Most cash-sensitive small companies don't want to hire new people until it's absolutely necessary—or until it was absolutely necessary about a month ago. This mismatch means that the hiring manager is even more overworked than usual by the time the organization has decided to add someone, and can't find the time to go through the whole process of job definition, recruiting, interviewing, and training. This is one of the biggest traps I've seen startups fall prey to, and the only way to break the cycle is for hiring managers to make the new hire process their number one priority. Prepare your colleagues to accept reduced output in exchange for longer-term gains of leverage and increased responsibility.
- *Remembering that the hiring process doesn't end on the employee's first day.* I always think about the employee's first day as the midpoint of the hiring process. The things that come after the first day—orientation (where's the bathroom?), context-setting (here's our mission, here's how your job furthers it), goal setting (what's your 90-day plan?), and a formal check-in 90 days later—are all make-or-break in terms of integrating a new employee into the organization, making sure they're a good hire, and making them as productive as possible.

Hiring Friends and Family

Hiring friends or family members can be great for you and for the organization. You want people around who you trust. You want people around who you've seen work before, who you've already gone through a war or two with. If you're going to work a million hours a week on a startup, doing it with friends can make it much more worthwhile and fun.

That said, if you don't handle it correctly, hiring friends or family members can be a disaster for you and for the organization.

When you bring friends and family members into your organization, you need to be up front and transparent with other employees about it. You need to let them help you make the decision about who to hire—even more so than usual in this case. And you need to let them know up front that your intent is to treat these people just like any other employee, and that you want everyone else's input if they feel like you're not doing just that.

Before you hire friends or family members, you have to tell them that there won't be any difference between how you manage them and how you manage everybody else at the company. They are going to be held to the same standards as everyone else, and you are their boss just like everyone else, and they shouldn't join in the first place if they're uncomfortable with those realities. Even if you have this "prenup" conversation, firing a friend or family member is an agonizing process. You need to prepare extra for these conversations; make damn sure you're making the right call; but also be wary of taking too long to make the call, because your credibility as CEO hinges on it, 10 times as much as if the person *weren't* a friend or family member.

I've never hired a family member other than having my brother Michael intern for us for a semester while he was in college and having Mariquita do a little bit of highly specialized consulting for us. I don't think I ever will ever do more than that. It's difficult enough for other employees to come to you as the CEO and criticize your friend, let alone your wife or sibling.

RECRUITING OUTSTANDING TALENT

Most of the managers on your team are making tactical decisions that can be forecasted and planned for in advance. This includes hiring: if you're planning to roll out a mobile app in the following year, you need to start recruiting mobile developers 6 to 12 months ahead of time. CEOs, by contrast, focus on long-term, strategic planning. When those plans change or go into a new phase, you'll find yourself needing an entirely new set of talent on very short notice. You can either scramble to find those people at the last minute, or you can go back to a contact you made years ago—just in case.

Return Path Head of Recruiting Jen Goldman on the CEO's Role in Recruitment

Jen Goldman is Return Path's long-time lead recruiter extraordinaire. Given how much of a CEO's time is devoted to recruitment, it's no exaggeration to say that she's played a significant role in any success I've had. Here, she discusses how CEOs can help recruiters succeed in their roles.

At all companies, of all sizes, recruiting is the responsibility of every employee. A key attribute of recruiting success is having everyone in the company understand their role in finding, attracting, and selecting great talent. The CEO's role is particularly important, and very unique. There are three areas in particular that CEOs should focus their efforts.

1. *Maintain a public persona.* Many CEOs have blogs and social media accounts or participate in groups outside of their organization. This is where a CEO can be a big part of sourcing great talent. Candidates typically "follow" a CEO on Twitter, LinkedIn, or other social media, and these are all great avenues for finding and attracting talent. They give candidates a very good sense of a company's culture and whether they want to work for it.
2. *Interview as many candidates as possible.* In Return Path's early stages, Matt was the final interviewer for every new hire, and he was also part of many interview teams. As we grew to about 200 employees, his role changed to being a quick final-stage interviewer for most positions only. At around 300 employees, he delegated this responsibility to his executive committee members, and now interviews only for specific roles in the organization (managers, senior individual contributors, and other high profile positions). While it sometimes makes junior candidates nervous, most of them are impressed by the opportunity to interview with the CEO.
3. *Check references.* Another area where a CEO can play an important role is in reference checking. I always recommend getting "informal" references—someone who knows the candidate but wasn't part of the reference list they provided—and CEOs typically have a strong network that can be helpful when trying to do this. You can learn a lot more about someone from these types of references (good or bad) than from a reference the candidate provided who has already prepped for the call, and CEOs can often get "the real scoop" on a candidate over the phone in a way that an HR-driven reference check cannot.

Recruiting, sourcing, interviewing, and checking references are all a part of the hiring process that a CEO can make a big impact on at any time, and especially as a company is in growth mode."

Jen Goldman, Head of Recruiting, Return Path

Staying "In-Market"

For the most part, your managers can focus their recruitment efforts around specific needs: your chief financial officer (CFO) needs a new controller, your chief technology officer (CTO) a database specialist, your head of sales needs two new reps. CEOs have to be engaged in general recruiting all the time.

This is a subset of being "in-market," and it's just as important as keep tabs on your customers and your competition. If a friend, board member, or colleague recommends somebody, meet with them—even if you don't need someone with their skill set at the moment. If you don't have the time, send one of your senior people. You never know when you'll find a great executive that you want to hire now and find a home for later. This is the same philosophy as Jim Collins's "Get the right people on the bus" theory from *Built to Last.*

There's nothing disingenuous about taking these meetings even if you're not hiring: when a need arises that this person might fill, you will get in touch. (It's important to be up front about this: don't give people the impression that they're interviewing for an active position if that's not the case.) You're just being honest when you say that you don't know when that will be. We've been able to fill more than a few key senior roles over time very quickly, and without having to use expensive recruiters, by being actively in-market all the time.

Recruitment Tools

In addition to reference from trusted colleagues and friends, there are five major areas you should focus on when thinking about recruitment:

1. *Your values.* I've already spoken about the importance of using your culture and values as hiring filters: if someone doesn't adhere to your values or fit in with your culture, don't hire them. On the flip side, your culture and values can be a great recruiting tool. If someone *is* a great cultural fit, they're likely to be as aware of that fact as you are. They're the type of employee you're looking for—and you've founded the kind of company they want to work at. It's a win-win.
2. *Your old jobs.* The simplest way to recruit is to go back to people you know from prior jobs. Everybody on your team should do the same. Why take the risk of bringing on an unknown entity—and

it's always a *big* risk—when you can recruit people you've already seen in a professional environment?

3. *Your team*. The bigger your team gets, the more leverage you have in using it to help with recruiting. You don't just have your own former colleagues to call on—you have everyone's. If you've done a good job building a high-purpose and high-performance organization, your employees will want to pull in the best people they've ever worked with at prior jobs. We consistently source between 40 and 50 percent of our new hires from existing employees, which keeps our recruiting costs down, our standards high, and our culture consistent. We pay employees a $2,500 bonus for every successful referral they make (other than executives and direct hiring managers), although sometimes I think we'd be almost as successful in getting employees to refer talent into the organization even if we didn't.
4. *Your company's reputation*. Nobody wants to work for a company with a bad reputation, no matter how innovative and disruptive their offering might be. *Everybody* wants to work at companies with reputations as great places to work. (Just ask anybody who's applied for a job at Google.) Return Path has made it onto "Best Places to Work" lists at *Colorado Business* magazine, *Crain's New York Business*, *Inc.*, and *Fortune*. Every one of those commendations has been an amazing recruiting tool.
5. *Your sales skills*. As I mentioned earlier, when you ask someone to come work for you, you're asking them to spend half or more of their waking hours devoted to your company. It better be worth it! Comp and perks are important, but you also have to sell your vision for the company, why it's important, and how your recruit is going to contribute to its success.

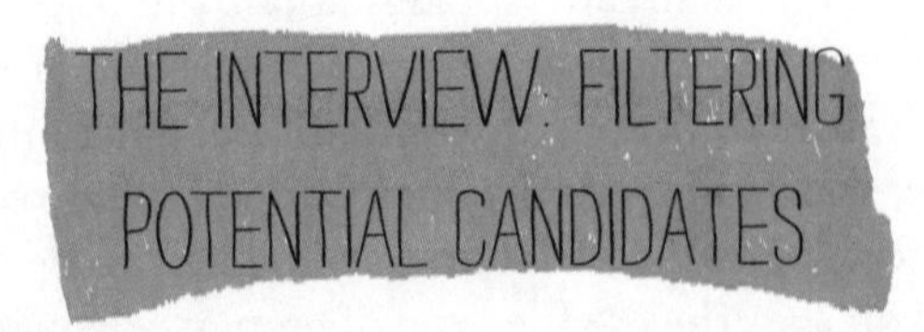

The recruiting process usually focuses on the skills and requirements listed in your job listing. Is this person a good developer? A high-performing salesperson? A talented marketer? *Ask* a potential hire, and they'll certainly say yes. If you want the real answer, you have to depend on two things: references (both on and off the list provided by your recruit) and domain experts. As Opsware co-founder and technology VC Ben Horowitz once pointed out, you can't determine whether someone is going to be an effective head of Japanese sales if you don't speak Japanese. Find a domain expert, and let *them* answer that question.

As a CEO, your goal should be to look for cultural fit and engagement—the X factors. The best way to do so is by interviewing candidates yourself.

The Cleveland Airport Test

Most years, we have a board/management offsite for a full 24 hours. It's a great time, and the conversation is always a nice blend of business and personal.

It was during one of those offsites that I realized just how much I genuinely enjoy the company of the people I work with. Whether it's my senior staff, our board, or anyone else at Return Path, we are not all the same personality type, but we can manage to have fun together as well as productively thinking about and discussing work.

With generic assumptions of eight hours of sleep a night and eight hours of work a day (neither one being true of course, but canceling each other out somewhat), we spend half our waking hours on the job. So we might as well choose to work with people that we get along with! That doesn't mean everyone we hire at Return Path has to be like-minded or have the same sense of humor. But it does mean that we look for people who have that spark in their eye that says "I get it"; it means we want to find people who are articulate, have strong convictions and aren't afraid to speak their mind; and it means we screen for people who can be lighthearted and don't take themselves too seriously when we recruit, interview, and hire.

Think about that "half your waking hours" thing the next time you're hiring someone. Which candidate would you rather spend your day with? In my former career in management consulting, we used to call this the "Cleveland Airport test": if you were stuck in the Cleveland Airport with this candidate, would you be happy about it or miserable?

Two Ears, One Mouth

There's a phrase I'm going to repeat a couple of times in this book, a favorite of our head of sales, Anita Absey: "You have two ears and one mouth for a reason." You should always listen more than you speak, especially when you're interviewing somebody. Lots of senior people spend all their time talking when they're interviewing a candidate for a job. Maybe they love selling, maybe they just love hearing their own voice. Either way, it's a mistake.

Perhaps the most important interview question you can ask is "What do you think of our business?" If the interviewee doesn't have a cogent response by the time they get to you, you don't want them. And it doesn't matter what job the person is applying for. Why should you hire an accountant who didn't take the time to read your web site or learn more about your company throughout the interview process and develop a point of view on your business? Find the candidate who cares enough to do that. With that question, you're still leading the conversation. For at least half the time you spend with someone, you should let them lead it instead. What are their questions? Are they focusing on the right areas or sniffing after red herrings? Did they show up prepared for 15 or 30 minutes' worth of questions or just a handful of generic concerns? Spend most of the interview listening, and you'll quickly find out.

Three Key Interview Questions

Most of the conversations you'll have with potential candidates are going to be specific to the position you're interviewing for. There are some things you want to know about *every* candidate, whether they're applying to be a sales intern or a chief marketing officer (CMO). These are three questions I always ask:

1. *What do you think of our business?* This tells me whether candidates have done their homework on us and developed a point of view about what we do. They don't have to be an expert, but they need to have done some work and thinking.
2. *What do you think of our company?* This gives me an opportunity to see how much attention they've paid during the interview process to the people they've met, the work environment, and so on.
3. *I'm sure, like all of us, you have had a development plan at jobs in the past. What items keep showing up?* Asking "What's your greatest weakness" usually shuts people down. This question is more specific and requires an equally thoughtful answer. If someone gives a B.S. answer ("My greatest weakness is that I care too much"; "People say I work too hard")-they aren't self-aware enough to handle our feedback process.

Whom Should You Interview?

I interview a lot of people: I probably interviewed 60 people last year and will interview at least that many this year. Until the year we hired over 100 people for the first time (which brought our team to about 275), I interviewed *everybody*. Not just direct reports—or even reports of reports—but every last intern.

Usually, these were on the phone or Skype. In most cases, they lasted for only 15 to 30 minutes. For the most part, I only wanted to meet what were almost certain to be new employees and validate my managers' decisions. It was only in *extremely* rare cases that I overrode a hiring manager's decision and dinged a recruit. In those cases, it was clear that the manager was rushing the process to fill a seat—which didn't happen often and needed to be stopped when it did.

These short interviews have been great mechanisms for collecting data about the organization, for making a personal impression on the culture, and for continuing to get to know all employees, at least a little bit. Moreover, it was a great recruiting tool: good candidates really appreciate the fact that the CEO is interested in them, even if you give them only 15 minutes of your time.

It was a bittersweet moment when I stopped interviewing everyone: while it was great to be growing fast, I immediately started missing the personal connections with everyone, and it's harder to remember names as I walk through the hallways now.

Topgrading Your Team

One of the best business books I've read in recent years is *Topgrading* by Brad Smart. The book is all about how to build an organization of A players and only A players, and it presents a great interviewing methodology. It's very long for a business book, but also very valuable. Buy a copy for anyone in your company who's doing a lot of hiring, not just for yourself or for your HR person.

There's been much talk lately about "the importance of B players" in the *Harvard Business Review* and other places. I share the Topgrading perspective, which is that you should always hire A players—the definition of which is "one of the top 10 percent of the available people in the talent pool, for the job you have defined today, at the comp range you have specified." The *Topgrading* methodology, though, splits out A1 players (future executive material) from A2 players (promotable) to A3 players (great at the role, could do it forever). Why would you ever settle for less than an A player in every role?

ONBOARDING: THE FIRST 90 DAYS

The hiring process doesn't end on an employee's first day. It ends 90 days later.

Perhaps the single most important part of the recruiting process is onboarding. Nothing has a greater impact on a hire's viability. Sure, you have to get the right people in the door. But if you don't onboard them properly, they may never work out. This is where all companies, big and small, fail most consistently.

Remember your first day of work? Did you (or anyone at the company) know where you were supposed to sit? Did you (or anyone at the company) know if your computer was set up? Did you (or anyone at the company) have a project ready for you to start on? Did you (or anyone at the company) know when you'd be able to meet your manager? Probably not.

Take onboarding *much* more seriously, and you'll be astounded by the results. We have a manager of onboarding whose only job is to manage the first 90 days of every employee's experience. You don't need to go that far (and won't be able to until you've scaled well past 100 employees), but here are some things you can, and *must*, do to ensure a successful onboarding process:

- *Start onboarding before Day 1.* Just as recruitment doesn't end until Day 90, onboarding starts before Day 1. At Return Path, we ask people to create a "Wall Bio"—a one-page collage of words and images that introduces them to the team—before their first day. It's a quick introduction to our company culture, and something the rest of our team looks forward to seeing as new people join. Your project can be different, but it's important to get new hires engaged even before their first day.
- *Set up your new hire's desk in advance.* There is nothing more dispiriting than spending your first day at a new job chasing down keyboards and trying to figure out your phone extension. We go to the opposite extreme. When new hires walk in the door at Return Path, their desk is *done.* Their computer, monitor, and telephone are set up. There's a nameplate on their office or cube. They've got a full set of company gear (T-shirt, tote, etc.). To show how excited we are, we even include a bottle of champagne and a handwritten note from me welcoming them to the company. In the early days of the business, we even had the champagne delivered to the employee's home after

they accepted the offer. (That didn't scale well, particularly outside of New York City.)

- *Prepare an orientation deck for Day 1.* There are certain things about your company that new hires will learn as they go along: nuances of culture, pacing, and so on. But there are some things that should be made explicit right away. What is the company's mission? What are its values? How is the organization structured? What is the current strategic plan? These details are common to every employee, and all new hires should hear them—preferably from the CEO. You can present these details one-on-one to your direct reports or do larger in-office sessions to groups of new hires over breakfast or lunch.
- *Clearly set 90-day objectives and goals.* Other details are going to be specific to an employee's position. What's their job description (again)? What are the first steps they should take? Resources they should know about? People they should meet? Training courses to enroll in? Materials to read and subscribe to? Finally, and most important, what are the major objectives for their first 90 days? They shouldn't spend their first quarter "feeling around." They should spend it actively and intentionally working toward a clear goal.
- *Run a review process at the end of 90 days.* Whether you do a 360 review or a one-way performance review, the 90-day mark is a really good point to pull up and assess whether the new hire is working out and fitting culturally as well. It's much easier to admit a mistake at this point and part ways while the recruiting process is still somewhat fresh than it is months down the road after you've invested more and more in the new hire.

With *that*, the hiring process is done. Now, repeat.

Management Moment

Exercise the Courtesy of Notification

In most startups, there's something in between asking for permission (in advance) and begging for forgiveness (after the fact). I call it the "courtesy of notification."

It comes down to practicality. A healthy organization is one where most of the players know the rules and framework and mission and are empowered to make things happen. Most importantly, people understand what they're in charge of. There are lots of circumstances where "just doing it" makes sense. Making sure that the relevant people at least know "it" is happening will save a lot of heartache down the road—and probably create a safety valve to make sure there are no radically adverse unintended consequences.

Teach your team to think about who in your organization is affected by the things they do. When they have to charge forward on their own, they should at least give their colleagues the courtesy of notification.

CHAPTER ELEVEN

EVERY DAY IN EVERY WAY, WE GET A LITTLE BETTER

Recruiting people to join your startup is essentially a sales pitch: you're convincing people to sign up for your dream. It's all flowers and chocolates. And while there's a crucial educational component to successful onboarding, it also involves more selling and evangelism for your cause. The hard part comes later, when you have to solicit and provide feedback on performance or fit (this is even more difficult).

Even the most self-aware and self-possessed among us don't like being told that we're not doing a good job, no matter how much positive feedback we might also be hearing. Communicating criticism is a necessary component of providing honest feedback. It's uncomfortable. It can lead to tears and firings and resignations, but it's the most important thing you can do as a CEO, both for yourself and for your team.

There is a variety of ways to give and receive feedback, but I've found it useful to divide all of them into a simple 2 × 2 matrix: informal 1:1s, formal performance reviews, ad hoc hallway chats, and annual 360s.

THE FEEDBACK MATRIX

There are many different opportunities for giving an employee feedback, and there are many types of feedback that you can give. To clarify things, it's helpful to reduce this variety to a simple 2 × 2 matrix: The Feedback Matrix (shown in Figure 11.1).

	Informal	Formal
Performance	1:1	Performance Review
Development	Hallway Hoc	360

FIGURE 11.1 Introducing the Feedback Matrix

Essentially, there are two types of feedback you can provide:

1. Feedback about an employee's performance relative to their goals and objectives.
2. Feedback about an employee's skill set, cultural fit, and way of getting things done.

You can deliver that feedback in one of two ways: formally or informally.

This matrix helps you be clear about what type of feedback you are providing (or soliciting) and what outcome you hope to achieve. It also serves another purpose: making the process of giving and receiving feedback more comfortable. Instilling a culture where feedback is wanted, expected, and doled out regularly is the best way to get over people's innate discomfort with feedback, and the feedback matrix helps provide that regularity. In addition to keeping you and your management team organized, it fosters a culture that values transparency; celebration (not all feedback is negative!); and honest, constructive criticism.

1:1 Check-ins

Informal 1:1 check-ins are a great way to take your team's pulse without creating an overly top-heavy (and intimidating) system of constant reviews. I find that these work best on a weekly basis, but the specific interval isn't important—as long as it's consistent. While it's important that you and your managers set the agenda for these meetings at a high level, the key to keeping them informal is allowing your reports to drive the specific content.

The standing agenda for 1:1s is simple. Each week, you and your reports will review goals, track progress against those goals (i.e., review metrics) and set short-term priorities. If your reports are managers themselves, you should also review those items with regard to the people they oversee.

By allowing your reports to drive these meetings, you're making it clear that you trust them with the responsibility of managing their own careers. In addition to setting the basic framework for these informal check-ins, there are two important functions you can perform: reacting with feedback, and providing organizational context. As CEO, you have a panoptic view of your company that nobody else in your organization shares. Your reports may simply be unaware of how their work complements—or conflicts with—other initiatives at your organization. This is your opportunity to fill them in.

"Hallway" Feedback

While informal performance reviews can be handled on a regular basis, informal feedback about other matters can take place anytime. This kind of feedback falls into two categories: quick corrections and congratulations.

On the negative side, there are behaviors that need to be corrected immediately: an employee has behaved in a way that violates your team's core values, alienates their colleagues, or has otherwise caused a problem. If matters like these aren't handled right away, they can poison your culture. It is essential that you (and your managers) not allow this to happen. On the positive side, if someone has done outstanding work, you want to recognize and reinforce that behavior as quickly and explicitly as possible. It only takes a minute, but employees tend to have long memories about positive feedback. As we've discussed, a culture of thankfulness is as essential to success as a culture of performance.

Even ad hoc processes have their best practices. The one I follow for these quick check-ins is from Ken Blanchard's book *The One Minute Manager*. To sum it up:

- Tell the person up front that feedback is coming.
- Give the feedback as soon as possible after the incident.
- Be specific.
- Stop for a few moments of silence.
- Shake hands at the end.

"Ad hoc" simply means that the meeting wasn't scheduled in advance. It doesn't mean that it should be sloppy and unproductive. The simple guidelines listed here will make it as high impact as your weekly check-ins.

Performance Reviews

Effort is important in life. Woody Allen says 80 percent of success in life is just showing up. If he's right, then perhaps 89 percent is in showing up *and* putting in good effort.

If you put forth a poor effort and still got to the right place, you got lucky. Ultimately, *how* you get something done *is* important. Wasting time or burning bridges with colleagues or clients along the way can have long-term negative consequences that outweigh any short-term gains. When all is said and done, results speak very loudly. Customers don't give you a lot of credit for trying hard if you're not effectively delivering a product or solving problems, and investors ultimately demand results.

Results can't be realistically gauged on a week-by-week basis, so they don't form a huge part of informal weekly performance reviews, but they should be central to the annual performance management process.

It's easy to overdo these processes. Don't. Keep them as short and light-weight as possible, and focus on the essential question: how are employees performing relative to their goals? For the annual performance review (as opposed to the comprehensive "360"), only two people should answer that question: managers and the employees themselves.

Every organization defines performance differently. If you communicate performance benchmarks clearly and frequently, employees should have no trouble evaluating themselves and others relative to those benchmarks. In other words, for each given area, whether employees are performing "At Standard," exemplifying a "Best Practice," or this is an "Area for Improvement." (At Return Path, we used the abbreviations "RPS" [Return Path Standard], "BP" [Best Practice] and "AI" [Area for Improvement]. Some sample performance assessment forms are available at www.startuprev.com.) If it's either of the latter two, provide space for more detail. The actual performance review can then focus on two things: exceptions (areas where an employee is outstanding or lacking) and areas of disagreement, where employees and managers aren't aligned about what's going well and what isn't.

The 360

A 360 doesn't have to be live to be effective. As your organization grows, performing live 360s for every employee obviously won't be feasible. At Return Path, live 360s are limited to VP-level team members and above. For other employees, we take the same "full view," but we do it with online forms. These include a self-assessment, an assessment by the employee's manager and any of their subordinates, and reviews from a handful of peers or other people in the company who work with the person. They're done anonymously, and they're used to craft employees' development plans for the next 12 months.

The live 360 review combines performance and development feedback into a single event. It's time consuming, but it produces fantastic results. This is how it works:

Before the live 360, the person being reviewed meets with an outside facilitator (such as an executive coach) and has an in-depth discussion. Potential questions for this discussion include:

- What were the critical incidents in the past year?
- What went well and what went poorly?
- Did you make progress against your prior year's development plan?
- What areas would you like specific feedback on?

The facilitator then joins a large group to lead another discussion. (At larger companies, this might just be the executive team or members of an employee's group. At early-stage startups, this could be the entire company.) The person being reviewed is not in the room. Sometimes a note taker will be present or the session will be recorded, which frees up the facilitator to engage in the discussion.

The sessions are confidential, so participants should feel comfortable that their thoughts won't be shared outside the room. Uncomfortable as it may be, transparency about someone's performance, especially for people in senior management positions, is a good thing. Everyone has things they can improve upon, and the open discussion around what those things are produces *much* better results for the people being reviewed.

It can be a bit unnerving to know that a room full of 15 people is discussing you, especially when you can hear them all laughing through the wall. But the results are incredibly rich. They add two main things that you don't get by looking at compiled data from an online form: a sense of priority and weighting to feedback, and a detailed look into conflicting feedback. My live 360s in particular have always been far more enlightening than the one-way reviews I received in prior jobs. The commonality in the feedback from different people is a little bit of what one former manager of mine used to say—when three doctors tell you you're sick, go lie down.

Note: One best practice that applies equally well to performance reviews and live 360s is to avoid scheduling them near major events like product releases, marketing pushes, or redesigns. I used to do my own live 360 following a board meeting, but found that the content of the reviews tended to be much more focused around the events discussed in that particular board meeting rather than taking a 12- to 18-month view of my performance. Feedback and postmortems are different processes with different goals. Keep them separate.

One final piece of advice: automate this process! At Return Path, we conducted 360s manually for years (primarily in Excel and Word). Then we moved to an online solution called e360 Reviews from Halogen Software, and now we use Workday. Automated systems have saved us 75 percent of the administrative time in managing the process and it made the process of doing the reviews much easier and more convenient.

Tell It to a Five-Year Old!

I heard this short but potent story recently. I can't for the life of me remember who told it to me, so please forgive me if I'm not attributing this properly to you!

> A man walks into a kindergarten classroom and stands in front of the class. "How many of you know how to dance?" he asks the kids. They all raise their hands up high into the air.
>
> "How many of you know how to sing?" he queries. Hands shoot up again with a lot of background chatter.
>
> "And how many of you know how to paint?" One hundred percent of the hands go up for a third time.
>
> The same man now walks into a room full of adults at a conference. "How many of you know how to dance?" he asks. A few hands go up reluctantly, all of them female.
>
> "How many of you know how to sing?" Again, a few stray hands go up from different corners of the crowd. Five percent at best.
>
> "And how many of you know how to paint?" This time, literally not one hand goes up in the air.

So there you go. What makes us get deskilled or dumber as we get older? Nothing at all! It's just our expectations of ourselves that grow. The bar goes up for what it takes to count yourself as knowing how to do something with every passing year. Why is that? When we were five years old, all of us were about the same in terms of our capabilities. Singing, painting, dancing, tying shoes. But as we age, we find ourselves with peers who are world class specialists in different areas, and all of a sudden, our perception of self changes. Sing? Me? Are you kidding? Who do I look like, Sting?

I see this same phenomenon in business all of the time. The better people get at one thing, the worse they think they are at other things. It's the rare person who wants to excel at multiple disciplines and, more important, isn't afraid to try them.

My anecdotal evidence suggests that people who do take this kind of plunge into something new end up just as successful in their new discipline, if not more so, because they have a wider range of skills, knowledge, and perspectives about their job. Alternatively, it could just be that the people who *want* to do multiple types of jobs are inherently stronger employees. I'm not sure which is the cause and which is the effect.

It's even rarer that managers allow their people the freedom to try to be great at new things. It's all too easy for managers to pigeonhole people into the thing they know how to do, the thing they're doing now, the thing they first did when they started at the company. "Person X doesn't have the skills to do that job," we hear from time to time.

I don't buy that. Sure, people need to be developed. They need to interview well to transition into a completely new role. Having the belief that the talent you have in one area of the company can be transferable to other areas, as long as it comes with the right desire and attitude, is a key success factor in running a business in today's world. The opposite is an environment where you're unable to change or challenge the organization, where you lose great people who want to do new things or feel like they are being held back and where you feel compelled to hire in from the outside to "shore up weaknesses." That works sometimes, but it's basically saying you'd rather take an unknown person and try him or her out at a role than a known strong performer from another part of the organization.

Who really wants to send that message?

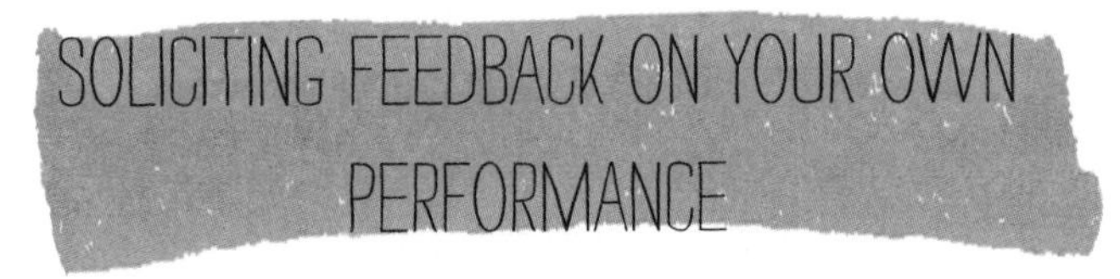

SOLICITING FEEDBACK ON YOUR OWN PERFORMANCE

As a CEO, one of the most important things you can do is solicit feedback about your own performance. Of course, this will work only if you're ready to receive that feedback! What does that mean? It means you need to be really, really good at doing three things:

1. Asking for feedback
2. Welcoming feedback
3. Acting on feedback

In some respects, asking for it is the easy part, although it may be unnatural. You're the boss, right? Why do you need feedback? The reality is that all of us can always benefit from feedback. That's particularly true if you're a first-time CEO. Even more experienced CEOs change over time and with changing circumstances. Understanding how the board and your team experience your behavior and performance is one of the only ways to improve over time.

It's easier to ask for feedback if you're specific. I routinely solicit feedback in the major areas of my job (which mirror the structure of this book):

1. *Strategy*. Do you think we're on target with what we're doing? Am I doing a good enough job managing to our goals while also being nimble enough to respond to the market?
2. *Staff management/leadership*. How effective am I at building and maintaining a strong, focused, cohesive team? Do I have the right people in the right roles at the senior staff level?
3. *Resource allocation*. Do I do a good enough job balancing among competing priorities internally? Are costs adequately managed?
4. *Execution*. How do the team and I execute versus our plans? What do you think I could be doing to make sure the organization executes better?
5. *Board management/investor relations*. Do you think our board is effective and engaged? Have I played enough of a role in leading the group? Do you as a director feel like you're contributing all you can? Do I strike the right balance between asking and telling? Are communications clear enough and regular enough?

Welcoming feedback is even harder than the asking part. You may or may not agree with a given piece of feedback, but the ability to hear it and take it in without being defensive is the only way to make sure that the feedback keeps coming. Sitting with your arms crossed and being argumentative sends the message that you're right, they're wrong, and you're not interested. If you disagree with something that's being said, ask questions. Get specifics. Understand the impact of your actions rather than explaining your intent.

The same logic applies to internalizing and acting on the feedback. If you fail to act on feedback, people will stop giving it to you. Needless to say, you won't improve as a CEO. Fundamentally, why ask for it if you're not going to use it?

Once you have formal feedback, the next step is to turn that feedback into a development or action plan. You may find that people want you to improve 34 different things. Pick the top three and start there.

Ideally, your feedback will be clear on this point. If it isn't, go back to your reviewers and ask them to help you prioritize. Then write a simple development plan that includes these top items and some specific actions you can commit to in order to improve. Table 11.1 shows my two most recent development plans.

The process is the same for your team: have them draft their own plans, and review and finalize them together with their facilitator.

Next, you have to make the plan come to life. Start by publicly sharing your plans with each other at an offsite meeting. That kind of sharing really builds trust and lessens the taboo on feedback. (Besides, the feedback originally came from the people around the table.) Then, at least once a quarter, reviews your plans with each other, starting with self-assessments of progress against the plan, then inviting comments from all. As long as your team is honest and authentic, this is a fantastic method for driving accountability against development plans.

For good measure, I publish my plan to the entire company—usually on my blog—and invite anyone who wants to comment on it to do so. The more public the commitment, the more likely I am to stick to it!

TABLE 11.1 Sample Development Plans

Skill	Action Items
Communication	Clarity in all communications, especially those with sensitive messages. Potentially run sensitive messages by others before delivering to whole group. Continue eliminating *um* from vocabulary. With both the team and the board, be sure to evaluate all feedback before making value judgments or decisions, keeping more of an open mind, and note predetermining outcomes.
Leadership	Continue to demand more accountability throughout the organization—don't focus on being loved so much as being loved + respected + feared. Consciously weave into senior staff meetings: organizational learnings, more dialogue around commitments and deadlines, and consequences of missing them, communication techniques and instruments that the senior staff has learned from Triad Consulting.
Job clarity	Ensure that organizational and task ownership is appropriate, clear, and consistent.
Support and development	Make sure people have actionable development plans and that they are making progress on those plans throughout the year. See people's weaknesses more quickly ... be more clear and crisp about hiring or termination decisions. Make sure to have more out-of-office time with New York senior staff.
Execution	Ramp up personal contributions to sales and marketing execution, bringing personal priorities in line with corporate priorities. Spend more time with the sales force and pitching new large accounts. Make sure marketing is where we need it to be—keep raising the bar on output to make sure we have an extraordinary public-facing effort.
Resource allocation	Be more entrepreneurial and scrappier about running the business. Make sure to treat it like I'm spending my own money. Solicit more outside reads on spending or cutting if I'm struggling with a particular decision. When possible, try to get some distance from the actual analytics to be able to react more to the work of others and use my gut to make decisions, rather than being too analytical personally.

Dev. Area	Dev.—Action Items
Institutionalize impatience and lessen the dependency dynamic on me.	Make others as impatient as I am for progress, success, reinvention, streamlining, and overcoming/minimizing operational realities. Drive deeper understanding of the core. Raise the bar on the team. Develop the team as a team. Practice relentless follow-through.
Focus on making every staff interaction at all levels a coaching/mentoring session.	Manager feedback loops. Inquiry versus advocacy. Develop a practiced understanding of the difference between managing, coaching, and mentoring, and be able to transparently communicate to the person that this (one of these three) is the relationship/transaction that you are both engaged in. Shift from providing tactical solutions to encouraging strategic thought in others.
Continue to foster deep and sustained engagement at all levels.	Evolve my signature "personal touch" items to fit a larger organization, while still trying to "know" everyone: training, management training, interviewing, onboarding, 90-day check-ins, roundtables. Work with HR lead and executive assistant on technology platforms to institutionalize engagement. What's the next major cross-functional project?

The Catcher Hypothesis

Here's an interesting nugget I picked up from a Harvard Business Review article entitled "Making Mobility Matter," by Richard Guzzo and Haig Nalbantian.

Of the 30 general managers in Major League Baseball, 12 are former catchers. A normal distribution would be 2 or 3. Sounds like a case of a Gladwellian Outlier, doesn't it?

The authors explain that catchers face their teammates, are closest to the competition, have to keep track of a lot of things at once, are psychiatrists to flailing pitchers, and so on—essentially that the kind of person who is a successful catcher has all the qualities of a successful manager.

What's the learning for business? Identify "training ground" positions within your organization. Sometimes, it's pulling people out of their current roles (fully or partially) and putting them in charge of a high-profile, short-term, cross-functional project. Another approach is developing a "mini-GM" role, which should develop a whole future generation of leaders as your company grows.

Who plays catcher in your organization?

CHAPTER TWELVE

COMPENSATION

One of the most important—and most contentious—parts of any CEO's job is managing compensation. There's an art to determining compensation, especially for startups with limited resources. Nonetheless, following a transparent set of guidelines will help you make fair, informed decisions. Individual pay can and should be private, but compensation *criteria* should be very public.

GENERAL GUIDELINES FOR DETERMINING COMPENSATION

Above all else, it's important to keep the following universal truth in mind: *most people, most of the time, feel undercompensated.*

There's almost no getting around it: good and bad employees are equally likely to think that they deserve a raise. The only thing you can try to do is make them feel *less* undercompensated, and to remember a corollary that should play a large role in how you determine compensation: *higher pay doesn't guarantee higher engagement*. If people feel *severely* undercompensated, you'll lose engagement. It sounds like a catch-22, but it's really just a balancing act.

To maintain that balance, use the following guidelines:

1. When negotiating compensation with a potential hire, ask what they expect early and often. For senior hires especially, be sure to do this *really* early in the process to screen out mismatches before you fall in love. I've interviewed some great candidates before for

senior roles, only to find out that their last job paid them 50 percent more than I could afford!

2. Make sure your top performers are earning enough equity to make them think twice before even picking up the phone when the headhunters invariably call.
3. Make sure team members who are at the same level and performance range wouldn't be pissed off if they compared notes at happy hour.
4. Make sure you don't get trapped by history. The person who started as an intern could someday be a VP, but not if you always think of him or her as an intern. Focus on how much equity employees are earning (e.g., vesting with respect to equity) relative to their level and performance as opposed to how much they have earned in the past or already vested. Pay attention to year-over-year data, but don't allow yourself to be handcuffed by it.

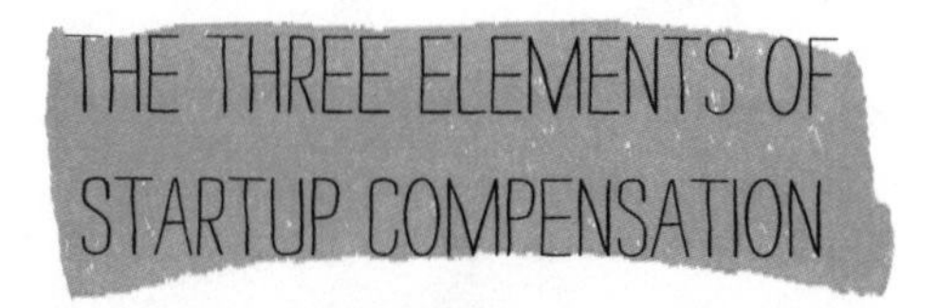

There are three typical elements to executive compensation: base pay, incentive pay, and equity. You need to pay attention to all three, every year, for you and your executive team. As your company grows, you need to pay attention to all three for a larger and larger number of employees.

Base Pay

This is probably the easiest of the three areas, especially as your company gets bigger and more benchmark data are available. In the early days, especially before any outside financing or post-angel financing, you typically just want to hold the number as low as the team can physically and emotionally handle, under the principle of "sweat equity." At Return Path, no one on the entire team (including me) made more than a $75,000 base salary for the first 9 to 10 months until we raised venture capital.

As you enter the revenue and growth stages, it's important to pay yourself and others a reasonable cash compensation package. Equity is awfully difficult to trade for groceries. (I've heard stories that would indicate the contrary, but they are limited to very small districts of San Francisco and Palo Alto from 1996 to 1998).

We use a few sources of benchmark data each year for our executive compensation process:

- Recruiting data—"market rates" are pretty easy to define if you're in-market.
- Published data from consulting firms like Mercer and Hay Group.
- Our own internal data from recruiting for comparable levels and positions.
- Internal comparables based on level and performance.
- The annual Venture Capital Executive Compensation Survey, conducted by Advanced-HR, Inc. and Opinion Impact and comparable public company data from 10K and 10K filings for senior positions.

A final note on this: you don't have to give senior executives pay increases every year. Maybe two out of every three years, but not every year. As one of our board members once told me, "It's not like someone making $200,000 year needs a cost-of-living increase. Sometimes someone who makes $150,000 is more insulted by the $5,000 increase than they are by skipping a year and then having a $10,000 increase."

Incentive Pay

There are lots of theories of nonsales incentive compensation. And we've tried a lot of them, coming nearly full circle in the end. In the early days of the business, we had no incentive comp. We felt like all employees in a pure startup were working for passion and equity, and the lure of a bonus wouldn't move the needle on the quality or intensity of their work, which was already high.

Then, at some point, we needed to cut everyone's pay to stay alive, so we cut everyone's base compensation by 10 percent in exchange for a 15 percent target bonus based on overall company financial performance because it seemed like an all-for-one-and-one-for-all philosophy of fairness. Of course, that just irritated a bunch of people who then felt that they had no control over the company's revenue or costs. It didn't do much to incent or align work.

So then we kept everyone's bonus target, but we made each person's bonus based on a combination of company performance as well as individual metrics and milestones. This seemed like a good compromise. But the problem here was one of governance. It was never clear that everyone had the same level of "stretch" in their personal goals or that managers had the same level of toughness in grading—and after a complex spreadsheet circulated among the executive team at the end of each quarter, almost all employees miraculously earned somewhere between 95 and 100 percent of their target. That seemed like a huge amount of effort for no benefit. It also had the unintended consequence of throwing our team out of alignment by creating too many separate incentives, especially at senior levels.

Then we came full circle at some point and abolished the 15 percent bonus targets and just increased everyone's base by 10 percent, back to where they were, other than senior executives and salespeople. We decided it would just be more impactful to instill a discipline of managing people to stretch goals and firing underperformers than go through all of the rigmarole of any of the legacy bonus programs we'd run through.

The major exception to this rule is sales compensation. There might be misalignment between individual development goals or marketing goals or accounting goals and your company's goals as a whole. But there really isn't any way that sales goals—which consist, in essence, of driving revenue—can be misaligned with top-line company goals. Reward salespeople for individual performance. In this case, it won't lead to any misalignment.

My conclusion from all of this is that incentive compensation is tricky in startups where passion and equity are big drivers. The best use of incentive compensation I've seen is to drive alignment or individual sales performance.

Equity

Equity is a much more challenging and nuanced topic than base pay or incentive pay. Like base pay and incentive pay targets, outside benchmark data can be helpful, but, unlike base pay, each company's cap table and financing history is different and independent of its size, stage, sector, and number of employees. We give equity to 100 percent of our employees in the form of stock options. We want everyone to think like an owner of the company and act like an owner of the company as they make decisions about time, resources, and money. The best way to do that is to make them owners of the company!

The type of equity you and others in the company receive has a lot of components to it—and they're all negotiable. As CEO, you want to make sure that you have a good deal, but you also need to manage your employee base to have deals that are fair for both employees and the company, preferably without many (or any) exceptions to standard policies for you to manage or worry about.

For most of our company's life, we've had an option pool (inclusive of all employees) of around 20 percent of the company on a fully diluted basis. I've heard of companies with as little as 10 percent and as much as 25 percent. The more important number, though, is the percentage of the company in the option pool that is either *unvested* or *ungranted*, which defines how much equity your current employee base is earning every year and how much equity you have left to give. Again, circumstances vary from company to company, but we've always tried to have the employee population earning about 2 percent of the company's equity each year, and we've always tried to leave at least 2 percent of the company ungranted for future employees (more in the early years).

Sizing individual equity grants for employees is really tricky early on, and the size of the grant is related to the next two topics:

- Different types of equity grants
- The vesting terms associated with the grants

I've heard two rules of thumb over the years that sound completely at odds with one another: "give out equity with an eyedropper" and "make sure your best people earn as much equity as you can possibly stomach." Usually, those two points aren't as far off from each other as they sound. In the really early days of a business, it's not uncommon to give senior hires as much as 2 percent of the company over time; even later, new senior hires still receive up to 0.5 percent. The biggest rule of thumb with equity, though, is that it's much easier to give than to take away, so you're better off starting with smaller grants and adding new ones over time.

There are several different forms that equity grants can take. I can describe some of the common ones here in brief terms—but be sure to consult an accountant or a lawyer for more specifics as they relate to your company's situation. If you just own founder's stock (regular old common stock) in your company, you don't need to worry about this—for now. Over time, assuming you take on investors, you'll probably receive incremental equity that can take other forms, and any employees who get equity will also take one of these other forms.

The most common forms of traditional stock options are ISOs (incentive stock options), which are available only to employees and likely have better tax treatment upon a gain than NQSOs (nonqualified stock options), which are the only kind of options you can grant to nonemployees like directors and advisers. Also, note that should you receive a big enough stock option grant in a given year, the IRS forces some of the options to be NQSOs.

Another important consideration is the vesting schedule associated with equity. The typical vesting schedule of a stock option grant, or even restricted stock (which usually has a claw-back provision, effectively the same as vesting) is a four-year evenly distributed vest with a one-year "cliff": no stock vests until one year, then the stock vests monthly or quarterly after that. I've seen other terms, though, from performance vesting (stock vests on a particular hurdle being met like profitability or a specific revenue target), to three- or five-year terms, to backloaded vesting (i.e., not 25 percent per year for four years, but a pattern like 10 to 15 to 25 to 50 percent). You can do anything you want here, but keeping it fairly consistent across your employee base and having a rationale for it are important.

Some companies also include some kind of acceleration of vesting on the sale of the company or IPO. Years ago, in the throes of the Internet bubble, lots of companies gave all employees 100 percent acceleration on a "single trigger," meaning if the company got acquired, all employees' shares would vest. This has fallen out of favor quite a bit in recent years as acquirers realized that having lots of the employees of an acquired company cash out and quit after they acquired the company was a bad idea. (As Brad Feld and Jason Mendelson point out in *Venture Deals*, smart investors push back on "single trigger" acceleration for exactly this reason.) Now, it's more common to occasionally see some minor acceleration of vesting (one year, two years) on a "single trigger" event if any; and occasionally full vesting on a "double trigger" of the sale of the company combined with getting fired or laid off in conjunction with the sale, but plenty of companies have no vesting acceleration provisions.

Note: There is one exception to the rule that you should generally avoid "single trigger" acceleration: your board of directors. Directors are always fired upon change of control, so their options should vest immediately.

What About Pay Reductions?

Nearly everything I've said in this section depends on the assumption that compensation always increases. What about scenarios—like a downturn in an employee's performance, a demotion, or a significant drop in company performance—where a pay *reduction* seems called for?

Individual pay reductions don't usually work out too well. It's not impossible to pull one off, especially with more senior people if it's clear that their roles are outgrowing them, but it's a huge demotivation, often leading to bad behavior and, more often than not, an employee's departure. The best you can do is "redline" compensation: keep it the same indefinitely, with no annual raise. Hopefully, your employee's performance or role scope will increase soon, and you'll be able to revisit down the road.

More troubling is the general situation where you can't afford to meet payroll at current levels. A couple of times over the years, we've implemented across-the-board pay freezes and even pay cuts. As long as they're temporary and impact senior people more than junior people (or at least equally), you can pull them off for a short period of time with a lot of solidarity. But you have to communicate like crazy about it, and it may not be worth it in the end.

If your company's performance has dropped to the point that you can't make the numbers work even with a temporary, across-the-board compensation cut, it's time to discuss the absolute worst thing you have to do at a startup, if not the absolute worst thing any manager has to do in any business altogether: layoffs.

Management Moment

Don't Let Casual Conversation Become De Facto Orders

Sometimes it's hard for CEOs—and especially new CEOs—to realize the impact of their words.

Often, a casual conversation can turn into a *de facto* decision because an employee takes your words and then acts on them. The same thing could happen inadvertently if an employee starts to incorporate your remarks subconsciously, thinking they are likely to become the law of the land.

It's also important not to create false expectations and disappointment if you decide *not* to pursue an idea.

The best antidotes to these misunderstandings are communication and judgment. Make sure to communicate early and often to your audience that you're trying an idea out, and follow up with people afterward to make sure your intent really sunk in. It's also critical to pick your target audience carefully. But even then, this can be risky.

Your words as CEO or any kind of a leader can be quite powerful. If you're not careful, trying something on for size can have real, unintended consequences.

CHAPTER THIRTEEN

PROMOTING

When people ask me how to get promoted, I always have the same answer: start doing the job you want to get promoted into, and do it well, while still doing your own job. Eventually, the title will follow you.

For a lot of managers and CEOs, it's hard to think of a marketing coordinator they hired as a potential marketing manager, director, or VP. It's a big trap to watch out for, and an important habit to break. Every organization should aspire to promote employees to more senior positions as the company matures and grows. This is especially true of startups.

RECRUITING FROM WITHIN

Whenever possible, groom and promote people from within your organization. It's good to keep talent within your company, and it's good for you to hire younger (and more easily molded) talent. And the *possibility* of a promotion is a great motivator. Hire all your senior staff from outside, and you'll be removing another incentive for more and better work.

While these considerations apply just as well to any company, big or small, there are other considerations that are more specific to startups.

When a major pharmaceutical company needs a new sales leader, they have an obvious and large pool of candidates to draw from: current or former sales leaders at *other* major pharmaceutical companies. What if a company that specializes in email deliverability needs a new consultant? Or a company specializing in 140-character updates needs a new SMS engineer? There aren't nearly as many "comparables" to lean on.

Many startups aren't simply building businesses; they're creating new marketplaces. If that describes your company, you have a particularly compelling reason to promote from within: you don't need a new hire to only acclimate to your culture; you have to train him in nearly every detail of your (brand new) business.

You can't always hire from within, and sometimes it's not particularly important that you do. (We recently needed to hire an international finance person; nobody in accounting took it the wrong way when we looked outside

Promotion Criteria

In order for promotions to feel like achievable rewards for outstanding performance, rather than ad hoc and arbitrary appointments, it is crucial to have clear criteria for promotions in place. At Return Path, we have "levels" that each job is mapped to, so it's clear when someone can become a VP, and when they're not ready. Don't make the system *too* rigid or too general: titles often fail to translate between departments, and you need the ability to make a promotion outside these criteria without being accused of violating ironclad rules.

At Return Path, each job falls into one of four broad levels—Learning (newer in a career), Applying (more senior, usually still an individual contributor), Guiding (senior individual contributor or manager), Shaping (senior manager and up).

Each year along with our performance management process, we evaluate every employee along five dimensions—each of which has several categories:

- *Growth*: Self-awareness, Incorporates feedback, Learns from experiences, Leverages strengths.
- *Professionalism*: Role models, Reliability, Builds community, Lives by RP values.
- *Execution*: Takes ownership, Reasons Analytically, Collaborates, Makes Decisions.
- *Impact*: Listens, Communicates, Builds Relationships, Develops others.
- *Strategic Thinking*: Develops vision, Instills passion, Prioritizes business levers, Drives innovation.

Employees need to show meaningful progress against each of the above dimensions and categories in order to be promoted to a new level.

For the full "Return Path Expectations" guidelines, go to the web site www.startuprev.com.

because no one had that skill set.) Before ever promoting someone within your organization, be careful that you're not about to create another instance of the "Peter Principle."

Back when I worked in management consulting, I always used to wonder how it was that all the senior people at the firm I worked at spent the majority of their time selling. They hadn't been trained to sell, and a lot of the people great at executing complex analysis and client cases hated selling.

Should a company take its best salespeople and turn them into managers?

There are those of us whose personalities don't work in a management context, and there is nothing wrong with not managing. The usual notion of promotion to management by merit has always been a curiosity to me. If I am good at my job, why does it mean that I would be good at managing people who do my job? In other words, a good "line worker" doth not a good manager make. Hiring people specifically to manage and lead teams is preferable to promoting someone in your organization who's ill-suited for such a position. The latter happens too often, to the detriment of many companies and individuals.

For those of you not familiar with the Peter Principle, the short of it is that "people are promoted to their level of incompetence." At that point, they stop being promoted. By then, every post in the company tends to be occupied by an employee who is incompetent to carry out their duties.

We've had numerous examples over the years at Return Path of people who are great at their jobs but make terrible—or less than great—managers. The problem with mistakenly promoting someone into a management role isn't only that you're taking one of your best producers "off the line." The problem is that those roles are coveted because they almost always come with higher comp and more status. If a promotion backfires, it generally (though not always) dooms the employment relationship. People don't like admitting failure; people don't like "moving backward"; and comp is almost always an issue.

Sometimes there's not much you can do about this, even if you know it's a mistake to promote someone. We had a top-performing sales rep once who was dying to be a sales manager. She begged for the job. We didn't think she would make the shift to manager well based on how she interacted internally.

At some point she begged enough—and threatened to leave if she didn't get a management position—so we gave it a shot, with all the caveats and training in the world. What happened? It didn't work out. In the end, she left the organization because she couldn't handle a demotion.

What can be done about this? We have tried over the years to create a culture where being a senior individual contributor can be just as challenging, fun, rewarding, impactful, and well compensated as being a manager, including getting promotions of a different sort. But there are limits to this. One obvious one is at the highest levels of an organization, there can only be one or two people like this, at most. A CEO can only have so many direct reports. Another limit is societal. Many companies define success as span of control. You get a funny look if you apply for a job with 15 years of experience and a $100k+ salary yet have never managed anyone. After all, the conventional wisdom mistakenly goes, how can you have a big impact on the business if all you do is your own work?

The fact is that management is a different skill. It needs to be learned, studied, practiced, and reviewed as much as any other line of work. In most ways, it's even more critical to have competent and superstar managers, since they impact others all day long. Obviously, people can be trained into being managers, but the Peter Principle is spot on: just because you are good at one job doesn't mean you should be promoted to another one.

There are lots of ways of meeting this challenge, but the one I've found most successful is moving people to new and interesting roles within the organization, though not necessarily management ones. We call it "scaling horizontally."

SCALING HORIZONTALLY

As important as it is to help people scale by promoting them whenever possible, it's also important to recognize when that can't work, and figure out another solution to retain and grow those people.

The traditional way to promote people is to scale them "vertically": to senior or management roles within their existing function or department. As I just wrote, this approach is highly susceptible to the Peter Principle. Another approach is to scale employees "horizontally" by moving them into different roles on different teams. This allows them to grow, develop, and, over time, become more senior and more valuable to the organization.

We've had instances over the years of engineering managers becoming product managers; account managers becoming product managers;

product managers becoming sales leaders; client operations people moving into marketing; account managers moving into sales—I could go on and on. We've even had executives switch departments or add completely new functions to their portfolio.

Moves like this don't always work. You do have to make sure people have the aptitude for their new role. When moves like this *do* work, they're fantastic. You give people new challenges, keep them fresh and energized, bring new perspective to teams, and retain talent and knowledge. When you let someone scale horizontally, make sure to celebrate the move publicly so others know that kind of thing can be available. Also, be sure to reward the person for their knowledge and performance to date, even if they're moving laterally within your org chart.

PROMOTING RESPONSIBILITIES RATHER THAN SWAPPING TITLES

A couple of years ago, Brad Feld wrote a post on his blog *Feld Thoughts* about how title inflation had infected startups with the same virulence with which it proliferates through major corporations:

> Suddenly, title inflation is everywhere. I've seen more business cards or email sigs lately with adjectives like "executive" or "senior" or "senior executive" or "special" or "chief" in front of more traditional titles (e.g., "vice president"). The "chief" one is especially bizarre since it's not always obvious whether the CSO is a "Chief Sales Officer" or a "Chief Security Officer," which in and of itself is a problem.

I first saw this in my previous job at MovieFone, where I was struck that people at Hollywood studios had titles like chairman of marketing (really?). There are lots of problems with titles: they don't translate well from department to department, they don't track to comp in any consistent way, and they create the wrong kind of pretty meaningless set of incentives.

Brad suggested a radical alternative: think of every senior member of an organization as the "head" of something. Is your controller a director or an SVP? Does it matter? He or she definitely is the "head of accounting and financial reporting quality supervision."

I'm not ready to make that switch altogether or to eliminate titles as some companies have. I do think about Brad's proposal every time I make a promotion. Am I simply turning a "director" into a "vice president," or am I putting someone in charge of a new responsibility? If it's the former, it's a waste of time—with one key exception, which, as I said at the beginning of this chapter, is when the person is already doing their "next" job.

Reversing a Promotion

Like reducing someone's compensation, demoting an employee—specifically, reversing a bad promotion—almost never works. It's not impossible, but it's hard enough that you should try something else. The easiest solution is to move the person into a completely different role. If they got a promotion in the first place, they were probably talented, valuable employees. They were just put in the wrong role. Move them into a more appropriate one. The one exception to this role is with somewhat senior people where the rapid growth of the company may have just outpaced their development, but where they're still excellent in their department.

CHAPTER FOURTEEN

REWARDING: "IT'S THE LITTLE THINGS" THAT MATTER

The old adage, "It goes without saying . . ." should never be spoken inside the walls of a well-run startup. Communication—real communication, not implied communication—is the foundation for a successful business. Good CEOs know this but even the best CEOs often fail at one crucial piece of communication: rewarding good performance.

It *never* goes without saying because it's the little things that count. Have you ever finished doing something and thought, "Wow, that was a thankless task"? Right. No fun. Why should your employees ever feel that way?

IT *NEVER* GOES WITHOUT SAYING

We human beings live for "moments." We mark time by observing regular occasions like birthdays, anniversaries, and holidays. While religions and cultures differ on the details, we mark the cycle of life with things like baby namings, bar mitzvahs, confirmations, first communions, weddings, and funerals.

There's no reason the workplace should be any different. Think about a few examples where it could "go without saying," but where you're so much better off creating a "moment":

- Publicly acknowledging a member of your team for reaching an employment anniversary (the bigger the number, the heartier the acknowledgment).

- Marking the end of a project or a transition period with a celebration.
- Meeting two weeks after the end of a project or a crisis to do a post-mortem or after-action report, analyzing what went well and defining lessons learned for the next time.
- Publicly thanking a colleague for helping out on something—anything.

Clear, simple communication is the cheapest and easiest way to create a fun, rewarding, accountable, and focused work environment.

The Spiff

A very personal gift is worth 10 times its monetary value. If you have an employee who loves home improvement projects, a $250 gift card from Home Depot will mean much more to them than a $250 check—unless, of course, a $250 gift card from Home Depot is your standard gift. Gifts can't be generic; they have to be personalized demonstrations of your gratitude and signs that you've listened well enough to know your employees' interests.

BUILDING A CULTURE OF APPRECIATION

What does creating a thankful atmosphere get you? It gets you great work, in the form of people doing their all to get the job done. All of us, including CEOs, appreciate being recognized when we do good work. I love what I do and would do it without any feedback, but nothing resonates with me more than a moment of thanks from someone on my executive team or our board. Why should anyone else in the organization be any different?

This is not about giving everyone a nod in all-hands by doing shout-outs. That's not sustainable as the company grows (and not everyone does great work every week or month!) It's also not about remembering to thank people in staff meetings either—although that's never bad. It's about informal, regular pats on the back. To some extent inspired by the great Ken Blanchard's book *Whale Done!*, it's about enabling the organization to be thankful.

Years ago, we created a peer award system on our intranet/wiki at Return Path to enable peer recognition. The idea is simple. We have an "award request" form on our company intranet that any employee can use to request one of five awards for one or more of their colleagues, and the list evolves over time. (You can see our latest version at www.startuprev.com.)

Our office manager does a quick review of the submissions to make sure they are true to their definitions and that people aren't abusing the system. In the early days, we read these out each week at our "all-hands" meetings. At our scale today, we announce these awards each week on the wiki and via email. The leaders of the business regularly read the awards list to see who is doing good work and who needs to be thanked separately on top of the peer award.

As of late, with about 350 employees, we probably have 30 to 40 of these every week. They typically carry a $25 gift card award, although most employees tell me that they don't care about the gift card as much as the public recognition.

It's not a perfect system. (The biggest shortcoming is that it's not used evenly by different people or different groups, but it's the best thing we have come up with so far to allow everyone in the company to give a colleague a virtual pat on the back, which encourages great teamwork!

- *EE (Everyday Excellence)* recognizes those who demonstrate excellence and pride in their daily work.
- *ABCD (Above and Beyond the Call of Duty)* recognizes the outstanding work of our colleagues who go above and beyond their duties and exemplify exactly what Return Path is about.
- *WOOT (Working Out of Title)* recognizes those who offer assistance that is not part of their job responsibilities.
- *OTB (On the Business)* is about pulling ourselves out of day-to-day tasks and ensuring that we are continually aligned with the long-term, strategic direction of the business. We make sure we're not just optimizing our current tasks and processes but that we're also thinking about whether we should even be doing those things. We stop to think "outside of the box" and about the interrelationship between what we are doing and everything else in the organization. In doing so, we connect the leaves, the branches, the trunk, the roots, and soil of the tree to the hundreds of other trees in the forest. We step back to look at the big picture
- *TLAO (Think Like an Owner)* means that every one of us holds a piece of the company's future and is empowered to use good judgment and act on behalf of Return Path. In our day-to-day jobs, we take personal responsibility for our products, services and interactions. We spend like it's our own money and we think ahead. We are trusted to handle situations like we own the business because we are smart people who do the right thing. We notice the things happening

around us that aren't in our day-to-day and take action as needed even if we're not directly responsible.

- *Blue Light Special* recognizes anyone who comes up with a clever way to save the company money.
- *Human Firewall* is awarded if you catch a colleague taking extra care around security or privacy in some way, maybe a suggestion in a meeting, a feature in a product, or a suggestion around policy or practice in the office.
- *Coy Joy Award* is in memory of Jen Coy (a long-time employee we very sadly lost to cancer), who was positive, optimistic and able to persevere through the most difficult of circumstances. This award is designed to recognize individuals who exemplify the Return Path values and spread joy through the workplace. This can be demonstrated by going above and beyond to welcome new employees, by showing a high degree of care and consideration for another person at Return Path, by being a positive and uplifting influence, and/or making another person laugh out loud.

Beyond institutionalizing thanks, there are lots of ways to give thanks that are meaningful. Some are about maximizing moments of truth. Another thing I do from time to time is write a handwritten "thank you" note and mail it to homes rather than passing it to someone at work. There are lots of genuine ways to express your appreciation. Find ways that work for you and be consistent.

Management Moment

Manage Your People by Their Needs, Not Yours

Different people and different teams require different management styles and approaches. This is what I call management by chameleon. As a chameleon has the same body but shows it differently as situations warrant, you can have a consistent management philosophy but show it differently when you are with different direct reports or teams.

On a team of five direct reports earlier in my career, I had five incredibly different people to manage with five incredibly different functions and teams under them. Trying to manage those people identically was counterproductive. A small example: 8 A.M. meetings never worked well for the insanely creative insomniac. A bigger example: diving into strategic topics with the former consultant who just joined the team and had never managed anyone before was a little bit of focusing on the forest and forgetting about the trees.

At the end of the day, you are who you are as a manager. You are hard-charging; you are great at developing individuals; you seek consensus. But how you show these traits to your team and how you get your team to do the work you need them to do can differ greatly person by person. Manage people based on their needs, not your own.

CHAPTER FIFTEEN

MANAGING REMOTE OFFICES AND EMPLOYEES

If I had to do one thing over again with Return Path, I'd have kept the entire company in a single office for as long as possible.

Today, we have 12 offices in seven countries on four continents. We have been in business well over a decade and have a significant international sales force, so that's probably to be expected, but even in our early days, our team has been split across multiple locations: we started in New York and San Francisco simultaneously to attract good talent; then an early merger led to offices in New York, San Francisco, and Boulder within two years of the company's founding.

There are situations where remote offices are actually the *ideal* situation, especially with international sales, and there are ways to mitigate the challenges of having a highly dispersed team. The key is recognizing the value of physical proximity—as old-fashioned as that sounds—and doing what you can to sacrifice as little of that value as possible as your team expands.

BRICK-AND-MORTAR VALUES IN A VIRTUAL WORLD

As buzzwords go, *telecommuting* sounds pretty old-fashioned. That's partly because the practice it describes is no longer a distant promise of this new thing called the World Wide Web but a reality that most of us take for granted, at least during part of our lives. Employees at high-tech startups are liable to work from home more than ever these days (although as I'm writing this book, new Yahoo! CEO Marissa Mayer just banned working from home), or to communicate with colleagues at home or at other offices on a daily basis. Business travel is still essential but with online collaboration and videoconferencing tools at our disposal, the bar for approving a flight is much higher than it was a decade ago.

And yet, there is still real value in having an office. To name just a few:

- *Human connectivity.* Every month seems to bring a new feature article about whether the Internet—and social media in particular—is making us lonelier. Without getting into the details, there's an essential point we have to address: clearly, a global web connecting billions of people *virtually* hasn't yet met all the needs that prompt us to connect in person. We need look no further than at the growth of "co-working spaces" in recent years to understand this need. Someday, a company composed entirely of remote employees connecting virtually may be a practical reality. It isn't one yet.
- *Collaboration.* Online collaboration tools are fantastic: Dropbox, Google Drive, and Basecamp continue to change the world in remarkable ways. What they *haven't* done is replace in-person meetings entirely. An old practice at Intel demonstrates the point: after managers noticed how often employees would stop each other in the hallway to discuss ad hoc ideas, they put up whiteboards to facilitate those conversations. Structured online collaboration is great, but it still can't produce that kind of synergy. (How's *that* for an old-fashioned concept?)
- *Focus.* There's a curse that comes along with the blessing of immediate access to everything and anything. It's the immediate access to *every*thing and *any*thing. Part of building a culture of trust means not tracking or blocking URLs on our servers—Facebook and YouTube are always just a click away. Nevertheless, the temptation to make a quick status update is always greater away from the office, to say nothing of the myriad other distractions that working from home (to take the most extreme example) brings with it.

All of that said, the world is growing more virtual, not less. One of the main consequences of this fact is that people are less willing than ever to move for work. Given the hiring challenge I addressed earlier, this forces you to make a difficult decision. Or, to make it a bit less dramatic and binary, it forces you to perform another of those balancing acts that define the job of the CEO: *you want the best people for your team, wherever they are.* Ideally, you want them all in the same place. When that can't happen, you have to open and operate remote offices or let people work from home. It will be interesting to see what happens to or as a result of Marissa's policy change at Yahoo!.

BEST PRACTICES FOR MANAGING REMOTE EMPLOYEES

Managing remote employees presents a unique set of management challenges. We have had more than our fair share of experience with this at Return Path. I have people on my executive team in four offices and a fifth person works from a co-working space in a city where we have no presence at all.

We give our remote employees a series of guidelines to help them work as effectively as they can from home or from a co-working space. These guidelines include:

- *Setting up appropriate work space.* We advise remote employees to set up an adequate work space with all the necessary equipment and supplies. Work areas should be quiet and free of distractions, ideally with a door so there's a clear separation of "work" and "home." We also insist that remote employees have enough bandwidth to support high-intensity business applications, including Skype or a videophone.
- *Expenses.* We allow remote employees to expense a fixed amount each month to cover supplies and incremental bandwidth charges. Remote employees who want to use a co-working space need to get that approved since it usually costs more than supplying a home office, but we encourage it whenever it makes sense.
- *Customizing their operating system.* We advise employees who work remotely—particularly those who are not accustomed to doing so—to carefully review and change the way they work to make it match their virtual status. For example, we remind employees that they need to work harder at communication since they're remote, probably using voice and video more as well as having more frequent, shorter meetings with colleagues and managers. When remote employees do go to an office, we make sure they make the most of their time there by scheduling key meetings in advance.
- *Implement regular meeting routines.* Without necessarily realizing it, you have frequent informal "meetings" with employees who work in the same office with you. You will bump into them in the hallway, they'll swing by your office, you will chat at the proverbial "water cooler." These interactions are extremely valuable—and you can't have them with your remote employees. To offset this loss, set up frequent,

regular meetings over Skype with your remote team members. You can't exactly replicate the serendipity of in-office interactions but you can avoid the mistake of ignoring your remote employees altogether.

As CEO, whether or not you directly manage a remote employee, you can do a lot to reinforce the fact that your company's values don't only apply to employees who are in offices or company headquarters. Teach your managers to modify the way they work and the way they manage to build the extra trust and information flows required to get the most out of remote employees.

Discrete Teams in Separate Locations

Most of what I written in this chapter has to do with having a single team in multiple offices. Having discrete teams in separate locations is different. If you have developers in India or back-office employees in Ireland, the cultural concerns and rotations don't make as much sense. In these scenarios, you're the consumer of a service rather than a manager of team. (The distinction is a bit blurry with development teams.) Offshoring a function is more like a vendor relationship: set expectations clearly and manage according to them. If they aren't met, change vendors.

When sales is in New York and engineering is in Colorado, that's a bigger challenge, and it can't be managed like a vendor relationship. It's easy for those relationships to devolve but you have to learn to work around that and make it a nonissue. Don't be overly reliant on email, especially with difficult conversations. Pick up the phone or use Skype.

CHAPTER SIXTEEN

FIRING: WHEN IT'S NOT WORKING

I hate to end this section on this topic but it's unavoidable: sometimes, you have to fire people. On the worst days, you have to lay them off.

NO ONE SHOULD EVER BE SURPRISED TO BE FIRED

One of our most important management training mantras is "No one should ever be surprised to be fired." As hard as it might be to actually fire someone, the *really* hard conversation should have taken place weeks or months prior. Here are some stages that should always precede firing someone:

1. *Alert the employee that his or her job is at risk.* Every employee you or one of your managers fires needs to have heard the following sentence weeks earlier: "Things aren't working and here's what you have to do to fix them—*or you will be fired.*" That last phrase needs to be explicitly stated and repeated in writing. I can't stress this enough. No euphemisms. Don't say "part ways," or "move on." Say "or you will be fired."

   Note: There is one exception to this rule: if someone commits an egregious violation—for example, theft or assault—there are no intermediate steps. Fire them immediately.
2. *Institute a performance improvement plan (PIP).* PIPs should be as specific and quantitative as possible. Sometimes, the criteria you have to set will be impossible to meet: an underperforming salesperson just won't be able to close X dollars in 30 days. Nonetheless,

PIPs make it clear that firings aren't random and if they really do seem out of reach, employees will often quit of their own volition.
3. *Radically increase supervision of at-risk employees.* If you meet with your direct reports for weekly check-ins, meet with at-risk reports twice or three times a week. This sends an important message: you're trying very hard *not* to fire this person. The onus is on them to improve.

The first time I ever had to fire a person while I was at MovieFone was one of the most awkward and awful experiences of my professional life. I think it was harder on me than it was on her. I'm not being glib: *she* told me that. It was a lay-up: she was being fired for cause!

It's hard for an empathic person to look people in the eye and tell them they don't have a job anymore, whatever the reason. I also think that people are generally well served, even if they don't think about it that way at the time, if they can understand why they're being let go. That allows them to constructively develop their careers going forward and seek out jobs in which they might be a better fit.

TERMINATION AND THE LIMITS OF TRANSPARENCY

Transparency is one of our most important values at Return Path. There are a number of reasons why I wish I could extend that to cover every termination at the company:

- *Explanations make terminations look less random.* You don't want high-performing employees to think they could be fired at any point, without real cause. If the circumstances of one or many terminations are a mystery, they might start to believe that there was no good reason.
- *People create their own explanations.* Human beings need meaning, even if they have to create it. If you don't explain *your* reasons for firing someone, your team isn't going to be satisfied with a lack of explanation altogether. They will just come up with their own reasons—and that alternate reality could send exactly the wrong message.
- *Terminations reinforce company values.* When you explain your reasons for firing someone, one of the messages you're sending is that you're serious about your company's values. Violate them and

you're out. That message may not come through with a quiet, discrete termination.

Given all those advantages, why not be transparent about terminations? It's a liability issue. Put your reasons for firing someone in writing—or broadcast them to a large group of witnesses—and you give the recently fired employee ammunition to pursue legal recourse against you. I hate to retreat behind a wall of lawyers but this is a very real risk. The best you can do is to communicate your reasoning to controlled groups, which is probably more than half the battle anyway. Additionally, you should be able to trust your senior staff: if anything, they would probably respect you less if you *didn't* fire someone who was underperforming or violating your core values. Uncomfortable as terminations are, they validate everyone else's work.

Severance Pay

As I mentioned earlier, you should avoid contracts whenever possible. You want to create relationships built on trust—and you want the flexibility that the lack of written terms gives you. If one of your employees does have a contract, it will include severance terms—probably between three and six months' pay. If you don't have a contract, have a policy and stick with it. (At Return Path, we give two weeks' pay per year served, rounded to the nearest week.) You can be more generous than your policy stipulates—but not less. Keep that in mind when you formulate it.

Sometimes, this can be a hard nut to swallow. Employees fired for cause have either woefully underperformed or really violated your company's values. Sending them off with a check might seem like a bit much. Do it anyway. If there's bad blood and you end up in court for violating a severance policy, you will pay significantly more in legal fees, no matter who wins. End the relationship with a clean break. Pay up.

One thing I've increasingly seen in employment contracts is something called the "salary bridge." It's intended to reinforce the concept of severance as a payment to tide someone over between jobs, not as a fixed payout. You can always offer someone X weeks of severance plus Y weeks of salary bridge (payment if they haven't found a new job) if you would like to be more gracious on someone's exit but not create an entitlement if the employee finds a new job.

LAYOFFS

Short of declaring failure and shutting down your company, there is nothing worse you will ever have to do as a startup CEO than lay employees off. This isn't firing for cause—employees aren't being asked to leave because of *their own* failings. They're being asked to leave because the company can no longer afford to keep them. It's not their fault. It's yours.

I had to lay people off on three separate occasions early on in the life of the company. They were the worst days of my professional life and probably in my top 10 worst days period. You don't want to do it any more than is absolutely necessary, so follow these guidelines to get it right the first time:

- *Cut earlier than you have to.* Things are always worse than they look, even when things look *this* bad. Financing will take longer to come through, receivables will dry up, and so on. Assume you have less runway than expected and cut early.
- *Cut deeper than you have to.* You really, really don't want to go through this a second time. Cut more employees than you think you have to and reduce the risk of a second round.
- *Use the occasion to remove* ***all*** *poor performers.* You have no choice but to remove people if their positions are being cut altogether. However, you can also take this as an opportunity for some major housecleaning. Just be sure to work with someone who can help you navigate the legalities.
- *Plan talking points in advance.* A round of layoffs is likely to be one of the most emotional moments of your career. Don't wing it. Plan everything you're going to say in advance, both to the individuals being let go and to your team as a whole.
- *Follow layoffs with an all-hands meeting.* Layoffs are emotional for the entire team. Follow them by an all-hands meeting explaining why they happened—preferably an explanation backed by metrics—what's next, and whether people who *weren't* laid off are at risk. (Be honest!) Ideally, the people you're laying off will be there, too. You want to honor and thank them in as public a forum as possible.

In the end, the only positive thing that came from having to lay people off (other than saving the company!) is that the mere thought of ever having to do layoffs again drives my thinking about everything from business model to profitability.

Management Moment

Nip Problems in the Bud

As Einstein once said, "A clever person solves a problem. A wise person avoids it." At your best, you're wise, preventing problems before they arise. More often, you will have to be clever and solve problems *after* they come up. You have to nip problems in the bud immediately but that means you have to look out for them. Do you have an employee who has shown up late for work a few days in a row—and are they better dressed than usual? They might be interviewing for a new job. Do the complaints about a new employee have a consistent theme, regardless of the source? They might not be fitting in. Make sure you and your team spend enough time thinking about your business's vulnerabilities. Call on your inner paranoia once in a while to make sure you're cognizant of the major potential threats to your livelihood. Learn to spot smoke as an early warning detection of fire.

Etsy CEO Chad Dickerson on How a CEO's Role in Talent Changes Over Time

One of the only constants for startup CEOs is the fact that building and fostering talent will occupy a significant percentage of your time. How you spend that time—that changes. Etsy CEO Chad Dickerson gets the last word on how a CEO's role with respect to talent changes over time.

There are three stages to a CEOs role in building out talent:

1. Articulate your values.
2. Scale trust in hiring.
3. Evolve into the "closer in chief."

Articulating Values

Every CEO says some variation of, "I want to hire smart, motivated people," but in your company does "smart and motivated" mean successful candidates will be able to endure Darwinian contests among team members to achieve goals? Or does it mean the ability to operate in an open and collaborative culture where people are expected to work together to make each other, their ideas and their execution better? I prefer the latter, but every CEO must clearly articulate and communicate *their* cultural values before hiring anyone. Culture is the baseline for everything you do and determines what kind of organization you want to build.

Scaling Trust in Hiring

With cultural values articulated, the CEO should focus on hiring talent that fits those values in each functional role: marketing, engineering, product, HR, and the rest. Filling these roles well is all about scaling trust, since the CEO needs to be able to trust these functional experts to hire *their* team members and build out their teams. When you hire someone, ask yourself if you trust that person to hire people in that functional area without your input. If you do, you're in good shape. If not, you don't have the right person for that role—and it will be difficult to scale your talent efforts.

Becoming the Closer in Chief

In the early days of a startup, the CEO might interview every person who gets hired. As a company climbs into the high double digits and puts trusted functional leads in place, having the CEO interview everyone becomes logistically difficult. The CEO could be creating a bottleneck that slows progress, frustrates candidates and subtly suggests mistrust of the hiring managers.

There is a way to stay involved broadly and productively, though, as "closer in chief." No matter how big a company gets, the CEO should always make him- or herself available to close key candidates at all levels. This does two important things for the company and the CEO:

- Closes candidates, of course, and
- Keeps the CEO's recruiting pitch sharp.

It's also the perfect way to meet the future stars in the company and establish relationships beyond the immediate management team.

Chad Dickerson, CEO, Etsy

PART THREE

EXECUTION

Execution is where the battle is won or lost. It's working with the team you have built to bring your stories to life. As I said at the beginning of the book, it's not "the big idea" that's important; it's what you and your team do with the idea once you have it. You get it funded and then you have to make it work.

Part Three of this book will go into some of the key elements of execution, from specifics around financing the company, to budgeting, to running great meetings and setting goals, to creating a learning environment so you can improve future execution based on past results.

CHAPTER SEVENTEEN

CREATING A COMPANY OPERATING SYSTEM

Startup CEOs need to make rigorous predictions about their cash flow and their budgets, despite the overwhelming uncertainty that makes it impossible for either of those predictions to be accurate. While you and your team simply have to accept market uncertainty as a part of startup life, you can mitigate it by maintaining a high degree of regularity in how your company operates. You do this by creating a *Company Operating System:* a regular set of behaviors and rhythms upon which your team can depend as they make that daily leap into the unknown.

CREATING COMPANY RHYTHMS

Whatever uncertainty the day holds, the sun rises when it rises, sets when it sets—and the moon accordingly appears on a regular schedule of waxing and waning. The same holds for weeks, months, and years. None of us know what surprises 2020 has waiting for us—but we know December 21 will be the shortest day of that year, like every other.

There's a way to bring the same regularity to the chaos of startup life. Is your latest product release going to ship on time? Is your new sales lead going to triple customer acquisition? Is your new marketing approach going to gain traction in the marketplace? Nobody knows—not you, not the head of product, not the head of sales, not the head of marketing. That said, there are some things every member of your team *can* depend on:

- *An advanced schedule of major meetings.* What you will discuss at your next quarterly board meetings or your next annual strategy session is anyone's guess. The date and time of those meetings should be common knowledge well in advance. It may seem like a minor point, but these types of meetings often result in significant changes in direction. By knowing the schedule, everybody will know exactly when to expect a potential change of course.
- *A consistent format for major communications.* At Return Path, we share our Board Book—the full presentation we give our board on a quarterly basis—to the entire company (excepting a few sections that need to remain "confidential"). The content is always different; the format is (almost) always the same. If there's major news, everybody will notice it right away, because they won't be trying to decipher some new layout. You can vary the format once every year or two, but try to keep all your reports in a consistent format and you will reduce the possibility of major miscommunications.
- *Clarity around leadership groups and decision making.* Even if your organization is flat, it will invariably have some kind of leadership team that steers the ship, possibly one with a few layers to it. Making sure those groups are known and their roles are clear is key. They should also have a name, a regular meeting time and an email distribution list (and other group lists on social media vehicles) so that people in the company know how to reach that group if needed.
- *A rigorously enforced open-door policy.* Given the degree of uncertainty that's inevitable with every startup venture, don't create new uncertainties by being cagey or closed off from your employees. If they have questions, answer them—and demand that your executive team does the same.
- *A single set of IT systems and operational procedures.* I mentioned this when I discussed the challenges of managing remote offices and teams but it bears repeating: don't slow down your team's productivity with insufficient or inconsistent infrastructure. The only challenge in sending an email should be crafting thoughts in a clear and persuasive manner—not getting attachments to work.

Keep these pieces of your Operating System in good working order and your team can be alert and ready to deal with the challenges that really matter.

A MARATHON, OR A SPRINT?

My Grandma Hazel had a Yiddish saying that she used to describe me from time to time: *Oder gor oder gornisht*, which means "all or nothing." My dad has a Greek saying that he uses to describe me from time to time: *meden agan*—μηδὲν ἄγαν to the real sticklers—which means "everything in moderation." These two approaches to life seem diametrically opposed. Which one is right?

Being a successful entrepreneur requires *both* approaches, each at different times. More importantly, it requires the ability to shift gears between the two and to be clear about the shift to yourself and to others.

There are periods of time when you need to be in "all-or-nothing mode." Push extremes. Demand more from your team. Drop lots of the items from your to-do list and focus on the One Big Thing. Don't go for a light jog—train for a marathon.

Then there are periods of time when you're in execution mode. The path has been defined. Things are working. Put the "life" back in your "work-life" balance. A marathon? Are you nuts? Just run three miles a day and stay in shape.

It's hard enough to manage yourself through extremes like that. You're also responsible for making sure your entire organization is able to shift gears between the two modes. An organization that never goes through extreme periods is in grave danger of stagnating. No one in an exciting company ever has "business as usual" emblazoned on their to-do list 365 days a year. Organizations tend to take their biggest leaps forward when there's an extreme situation, an all-hands on deck, a crisis.

An organization that *only* knows how to exist in crisis mode can be miserable. Trust me, I've worked in one before. There's a shiny new object every week that everyone has to drop everything to pursue. Everything gets started; nothing gets finished. People are frustrated. They burn out. There is yelling. Sometimes tears.

Companies and people have to go through periods of time where they thrive on the routine and celebrate their every day achievements. The trick to getting this duality right is to make sure you are clear to yourself—and, when necessary, to others—about when you're shifting gears. For yourself: when you go into *gor oder gornisht* mode, clear that calendar and set aside the time to do the job right. For others: don't make them guess where you're coming from. If you're hitting an extreme patch, let them know by meeting or email. Make sure you're fair to them as well. If you're forcing people in the organization to focus on the One Big Thing, make sure you recognize the changes in their goals, their deliverables and their external commitments. Give them the flexibility they need to succeed. Going back into *meden agan* mode is easier but still requires a note of closure to your team, celebrating the success of the big push and probably giving everyone a day off.

CHAPTER EIGHTEEN

CREATING YOUR OPERATING PLAN AND SETTING GOALS

In my observation over the years, most companies explode when they try turning their strategic plans into operating plans. They have good ideas and capable workers, just no cohesive way to organize and contextualize the work. That is the purpose of the operating plan.

Just as my favorite framework for internal "business plans" is Ash Maurya's "Lean Canvas," my favorite framework for "organizational goals" comes from Patrick Lencioni's book *The Advantage*. I introduced that framework when I described how to define an organization's mission, vision and values in Part One. The second part of the framework is more relevant to execution and goal setting. Lencioni divides it into three levels: "Thematic Goals," "Defining Objectives," and "Standard Operating Objectives." Those are a little different from my presentation of the process in this chapter but the spirit is the same.

TURNING STRATEGIC PLANS INTO OPERATING PLANS

There are many different formats that operating plans can take and a variety of acronyms to go with them. No one of these formats is "right," but I'll share the key process steps my own team and I go through to turn our strategic planning into action plans, synchronizing our activities across products and groups.

- *Theme.* Pick a theme for the year that encompasses the bulk of your strategic plan. A good place to start is your elevator pitch.
- *Initiatives.* Recognizing that lots of people on our team do lots of routine work, organize a small number of major cross-functional efforts into specific initiatives. These projects give nearly all employees direct ownership of a concrete piece of the strategic plan.
- *Plans.* Involve others in the process to gain the benefit of their ideas as well as their ownership over the outcome—this is the place for individual teams and divisions to play a significant role in laying out the long-term road map. Every initiative team and each department within your company (they will probably be different) should work together to produce a one- to three-page plan on a common template if possible. It should include a mission statement, a list of direct and indirect participants, important milestones, and key performance indicators and metrics. This is also the place to capture all the activities in your organization that aren't directly related to the theme—like accounting, legal, HR, and IT.
- *Synchronization.* However realistic the plans may be in themselves, they might require overlapping resources or have dependencies and sequencing requirements. It's up to you and your management team to make all of these plans work well together. Review all of the plans, making edits to both substance and timing. We have started posting these plans on Google Docs and creating an "open comment" period for all managers in the company to read, comment, respond, and reshape plans to make sure they all line up.
- *Communication.* Unveil the theme and initiatives at an all-hands meeting. This should be fairly high level. It's the rallying cry that will get everyone's head around the work to be done in the upcoming year. Keep communicating as you go into more and more detail as the theme soaks in.
- *Scorecard.* Build a simple scorecard for the year to reflect the grading on each initiative and visually display their most important metrics. (We use a "green/yellow/red" system but you can create your own.)
- *Ongoing reporting.* Every quarter, update each of the initiative plans for presentation to your board and your team (more frequently, if you're smaller and younger as a company). When you do so, publish it alongside the current scorecard for each initiative.

As I said, there's no single recipe for success here. This is a variant on what we have done consistently over the years at Return Path—and it seems to be working well for us.

FINANCIAL PLANNING

As I said earlier, the predictable uncertainty of startups is no excuse to avoid the work of making *educated* guesses—especially about the next quarter. This is particularly true in the realm of financial planning. An operating plan without rigorous financial predictions—on both income and expenses—is just another bit of storytelling. The financials start you on the journey into execution.

Your financials should be very detailed for the coming months but don't need the same degree of precision for one to three years out. You should be able to produce a full set of financials (income statement, balance sheet, cash flow) on a monthly basis for the first year and on an annual or quarterly basis for two years after that. Essentially, you need to answer three questions: How much is this going to cost? How and when is this investment going to pay itself back? What is the capital required to get there and what are your financing requirements from where your balance sheet sits today?

The costs are easier to forecast, especially if you carefully articulated your resource requirements. As everybody in the startup world knows, ROI is trickier. You're not leading an enterprise that has extremely detailed historical performance metrics to rely on in their forecasting. When Schick or Gillette introduces a new razor into the marketplace, they can very accurately forecast how much it's going to cost them and what their return will be. If you're creating a new product in a new marketplace, that isn't the case.

While monthly burn and revenue projections will inevitably change, capital expenditures can be more predictable, though you need to make sure you understand the cash flow mechanics of capital expenditure. Sometimes vendors will provide financing, sometimes they won't. Usually, you pay cash out up front, so it's a balance sheet event. You depreciate the expense over many years, so the impact on the income statement is very different.

BRINGING YOUR TEAM INTO ALIGNMENT WITH YOUR PLANS

If you're writing your first operating plan for a raw startup off of freshly validated hypotheses from your Lean Canvas, odds are that your team is pretty solidly in alignment to begin If your operating plan is for a business that's been running for a couple years or more—and assuming that plan isn't to do more of the same for the next three years, it will likely be somewhat disruptive. Your company is about to pursue a new or modified set of goals. You will either be ramping up on existing business lines, adding new ones or dropping products and services altogether in order to focus on your core business. There might be another round of investment coming, a merger or acquisition, a divestiture, or a public offering.

What impact will your new plan have on internal resource allocation? Answering this question requires considerable finesse. As startups don't have the enormous resources of major enterprises, almost every decision to pursue one direction requires a decision to abandon—or significantly cut back on—another. Are marketing dollars going to be increased or reassigned? Are some departments going to get significantly more funding in order to bring a new initiative to fruition? Are other initiatives being put on the back burner or cut altogether? Is Sally or John going to have to start doing a slightly different job tomorrow? A radically different one? Will you end up doing layoffs because the complexion of your staffing needs has changed?

Whatever your plan, it may have a real impact of the day-to-day lives of your employees. The first question you'll need to answer is: "What is that impact going be on every stakeholder? Answer that question explicitly. In particular, you need to set clear guidelines for each of your functional departments, including:

- *Strategic goals.* What is each department's specific role in securing your company-wide goal? Work with your executive team to break your overall strategic plan down into a series of department-specific goals and help them communicate those goals to their teams.
- *Business goals.* What kinds of operating changes will departments need to make to reach the company's goal? Will there be new hires? Promotions? Reassignments? Will resources be moved from one department to another? This is where you explain the impact of your goal on your team's day-to-day operations. Be *very* clear about what's going to happen.
- *Milestones and metrics.* The ultimate measure of your success is whether you achieve the business goals—revenue, sign-ups and so on—laid out in your strategic plan. How are you going to measure each department's progress? What specific milestones do they have to reach to support the overall goal? What metrics are you going to use to measure their success? These metrics should be appropriate to specific departments but everybody should be clear that their

efforts ultimately serve the company's success as a whole. (For more on this topic, see Chapter 26, "Driving Alignment.")

Everybody in your company can and should feel included in the new direction. The solution often lies in savvy reallocation. The fact that somebody's project is being cut doesn't mean their contribution has to come to an end. They'll simply need to contribute elsewhere. Tell them where that will be. More important, a well-communicated strategic plan should make it clear that the new direction is going to benefit *the company as a whole*. If a particular employee or department's incentives don't align with your overall company's health—you have a bigger problem.

The primary emotion associated with your plan should be excitement about what's coming next for your company. That can only happen if you overcome anxiety about what's coming next for your individual employees. Doing so requires a high degree of clarity about short-term changes. Provide it—then move on to the big picture.

Prepare to Win the Peace

As important as it is to prepare for the worst, entrepreneurs and politicians alike need to make sure they're also planning to win the peace—in other words, planning for a successful outcome. Great to invade another country if the situation warrants—even better to know ahead of time what you're going to do when you topple the dictator. Budget like you're going to miss your goals but plan for how to reinvest the extra cash if you find yourself with it.

CEOs need to put some cycles against scenario planning for successful outcomes so they're not caught flatfooted when things go well. How can lack of planning to win the peace come back to bite you? Here are a few ways:

- You're not staffed properly to support a big contract that comes in—and you have no pipeline of candidates or contractors to backfill.
- You don't have media buys lined up for a marketing campaign you want to run as soon as the financing closes.
- You haven't started an integration plan before a tenuous acquisition closes, so integration doesn't happen quickly enough.

There are certainly other examples as well, in war as in company building, but what it all comes down to is the need to scenario plan for best cases as well as worst cases. It's all about avoiding costly lead times.

Return Path Board Member and Former DoubleClick and Oracle CFO Jeff Epstein on Taking a Metrics-Driven Approach to Your Business

Ideally, the goals you set and work toward should be quantifiable. That's not always possible but it usually is. Below, former DoubleClick and Oracle CFO (and current Return Path board member) Jeff Epstein describes the "OKR" approach to setting and tracking goals.

> Many of the things you can count, don't count. Many of things you can't count, really count.
>
> —Albert Einstein

As Peter Drucker, one of the world's most influential writers about management best practices, famously said, "Efficiency is doing things right. Effectiveness is doing the right things." Of course, we want to be both efficient *and* effective. To do so, avoid time-consuming activities that produce few results and focus on the handful of things that will produce real results. To quote Drucker again, "Do first things first and second things not at all."

Ideally, the question of whether or not something "produces results" should be quantifiable. But as Einstein's quote reminds us, that's not always the case. The practical solution is to measure things that are measurable, while also formally tracking important qualitative, hard to measure results. Intel and Google have developed a particularly effective process for doing so: The OKR.

In the OKR process, each company, department and individual sets three to five quarterly goals (the "Objectives") and specifies in advance how to measure success (the "Key Results").

At many companies, the CEO begins his or her quarterly board presentation with the company's OKR results from previous quarter and goals for the upcoming one. At the company level, these may include OKRs such as:

- Achieve generally accepted accounting principles (GAAP) revenue growth of 34 percent, to $20 million.
- Achieve earnings before interest, taxes, depreciation, and amortization (EBITDA) margin improvement from 10 percent to 14 percent.
- Grow global engineering team from 82 to 94 people.
- Achieve revenue of $2 million from new product X.

OKRs can also be department specific. For example:

- *Sales:* Sign $1 million in new customer contracts by March 31.
- *Product development:* Launch new product, with the following five features, by the end of Q1.

- *Product quality:* Reduce "Severity 1" customer support tickets from five to three in Q1 and reduce total customer support tickets by 20 percent in Q1.
- *International:* Open offices in Germany, Sweden and Korea by the end of Q1.
- *Financial process:* Reduce quarterly close cycle time from 14 days in Q1 of last year to 10 days in Q1 this year.

In order to focus on the few things that will produce the greatest results, limit each department's or individual's number of OKRs to between three and five. If you find yourself pushing past this range, select the most important five and ignore the rest.

In general, I have found that the best results come from making OKRs broadly available to employees but there's a trade-off between effective internal communication on the one hand and keeping key information confidential from competitors (and sometimes customers and suppliers) on the other. Communicate OKRs and results to your employees but emphasize their responsibility to protect confidential information.

At many companies that use the OKR system, 80 to 90 percent of employees achieve their goals. Former Intel CEO Andy Grove suggests a different approach in his book *High Output Management*: only 50 percent of employees should achieve their goals. After all, professional sports teams are among the highest-performing results-oriented organizations in the world and 50 percent of all teams lose every day. This requires a CEO and corporate culture with a harder edge than many U.S. companies have today. And yet, when we think about our best teachers in school and our best bosses, they were often the most demanding teachers and leaders—and the toughest graders.

Jeff Epstein, Former Oracle CFO

GUIDELINES FOR SETTING GOALS

There are no general guidelines for *what* goals you should set: companies and industries are simply too varied for that. There are guidelines for *how* you set goals and how to work toward them.

- *Underpromise and overdeliver*. Being ambitious is what building a startup is all about but consistently missing goals quickly becomes a drag on productivity and morale. Set ambitious goals—big, hairy, audacious ones—but don't insist on setting goals that you will never meet.

- *Meet commitments or renegotiate and communicate.* This is especially true of individual goals: if you know in advance that you're not going to hit your goals, quickly communicate that to your team. Don't force people to scramble when it's too late. Give them time to adjust expectations, make new plans and communicate them.
- *Get broad buy-in from multiple stakeholders up front.* Rallying cries don't work if people are shouting different phrases over each other. Major stakeholders across a wide spectrum—including executives, board members and even some key junior people—should be ready to back you up when you make the big announcement.

This is much more likely to be a struggle in the life of a company. But as you mature, you will have a clearer sense of what you can achieve and what your company can rally behind. It's the same cycle you will go through in your forecasting and budgeting: Try, Learn, Adjust, and Try Again.

How to Impress Your Boss

No matter what area of the company you work in, ask yourself these three questions every time you are about to review something you did with your boss:

- What am I trying to accomplish with this piece of work?
- Is this the best/only way to accomplish that mission?
- Is this my best work?

I guarantee you two things if you get into this habit. First, you will frequently stop and do more work on something before handing it into your manager. Second, you will get a raise and a promotion sooner than your friends.

And, yes, it really is that simple.

Management Moment

Assign Yourself Deadlines for Tough Decisions

If you have a tough call to make, you're the right person to make the decision. If you have gathered all the input you need and you're still not sure what to do, give yourself a deadline for making the decision. Try bouncing the decision off a couple of people who you trust to see how it feels to articulate the decision and explain its consequences. Then stick to your deadline and decide one way or the other. No extensions.

CHAPTER NINETEEN

MAKING SURE THERE'S ENOUGH MONEY IN THE BANK

Running a business is very different from managing your personal finances. The revenue is less predictable than a salary; multiple people contribute to expenses; and there's a lag time between revenue/expense and cash impact.

Keeping a watchful eye on cash is *especially* important for two reasons: funding requirements and funding availability don't always go hand-in-hand and most startups regularly have to deal with the fundamental quandary of rapid growth being at odds with profitability.

SCALING YOUR FINANCIAL INSTINCTS

Return Path received its first institutional financing in late 2000 (we did a large "angel" round in late 1999) and our first "real" board meeting was in November of that year. It was a memorable experience all around but there is one piece of advice that I'll *never* forget hearing. Without the slightest bit of sarcasm or irony, one of our board members insisted that I never let the burn rate get above $1 million per month.

I had started Return Path almost a year before and we didn't come close to an *annual* burn rate of a million dollars. A million dollars a month?! Of *course*, I would never spend money so irresponsibly. You've probably guessed by now that I'm the type of person who kept careful tabs on his first checkbook, obtained at age 10 by riding to the bank on a bicycle with a piggy bank in tow. Is someone who takes care about every $100 really going to drop the ball on $100,000? Shockingly, the answer is often "yes."

Even if you're frugal as hell and build desks out of doors, nobody has the precision instincts about $500,000 versus $750,000 that you would have about $500 versus $750 in your personal life. Some people simply *do* lose their heads: what's $10,000 when you have a million? (It's $10,000.) The more important point is that nobody has developed *instincts* about how to handle this kind of money.

All of us have had a few hundred dollars or more in our accounts for quite some time now and have a sense of what it would mean to spend $200 on dinner instead of $30. When was the last time you had to manage multimillion-dollar budgets? And even if you did have some oversight over a major budget (as I did at MovieFone), when was the last time you were the *final decision maker* about how that money was spent? Unless this is your second go at being a startup CEO, the answer is probably "never."

Without instincts, financial problems can creep up on you. In fact, there's a famous parable every businessperson knows about exactly this issue.

BOILING THE FROG

It's an old story, most likely apocryphal, but every management consultant in the world has told it a couple hundred times:

If you throw a frog into a pot of boiling water, it will leap right back out. If you put a frog in a pot of water on the stove and then heat it up to boiling, you'll "boil the frog" because it doesn't realize that it's being very slowly cooked until it's too late.

We've boiled frogs at Return Path more than once. In one case, we let a staffing problem sneak up on us in a critical department. We were short one person in accounting and business operations and we decided to control costs by going without the extra person for a month or two. Then, another person in the group unexpectedly left. Then, another person in that group got seriously sick and was out for several weeks. We were now down three people in a critical area, without a proper pipeline of candidates coming in the door for any of the open positions. For a period of time, we weren't getting what we needed out of that group, despite the heroic efforts of the remaining team. It wasn't until the last person had already been out with an illness for a few days that we realized we had a serious problem on our hands.

The second time was a few years ago. We were working on doing a financing to fund our rapid growth and calculated that we had six months of runway left before we'd need more cash. Then, new expenses popped in that we hadn't focused on. We'd already stopped hiring, the biggest lever. Our ops team did a major hardware purchase (the kind that affects cash but doesn't hit the income statement, so we weren't thinking about it). Then we did annual salary increases (which we forgot to specifically add into the budget midyear). Then we had an unusually high Travel and Entertainment month with a few conferences (T&E is budgeted evenly across the year, even though it really has peaks and valleys). Then revenue was a little short of plan. All of a sudden, that six-month runway turned into three months! And the financing process, which was going fine, became rushed and hurried. We got it done and we probably didn't leave a lot on the table, but it was unnecessarily harrowing. And, like the other example, there was never a moment where it was obvious that we had a problem until we did.

How do you stop yourself from getting boiled?

- *Recognize when you're in a pot of water.* What areas of your company are so mission critical that they're always at risk? Have you done everything you can to eliminate single points of failure? As long as you're losing money, are you comfortable that you know every source of spending?
- *Recognize when someone turns on the burner.* Do you know the early warning signs for all of these areas? Can you really live without an extra person or two in that department? Is it really okay that you forgot to budget in raises?
- *Recognize which frogs you care about.* You can't solve all of the problems all of the time. Figuring out which ones need to be solved urgently versus eventually versus never is one of your most important roles as a company's decision maker. Focus first on cash in the bank!

Care and intuition will take you far here but metrics will always take you farther.

TO GROW OR TO PROFIT? *THAT* IS THE QUESTION

There's an elite club of (former) startups that never have to debate the relative merits of growth versus profitability. Google can set out to scan every book ever written (129,864,880 by their last count) without having to worry about the cost of such a project dragging down the profitability of their search ads business. Steve Jobs allegedly ordered his product teams to build a number of complete, polished prototypes of every new product (a dozen iMacs here, a dozen iPads there) before choosing one—or mashing them up and sending his team back to work. If you're reading this book, I'm going to assume that you don't have that luxury.

Every time you have a budget meeting once you're out of the raw startup phase, you have to strike a balance between growth and profitability. *Every time.* Even when you're making money. Invest everything into new hires and more product features and you will fuel growth. Cut costs and halt new initiatives and you will put money in the bank. How do you decide which approach to pursue?

First, Perfect the Model

Before you can think about the trade-off between growth and profitability, you have to get your business model right. Not just on your first Lean Canvas, but on your second, and your third. Get out of the startup phase and into the revenue phase. During this phase, you have to focus on neither growth nor profitability, but rather on frugality, on staying alive until you get to the point where you're ready to start scaling your business.

Choosing Growth

Once you have a model that's working, choose growth. Growth in revenue, growth in user base. Sometimes this doesn't make sense—if your business is mostly professional services, for example. As long as you're selling some kind of product or technology with high gross margin and a large and expanding market in front of you, early on, you have to choose growth.

Investors in those kinds of businesses aren't looking for steady annual profits that grow 10 percent a year. They aren't looking for a dividend. They are looking for a 3 to 10 to 50× return on their investment. That kind of return will happen only if you're growing your revenue or user base 30 to 50 percent per year, or even more in the early stages. Rapid growth companies are acquired at high multiples of revenue, or achieve ultra-successful IPOs. Even post-IPO, public market investors seem to be willing to value continued high growth over profits.

That said, you should be investing money in growth (at the expense of profits) only if you are reasonably confident that the investments you make will pay off. That confidence has to grow as your business gets larger—in the early days, of course you don't know if things will work at all. By the time you're in the revenue stage, though, you should be putting money to work in sales or marketing that you're fairly sure will pay back—or put smaller amounts of money to work to test things out first.

Choosing Profits

As your business matures (again, if you are running a high margin/high growth potential software or Internet business in particular), though, the lure of profitability starts to beckon. Why should you be constantly in fundraising mode with 70 to 80 to 90 percent gross margins? Why should you and your investors continually suffer from dilution? Those things might make sense in a world where your valuation is growing so fast that fundraising is easy and dilution is small, but that's not the case for most businesses.

It's also the case that strategic acquirers often value profits over growth—or at least a balance between the two—almost the opposite of the IPO market. Once you get to be $50 million to $100 million in revenue, other companies may start to look at you funny if you haven't actually demonstrated yet that you have the discipline to run a profitable business. It's one thing for strategic buyers to spend several million dollars on a neat piece of technology of team. It's another for them to spend hundreds of millions of dollars on a company that's going to be a drag on their earnings per share. This rule gets thrown out the window, however, if you are growing fast enough (e.g., >40 percent per year) and if most of your loss has a positive long-term ROI directly attributed to increasing customer acquisition.

Sometimes, though, the choice startup CEOs face isn't between growth and profits. It's between growth and *halting it in order to stay alive.*

If you have a solid product and an effective sales team generating somewhat predictable month-over-month revenue growth, achieving profitability isn't all that hard: just stop hiring. Lots of companies, including Return Path, did so in 2008–2009. The economy was melting down and completely uncertain, so we did our best to maintain top-line revenue and growth while preparing for the worst by cutting and freezing bottom-line expenses as much as possible. The result was that we went from very unprofitable to very profitable within six months. Once the world was in a better macroeconomic place, we felt more comfortable investing more money in our long-term growth once again.

The Third Way

Increasingly, some companies are trying to find a "third way" here in this debate, where they're not chasing growth at all cost but they're also not trying to maximize profits. They are declaring that they want to be in business for the long haul and while they're concerned about their investors' desires for liquidity, they don't want to rush to sell the business or to go public, with all of the accompanying challenges and headaches.

So they're exploring new financial models of long-term, private ownership. They're slowly starting to turn on enough profit so they buy out investors without slowing growth too much. And these include some great companies. It will be interesting to see how these companies pioneer new models in the coming years.

This is admittedly a very complex topic that could be the subject of a whole book. Suffice it to say that the trade-offs between growth and profitability are real and persistent throughout the life of a startup.

CHAPTER TWENTY

THE GOOD, THE BAD AND THE UGLY OF FINANCING

Making sure you have enough money in the bank is Step 1 in financing your business. Step 2 is finding the money when you need it. This is one of those topics that can take up a whole book (including *Venture Deals* by Brad Feld and Jason Mendelson) but the high-level overview here should get you pointed in the right direction.

Let's start with the premise that there are three forms of financing for your business: equity, debt, and bootstrapping. The difference is that selling equity is trading cash for ownership in your company; taking on debt means you need to pay the cash back; and bootstrapping means neither—but it might be impossible for you, depending on the business you're building. One of the most important principles to remember here is that debt is always senior to equity (meaning it always gets paid out first).

What kind of financing should you be looking for at the current stage of your startup? Review this matrix from Return Path Cofounder and CFO Jack Sinclair to find out (Figure 20.1).

	Type of Financing				
Stage	*Angel*	*Preferred Equity w/ Seed/Super Angel*	*Preferred Equity w/ VC*	*Venture Debt*	*Commercial Debt*
Idea	✓	✓			
Business model	✓	✓	✓		
Revenue with business model		✓	✓	✓	
Predictable revenue and profitability path			✓	✓	✓

FIGURE 20.1 What kind of financing should you be looking for at the current stage of your startup?

EQUITY INVESTORS

When CEOs think of equity investors, the first words that usually come to mind are *venture capitalists* (VCs). VCs aren't the only investors in the startup world. Inexperienced CEOs often learn this lesson too late, overexposing their idea to VCs who aren't ready to invest in something *so* early stage—and aren't likely to reconsider the idea further down the road.

I discuss VC economics in depth in this chapter and provide tips for negotiating with them in the following section. Here, I'd also like to introduce two other varieties of investors: angel investors and strategic investors. Again, if you want a lot more color on the nuances and different terms and security types associated with equity financing, read *Venture Deals*.

Venture Capitalists

VCs are professional investors who invest money on behalf of institutional investors.

The Good: VCs are the cream of the crop for startup investors. They're well-funded; they're experts in helping companies grow; and they're prepared for the risks and roadblocks that every startup venture entails.

The Bad: As a startup CEO, you will raise money a handful of times. VCs do this for a living. The combination of an inexperienced CEO and a savvy-but-cynical VC could be fatal—for the CEO. There are plenty of horror stories about VCs writing deals that are extremely disadvantageous for CEOs—mostly because these CEOs fail to get past the excitement of a multimillion-dollar investment and think through the consequences of various clauses—"Liquidation Preference," "Conditions Precedent to Financing"—that any experienced VC will include. (There's an easy fix: read *Venture Deals!*)

The Ugly: VCs essentially have a right of first refusal on the future existence of your company: if they don't invest in subsequent rounds, it will be *extremely difficult* to find other investors. (Why would anyone take a risk that the investors who know you best have chosen to pass on?) With Series A and subsequent rounds, this is a risk you may have to take. This is a good reason to avoid VCs in angel rounds. Throwing $200,000 into an idea is extremely low-risk for a

VC but they will only provide follow up investment for a handful of those deals. If yours isn't one they follow up on, you could be sunk.

Angel Investors

Though there are institutional "angel" groups, angel investors are typically high-net-worth individuals who put personal money into a company.

The Good: Angels are often your friends and family, so they don't play hardball when negotiating terms.

The Bad: Angels are typically your friends and family, so every dinner party you attend has the potential to morph into an ad hoc investor relations conference. You can blunt this by designating some social times as "work-free zones," but it's still there, lurking in the background.

The Ugly: Angels are typically your friends and family, so you will feel awful if you lose their money or radically dilute their investment in subsequent rounds. When you take money from friends and family, be sure to look them in the eye and tell them that they should be prepared to lose all of it but that you will do your best to avoid that outcome.

At the end of the day, not everyone is cut out to invest in startups. My biggest takeaways about nonfinancial/VC investors are:

- Be very selective about who you let invest in the early stages of your company.
- Make sure angel investors acknowledge to you verbally (above and beyond the accredited investor rep they give you) that they are totally comfortable losing all of their money.
- Make sure angels and strategic investors understand that in order to preserve the value of their investment, they may need to continue investing in your company if you end up raising multiple rounds of financing.
- Without being unfair, try to limit the rights (or assign them by proxy to you or to the board or to a lead investor) of less sophisticated financial investors who aren't and won't be close enough to your business to participate in major corporate decisions down the road. Along these lines, you should strongly consider selling common stock to both types of investors, especially if it's early in the company's life.

Above all, don't be tempted by dumb money. You want your investors to be partners, not blank checks. While you might get much better terms with angels—or even strategic investors who haven't made many investments—you will earn much more valuable partnerships when you bring a good VC onto your team.

Strategic Investors

Strategic investors are operating companies (not investment firms) that invest in other operating companies.

The Good: Strategic investors are typically some kind of business partner. If they have a stake in your company, they're more likely to help you.

The Bad: The person at the company who made the investment decision is usually a different person than the person with whom you conduct business, so the incentives are rarely aligned the right way.

The Ugly: Unlike institutional investors, strategic investors can change their philosophy about making other corporate investments for any reason or for no reason. While they might participate in subsequent rounds, they're far more likely than VCs to leave you without support in future rounds and with an unproductive player around the table. That makes securing subsequent funding—or a future exit—much more difficult. The best way to mitigate this is to insert some kind of "pay to play" provision in the financing but prepare for a fight on this front.

Dumb Money

There's nothing worse than dumb money backing a dumb idea or management team.

The dumb idea or team can destroy an emerging sector pretty quickly and the dumb VC behind the deal will just keep ponying up and muddying the waters for everyone else.

The classic dot-com version of dumb money is the company that decides to give away its core service for free in order to try making money at something undefined or untested. It could take two years and a ton of VC money before that company is out of business, having figured out that they needed to charge for their core business—and that process can wash out smarter and more conservative companies in the process.

So instead of just cheering that your competitor is dumb, dig in and look at how smart the money is behind the company. If the money is dumb, too, beware!

Smart Money

The converse of "dumb money" is that there's nothing better than smart money behind a great idea and solid team. Here, in no particular order, is my list of the 10 characteristics of great investors:

1. Great investors know how to give strategic advice without being in the operating weeds of a company.
2. Great investors get to know whole management teams, not just CEOs. In fact, great investors become part of the extended management team of their portfolio companies.
3. Great investors invite you to do due diligence on them by giving you a list of every CEO they've ever worked with and asking you to pick the ones you want to talk to.
4. Great investors ask great questions.
5. Great investors don't publicly take credit for the success of their investments, even if they were major drivers of that success.
6. Great investors show up for meetings on time and don't spend the meeting using their smartphone.
7. Great investors treat their portfolio companies' money as if it were their own money when spending it on things like lawyers or travel.
8. Great investors look for connections to make between their portfolio companies or relevant people but have a strong relevance filter and don't send junk.
9. Great investors never have a ready-made list of the ways they add value to companies—and they specifically never talk about the help they give in recruiting executives or making sales/biz dev introductions.
10. Great investors recognize when they have a conflict around a portfolio company and are clear to represent their points of view with proper context, recusing themselves from meetings or votes when appropriate.

You owe it to yourself to have great investors backing you. Find ones who meet every criterion on this list.

If you don't have access to high-net-worth individuals—and you don't have significant savings yourself—starting a company can be extremely difficult. There are a number of types of debt you can take on to finance your business. While debt typically makes more sense for mature business, there are times when debt can work for a startup.

Convertible Debt

Sometimes angel investors, or even early stage venture capitalists, will want to structure a deal as convertible debt instead of equity. That means you're taking on debt, which will have to be paid back per the terms of the loan, unless it converts into equity based on whatever triggers you agree to. The triggers could be around company milestones, like revenue or product shipping, but they could also be around financing milestones, like attracting other investors to the table, where the debt would convert to equity at the terms of that financing, or maybe at a slight discount to those terms.

The Good: Convertible debt isn't a bad deal at all for a young company. It makes particular sense if you are already working on a venture or strategic financing and want to pull in a little cash earlier but are nervous about setting the terms of that financing in a way that might spook the larger investor.

The Bad: A hastily written convertible debt agreement could convert *too much* of your debt into stock for your investors. This is an early stage strategy—too early to give away a significant chunk of your company.

The Ugly: This form of debt is a bigger drag on your balance sheet than most other forms of investment. In good times—economic and for the company—this isn't a major consideration. In hard times, it can limit your options.

Venture Debt

Venture debt is essentially a combination of debt and equity. It is cheaper in terms of dilution than preferred equity but it has to be paid back with interest in between one and three years. Because of the payment requirement, you will need some revenue and a proven business model in order to raise venture debt.

The Good: Early payments will often be mostly interest, with most of the principal paid near or at the end of the term. If you have a good venture partner they will often enable you to renew the principal at the end of the term for additional consideration.

The Bad: Venture debt investors don't require board seats, but they do have operational demands like standard reporting, senior liens on all assets including intellectual property (senior to any other equity but junior to commercial debt) and sometimes basic financial covenants. The equity piece is normally structured as "warrants" that enable the investor the right to buy a certain amount of shares at a fixed price, usually the price of your last round of venture financing.

The Ugly: "Interest-only" are interest-only for a specified term. If the underlying asset—your company—proves to be worth more than the size of the loan, this won't be a problem. Otherwise, you will be stuck with a significant principal payment down the road. If you think that's an unlikely scenario, just ask a homeowner who got stuck with a balloon payment in 2008.

Bank Loans

Banks are how most traditional companies get their financing. Traditionally, they're not the right place for startups. Startup investors take the uncertainty of startup business plans for granted. Those uncertainties will be nonstarters at your local branch.

The Good: Bank loans are relatively transparent and you're not likely to be surprised by a complex set of terms. They'll give you X, you have to pay back X plus interest on a regular schedule.

The Bad: Banks won't bankroll ideas that are years away from producing revenue. Business loans are great if you're opening a storefront or another traditional business but they won't patiently wait for your startup to hockey stick. Why should they? No matter how successful you are, their upside is fixed in advance.

The Ugly: You can't miss payments, no matter how big next quarter is going to be. Everything your company owns is potentially collateral and it won't take long for the bank to start calling it in—and many banks ask for personal guarantees. It's not exactly the *Goodfellas* "F*&% you. Pay me." But it's not that far off unless you're well into the growth stage, or at least the revenue stage of your startup.

Personal Debt

Maxing out your credit cards. Mortgaging your house. Mortgaging your parents' house. You hear about these things from time to time. They are part of the romance of startups. Once in a while, they work. There's also an extremely personal element to this decision that has a lot to do with one's family circumstances (both your own and that of your parents).

For me, I'd never really want to do this beyond a bare minimum of a few months' worth of Web hosting expense and some basic marketing materials (and forgoing salary). If your idea is that great, you should be able to find someone to help you finance it. If nothing else, see the next section on bootstrapping. 95 percent of startups fail and putting your personal credit score on the line to fund your dream is a higher-stakes game of poker than even the thickest-skinned entrepreneur should engage in.

BOOTSTRAPPING

Not every startup is founded with an infusion of capital, nor do they need to be. The other option is "bootstrapping": funding a company from your personal finances and your initial operating revenues. The two most common types of bootstrapping are customer financing and your company's cash flow.

Customer Financing

Customers don't lend you money; they pay for your services. Some are even willing to do so in advance. That's called customer financing. If you can pull it off, it's great.

The Good: If customers will pay for your products and services in advance (think Kickstarter or Indiegogo for business-to-consumer [B2C] and you can also sell something to a big enterprise customer ahead of delivery), it's incredible validation of the market value of your idea.

The Bad: Customers can react very badly when startups fail to meet milestones. VCs expect this but customers may never come back.

The Ugly: As diverse a group as "customers" may sound, the consumer end of this entire category may be eliminated by the failure of a few prominent, crowdsourced projects. It's too early to tell but this is a real danger that entrepreneurs in a hurry should be wary of. Business-to-business (B2B) customer financing, however, is much more like finding a strategic investor.

Your Own Cash Flow

Your own regular cash flow (not maxing out your credit cards) is another way to finance a new venture—for a while. This usually takes the form of starting a business off the side of your desk while you still have another job, or starting your company and then doing a bunch of consulting work on the side to pay some of the bills. (Consult an employment lawyer before doing this to understand the intellectual property risks you're incurring.)

The Good: You retain all the equity and don't take on any debt or customer expectations.

The Bad: You find yourself serving two separate masters at the same time, which is a difficult juggling act, at best.

The Ugly: You completely burn yourself out because you're effectively doing two jobs—then what happens to your new company?

After making a modest investment of your own time and resources, you really can't launch a startup without finding another source of funding. Let this sense of urgency drive your search for financing but don't let it lead you to the wrong *kind* of financing or the wrong investors. Whenever an opportunity presents itself, review the Good, the Bad and the Ugly in this chapter and make sure it's an opportunity that will lead to success and growth—rather than a short-term infusion of cash that will lead to long-term headaches.

CHAPTER TWENTY-ONE

WHEN AND HOW TO RAISE MONEY

The answer to both of these questions, of course, depends on the stage of your business. The general rule is that the best time to start looking for money is when you don't need it—but not so early that a potential investor can watch your business closely for too long a period of time before the deal. All startups have hiccups along the way and many investors are easily spooked by reality.

WHEN TO START LOOKING FOR MONEY

If you're looking for seed capital, you may not have too many options in terms of timing but it's best to do everything you can to keep bootstrapping things along with consulting or one-off projects. Why? At the proof-of-concept stage, the value of your company increases sharply with every new customer or new release, so it's best not to take capital too early—as long as you can live without it.

If you have a business that's generating real customer revenue, with a cash balance and a predictable burn rate and you have never taken in institutional capital before, you should probably start talking to VCs six months before you run out of cash. While you don't want VCs to anchor a valuation in their mind too early, the reality is that it takes time to get these your first institutional deal done. Furthermore, you definitely want to talk to several different firms, so a little more lead time is better. This is especially true if your window of time interferes with August or the holiday season, when not much new business gets done at VCs unless you have a super-hot deal.

If you're looking for expansion capital and are near or at profitability, deals will probably take less time to get done and valuations are likely to fluctuate less. In these cases, I'd say less lead time is required, although if you're in a volatile industry, you may need the capital sooner than you think!

Again, the best time to look for money is when you don't need it. Investors (even the nicest ones) aren't afraid to "market-price" a deal lower if they sense desperation—or, more important, a lack of alternatives. To that end, the most important piece of advice I can give you is—have a BATNA (Best Alternative to a Negotiated Agreement).

THE TOP 11 TAKEAWAYS FOR FINANCING NEGOTIATIONS

The most important part of the venture financing process is negotiating the term sheet. Although they're only two to three pages long, term sheets contain summaries of all the critical aspects of a financing and once they're signed, the remainder of the financing process is significantly more automatic.

For the real meat on term sheets, see Brad Feld and Jason Mendelson's *Venture Deals*, with my contributions on "The Entrepreneur's Perspective."

Based on the financings I've seen and worked on—both as a VC many years ago and as an entrepreneur and board member—my top 11 biggest takeaways for entrepreneurs are as follows:

1. *Get a good lawyer.* I mean a *really* good one. Not just one whom you are comfortable with and who is productive and doesn't charge you too much (as Brad and Jason say in *Venture Deals*, "your wife's brother's friend's neighbor") but one who knows venture financings like the back of his or her hand. No matter how many deals you have worked on, your lawyer has worked on more of them.
2. *Focus on terms that matter, otherwise known as "pick your battles."* A typical VC term sheet will have at least 20 terms spelled out in it. There are only a few that really matter in the end, although you should at least make sure your lawyer is comfortable that the others are reasonable and somewhat standard. Spend time on valuation, the type of security, the option pool, board composition, and your own compensation and rights.

3. *Sacrifice valuation for a clean security.* Everyone always thinks that price/valuation is the most important thing to maximize in a deal. However, the structure of the security can be much more important in the long run. Whether the VCs buy 33 percent of your company or 30 percent of your company is much less important than having a capital structure that's easy for an outsider to understand and want to join (e.g., investment banker or later-stage VC).
4. *Always have a BATNA (a fancy way of saying Plan B).* This is probably the most important piece of advice I can offer. This is true of any negotiation, not just a term sheet (see the sidebar at the end of this chapter).
5. *Be prepared to pay up for high-quality investors.* There is a world of difference between good VCs and bad VCs (both the individual partners and the firms) that will ultimately have a lot to do with how successful your company can become. The quality of your VC isn't more important than the quality of your product or your team but it's right up there. But—and this is an important but—you should expect to pay for quality in the form of slightly weaker terms (whether valuation or type of security). This is where having a BATNA really comes in handy.
6. *Ask for references.* Don't be shy: prospective VCs are checking up on you and you have every right to do the same with them. Ask them for references of CEOs they've worked with. Ask them for a CEO they've had to fire as a reference. The good ones will give you the full roster of everyone they've ever funded and tell you to call them all. The bad ones will give you two names and ask for time to prep them ahead of time.
7. *Don't let the VC get away with negotiating a point by saying "we always do it this way."* That's just not true. VCs may have a preferred way of doing deals or handling a specific term but every deal they've ever done is different—and they know it. If there's a compelling reason for them to insist on a particular term, you have the right to hear it, if it's important to you. (But remember to pick your battles!)
8. *If you have multiple investors in the syndicate, insist on a single investor counsel and a lead investor.* This is essential to (a) protect your sanity and (b) prevent you from paying zillions of dollars in legal fees. You have to make the VCs stick to it, though—they can't come back and retrade the deal after it's been negotiated. This is also

helpful in getting a syndicate cooperating with each other and aligning the members' interests, particularly if it has investors who have participated in different rounds of the company's financing. Do expect to play moderator constantly throughout the process, however, to ensure that it goes smoothly.

9. *Try to deal in advance with follow-on financings.* When an investor doesn't participate in a follow-on financing, it creates a total nightmare for you. Other investors will want to punish their wayward colleague and can create massive collateral damage in the process to common shareholders and management. Just as VCs will insist on something called "preemptive rights" (the right to invest in future financings if they want), you and your lawyer should insist on some protection in the event that one of your investors abandons you when you are raising more capital.
10. *Handle the term sheet negotiation carefully.* Whether it's an initial round or a follow-on round, how you handle yourself in this negotiation sets the tone for the next stage of your relationship with the VC. The financing is the line of demarcation between you and the VC courting each other and the VC joining your board and effectively becoming your boss.
11. *Don't forget to say thank you at the end of the process.* Whether you send a formal email, a handwritten note, or a token gift, be sure to thank your VCs after a financing. They're putting their butt on the line for your company; they're investing in *you;* and they're making it possible for you to pursue your dream. That deserves a thoughtful "thanks."

BATNA: The "Best Alternative to a Negotiated Agreement" (a.k.a. "Plan B")

It's often said that good choices come from good options. Sometimes, you have to walk away from a deal where you have invested a lot of time, energy, and emotion. As an entrepreneur, you can mitigate the number of times you have to walk away by developing good alternative options to a particular deal. That way, if one option doesn't pan out as you'd hoped, another very good option is waiting in the wings.

Dying to get a deal with a good VC? If you negotiate with one of them, you may or may not end up with a deal you like and it could suddenly change on you at the 11th hour. If you negotiate with two or three of them, you'll have a great backstop and won't let the emotional investment in the deal get the best of you. Trying to sell a company? You'd better have a couple of acquirers in mind to maximize price.

There's a very business school–sounding term called the BATNA, which stands for the "best alternative to a negotiated agreement." It's just a fancy way of saying Plan B. Sometimes, developing a good BATNA, or Plan B, can take as much time as working on Plan A. It's well worth it if it ensures that you will have multiple good options at the end of the process—which will invariably result in a good choice.

If you have two or three VCs who are interested in funding you, I can guarantee you will end up with better terms from the highest-quality investor in the group if you play the negotiation well. If you have one term sheet, you have zero leverage in your negotiation. Yes, you will spend twice to three times the amount of time on the process but it's well worth it.

CHAPTER TWENTY-TWO

FORECASTING AND BUDGETING

Like all elements of startup planning, the only thing you know about a budget or forecast when you finish it is that it's wrong. You just don't know how wrong it is or in what way it's wrong.

This is a difficult reality but it isn't a problem. Startups aren't about reading the crystal ball; they're about your ability to *react*. That doesn't mean you shouldn't make predictions, you just need to be willing to recalibrate them constantly based on new data. There are two things that you *can* predict: revenue will take longer realize than you expect and expenses will be higher than expected. Budget accordingly.

RIGOROUS FINANCIAL MODELING

Every CEO—startup or otherwise—should be able to roughly model their business and understand its main financial drivers. These might change over time. To be more precise, these *will* change over time, probably quite drastically. That isn't an excuse to avoid making predictions about your cash flow and your expenses. It's the reason why you have to continually adjust those predictions based on new realities.

Financial modeling is not only a task to be strictly delegated to your CFO. That person may *own* your financial model but you need to be extremely comfortable working your way around it, changing variables, understanding how little changes you make in those variables ripple through from concept to cash.

"That new client is going to be huge" isn't a satisfactory prediction of cash flow and "We're going to run a bit over this quarter" isn't a budget prediction.

If you want to be a CEO, you must understand the basic mechanics of balance sheet, cash flow, and P&L statements. These aren't distractions from the essential work of changing the world and disrupting the marketplace. They're the only ways that you can honestly—and rigorously—judge how close you are to actually achieving those goals. If you can't do the model yourself, you're going to have a very hard time understanding the levers when they're presented to you and you're going to have a hard time making critical business decisions as a result. If you want to abdicate all of those responsibilities, you should consider being Chief Product Officer or Chairman. You can still wear your founder badge with pride.

Forecasting and Budgeting in a Downturn

When Lehman Brothers failed in 2008, we were nervous. Everyone in the world was nervous. We have a recurring revenue model at Return Path, which makes revenue much more predictable than it is in areas like media and manufacturing, so were lucky. Nonetheless, we immediately forecast much higher customer churn, price reductions and slower customer adoption. The one thing we *failed* to forecast was longer collection cycles: every company we worked with started hoarding cash in late 2008 and we effectively found ourselves financing Fortune 500 companies so they could pad their cash balances for Wall Street. That proved to be a nightmare on *our* balance sheet—but the rest of our planning certainly helped.

Things change rapidly in an economic downturn. Make sure you reforecast monthly rather than quarterly, especially cash and cash flows. Develop your core revenue streams and make sure they're really your revenue—not just skimming tertiary revenue out of the ecosystem (like only making money on remnant online advertising inventory or affiliate fees). A downturn will really lay bare a revenue model that's unsustainable.

OF COURSE YOU'RE WRONG—BUT WRONG *HOW*?

If your internal financial models are as broadly stated as your pitch deck, you won't have good answers to these questions. If you went through the process of rigorously modeling every potential revenue stream or expense, you can check your predictions against reality. This allows you to do a few things:

- *Better understand the drivers of your business.* Keep things vague ("we need to accelerate customer growth") and you're understanding of your business will stay vague. Force yourself to work through a balance sheet and P&L statement and you will start discovering the *precise* drivers that move the needle in your business.
- *Measure success or failure against a baseline.* Even if your baseline predictions are wrong, they give you a less arbitrary way to measure performance than deciding after the fact whether you're happy with a given quarter's results.
- *Recalibrate your models based on outcomes.* Every model should be an improvement over the last one. What did you get wrong this time? How can you avoid the same blind spot or mistake the next time?

Startup business plans—and startup cash flow predictions and startup budgets—are essentially formalized guesses. There's nothing wrong with that. Formalize your guesses enough times and they will start turning into meaningful predictions. Skip the process and your decision making will never improve.

Former Quickoffice CEO Alan Masarek on Aligning Resources with Strategy

Alan Masarek is one of the most disciplined business operators I know. (Google must have thought so too: they recently acquired his company Quickoffice.) To open this section, I have asked him to talk about the nexus of resources and strategy.

The job of a startup CEO is generally tougher than that of running a more established company. Startup CEOs face a veritable Rubik's Cube of challenges, trying to run companies with constrained resources while operating in developing markets. This fundamental challenge is the essence of what this section attempts to define. Simply stated, how can startup CEOs align their constrained cash and human resources alongside business strategies that will inevitably change as their targeted markets evolve?

I believe most CEOs intellectually understand that their targeted market segments will change frequently. However, the failure of many of these same CEOs is to not synchronize their resources with this in mind. To achieve a successful outcome, CEOs must keep this continual change in mind.

The first thing to remember is that most startups fail simply because they run out of money. Cash for a startup is like oxygen for you and me. Without it, your business dies! While this is a widely understood fact, all too frequently we see startups pursuing overly broad business objectives without sufficient cash to stay in business long enough to achieve those objectives. In essence, their business strategies are not aligned with their funding realities and these companies fail without achieving the progress necessary to secure additional funding to keep going. In fact, they might have only accomplished 50 percent of what they needed to do to raise additional funding. Had they pursued a strategy that was half as broad, they might have accomplished 100 percent of their goal and been able to secure the funding required to continue.

Another common pitfall for startups relates to the timing and magnitude of spending. For example, it is common for startups to spend an inordinate share of their precious cash on marketing *before* their product or business model has proven viable. In the worst case, companies only serve to hurt themselves by attracting customers via aggressive marketing efforts but then disappointing them with products that are incomplete and unpolished. It's even more difficult and expensive to attract customers after a negative experience than it is to capture a new customer with a superior product or business model.

In my experience as co-founder and CEO of Quickoffice, Inc., we encountered these "business and resource" alignment challenges many times. In our early years, mobile was dominated by rudimentary mobile phones and PDAs, and our business struggled. Later, our business thrived with the explosive growth in high-end smartphones and tablets like the iPad. At each step along the way, we labored to align our resources with our market opportunity and financial resources. It was hard and we made mistakes aplenty but using a baseball metaphor, we managed to "hit with a high batting average." We were able to successfully navigate them by following many of the themes that Matt outlines below and our efforts were rewarded when we sold Quickoffice to Google in 2012.

The alignment of your business strategy with your resources is really tough and you will rarely know you have done it well or not so well, until after the fact. I believe your goal is to achieve that "high batting average" so your business will stay healthy enough to continue forward successfully. That's the lesson I hope you take away from this section.

Alan Masarek, Former CEO, Quickoffice

BUDGETING IN A CONTEXT OF UNCERTAINTY

A lack of certainty around revenue forecasts and budgetary needs should have one certain outcome: managing expenses on the assumption of worst-case scenario—or something close to it.

After a few quarters of laying out your predictions and checking them against reality, you will probably notice two consistent themes, as I mentioned at the beginning of the chapter:

- Revenue always takes longer to realize than you expect.
- Expenses are always higher than you expect.

Again, Brad and Jason made this point very well in *Venture Deals*: "Since your revenue forecast will be wrong, your cash flow forecast will be wrong. However, *if you are an effective manager, you will know how to budget for this by focusing on lagging your increase in cash spend behind your expected growth in revenue*" (emphasis mine).

Assume that your revenue will be lower than expected and you won't burn through your cash reserves ahead of schedule. Budget against the most optimistic scenario—and you will go broke.

FORECAST, EARLY AND OFTEN

I don't want the previous section to suggest that I'm unaware of how painful this process is. Even in industries without the radical uncertainty of startups, forecasting is a pain. To alleviate this pain somewhat when we were earlier in our revenue cycle, we adopted a 12-month rolling forecast model at Return Path, with quarterly reforecasts. Sometimes, there are simply too many moving parts in a business to provide enough visibility to produce an accurate 12-month budget. Four things in particular can make this extremely difficult:

1. *Investment and return.* You make investment decisions every day and you can get pretty good over the years at predicting return on investment. Predicting the *timing* of that return can be very difficult. Products ship late; customer seasonality can factor in; marketing campaigns can take longer to pay back than you expect.

2. *Competition*. By definition, you have even less of an idea what competitors will do—or for that matter, when new competitors will arrive on the scene. Any competitive activity can impact pricing and lengthen sales cycles in ways that are hard to predict.
3. *M&A*. Any acquisition you make throws the entire budget into chaos, both on the revenue side and the cost side.
4. *Revenue gaps*. No revenue model has perfect predictability. Media businesses are notoriously lumpy, cyclical and economy driven. For any business that has a recurring revenue model, missing your numbers in a given month or quarter makes it nearly impossible to get back on track for the rest of the year, since *next* quarter's number depend on making *this* quarter's numbers. This is what Fred Wilson calls the "New York Jets syndrome:" once you lose seven games, you know you're not getting into the playoffs.

Forecasting early and often is a great solution to this problem and it's a particularly effective tool to keep the team motivated. There's no shame in doing this: even large public companies consistently set new guidance to Wall Street at the end of every quarter for the following quarter and remainder of the year. Because it's a bit of a pain, I'd recommend that CEOs and CFOs follow a few practices we have learned over the years:

- *Make sure you have an incredibly flexible spreadsheet model that supports the process.* You can't reinvent the model four times per year. It has to be able to handle multiple scenarios with easy-to-use toggles and it has to be able to accept "actuals" as well as forecasts.
- *Manage expectations properly with the board and with the team.* As long as everyone knows what the process is, you can avoid a lot of confusion. The critical thing here is that neither constituency should feel like the system is being gamed or that numbers are being sandbagged.
- *Compare to originals.* Our model produces "waterfall" comparison charts showing how a given quarter's forecast changed over the quarters leading up to it and then how the forecasts compared to actuals. This is important mostly to produce learnings about how to forecast better in the future.
- *Plan to work your way out of the process over time.* Do quarterly budgets for a year or two, move to semiannual budgets for a couple of years and then try moving to full-year budgets.

This process has become much more important as the typical lifespan of a startup has grown from two to three years to exit, to a decade or more. As Fred Wilson has pointed out, the preponderance of Internet companies either get acquired early on in their life (e.g., for less than $50 million) or once they have achieved escape velocity—at which point IPOs are also common. He says that the space in between, "the valley," is where a lot of solid VC-backed companies sit and where good solid returns are made. I'd add that the valley is exactly where it's critical to forecast early and often; that's where businesses are working their hardest to grow from proof of concept to escape velocity, often with limited visibility 12 months out on their budget.

Management Moment

Follow the Facts

Successful teams know how to get outside of themselves. They have no personal agenda in mind—only the best interests of the company. They make every effort to see issues on which they disagree from the opposing point of view. They understand the difference between fact and opinion. There are so many memorable quotes on this topic, I'm not sure where to start, so I'll list them all in the hope that one sticks with you:

- Winston Churchill: "Facts are stubborn things."
- Various: "The plural of 'anecdote' is not 'data.'"
- Anonymous: "If we're going to base our decision on facts, let's hash them out. If we're going to base our decision on opinion, let's use mine."

If everyone on a team not only understands what is and what is not a fact and all team members are naturally curious to understand and root out all the relevant facts of an issue, that's when the magic happens.

CHAPTER TWENTY-THREE

COLLECTING DATA

Unless you're a sole proprietor, with every minute that passes from the moment you found your company, you know less about it. While you're never going to know everything, collecting data, both inside and outside your organization, is an important skill that only grows in importance as your company grows.

EXTERNAL DATA

Mike Mills, a long-time Return Path senior manager, frequently refers to the NIHITO Principle: Nothing Interesting Happens in the Office. Now that's not entirely true: running a company requires spending a huge amount of time with people and on people issues. Setting your company's vision and strategy means situating it into a larger market context. What problem are you solving? Whose needs are you meeting? Who else is trying to reach the same audience? You can't answer those questions intelligently without being "in-market." Spend time with customers and channel partners. Actively work industry associations. Get to know customers well. Walk the floor at a conference. Understand what the substitute products are and not only the direct competition.

In one year alone, I traveled nearly 160,000 miles around the world to meet with prospects, clients, partners, and industry luminaries. You don't have to be a road warrior to get this one right. You can attend events in your local area and develop a local network of people you can meet with regularly. If you're running a company with consumer products, it may be a lot easier. You do have to get out of the office.

Learning from Customers

One of the greatest gifts that you can give to yourself and your team is the insight that you get by spending time in the market with a few of your top customers or prospects. I have always found that to be one of the most valuable ways to shape the business, both strategically and operationally.

One of the most vivid memories I have to illustrate this concept is a meeting that I had with Crate & Barrel, a prospect, in the very early days of Return Path. I went in with a number of product sales specialists from our reseller, DoubleClick (back when DoubleClick was in the email business), for an all-day session with C&B's online marketing team. We collectively were pitching everything, possibly including the kitchen sink—ad serving through DART, buying online media through the DoubleClick Network, using Abacus to expand the reach of their catalog, sending email through DARTMail, renting email lists through DoubleClick's email list business, and, oh yes, using Return ECOA service to keep their email database clean.

The meeting was a mess. As far as I can tell, it didn't lead to any meaningful business, either for us or for DoubleClick. During this meeting, I learned two things the hard way but both were incredibly valuable lessons that continue to shape our business today.

First, we created massive confusion by bringing multiple salespeople in to each present a specific product to the customer, rather than sending in one senior, consultative salesperson to present a holistic digital marketing solution. Picture yourself as the head of e-commerce for a major retailer, expecting an insightful day with the leading vendor in the space. You walk into the meeting and see seven different salespeople introducing themselves—to each other! Since then, we have tried hard to run with a single sales force organized around our customers, rather than multiple sales teams organized around our own products.

Second, we discovered that the original version of our flagship ECOA product (which was still in beta at the time) had a couple of flaws that were probably going to make it a nonstarter in the retail vertical. We also learned, happily, that the client loved the concept. There were some details in the original product that had to be fixed if we were ever going to get traction with key customers in that key segment. We fixed these problems and were able to successfully relaunch the product later that year. More important, we now stay much closer to our customers as we develop new products and features, assuring that our design concepts are firmly market tested before they head into development.

I could have introduced this anecdote in chapters on "Sales" or "Product Development" but the specific lessons aren't the point. The point is that these key insights were gained in a single customer meeting. I could have spent months in our sales pit and it might never have occurred to me to reorganize the entire unit around customer solutions rather than Return Path products. Similarly, a significant investment into our beta testing operation would have yielded far less than the simple insight that we needed to test out our ideas in the market long before they became workable products. Again: both of these radical (and, in the long run, extremely valuable) shifts were the result of an hour or two spent with a customer rather than in the office. If that doesn't prove the value of the NIHITO principle, I can't imagine what would.

Learning from (Un)Employees

As I write this, Return Path has 400 employees in 12 offices around the world. That number has probably changed slightly as this book has gone to press but I can always call Angela Baldonero, our SVP of People, for the latest count. I'd have a harder time telling you exactly how many un-employees we have.

Un-employees are people in our industry. They are friends of Return Path. In some cases, they are people whom we have almost hired over the years—sometimes more than once, but we never have. They're friends of Return Path. Sometime they're clients or partners. Sometimes they aren't. Sometimes they have a token stock option grant as advisers. Sometimes they don't.

What all of our un-employees have in common is that they have played an incredibly valuable role in our company's development over the years. They're extra sets of eyes and ears for us. They often give us valuable information long before any of our regular employees hear anything. They make powerful connections for us with other companies in the industry. They know us well enough to know our products and strategy to give us sound advice—unsolicited but always appreciated. In truth, they're probably more valuable to us as un-employees than they would be as employees!

Our un-employees aren't industry luminaries or CEOs and they aren't classic advisers or board members. They never meet as a group and there's nothing formal about the relationship. In fact, formalizing the relationship would be a mistake: it would take them out of the market and put them into the company. That's where our employees belong and that's where startup CEOs are forced to spend a significant portion of their time. Un-employees are another connection to the world outside. There's no reason to sever it.

"The Nachos Don't Have Enough Beef in Them!"

Here's a story for you.

I'm sitting at the bar of Sam Snead's Tavern in Port St. Lucie, Florida, having dinner solo while I wait for my friend Karl to arrive. I ask the bartender where he's from, since he has an accent. Nice conversation about how life is rough in Belfast and thank goodness for the American dream. I ask him what to order for dinner and tell him a couple of menu items I'm contemplating. He says, "I don't know why they don't listen to me. I keep telling them that all the people here say that the nachos aren't good because they don't have enough beef in them." I order something else. Five minutes later, someone else pounds his hand on the bar and barks out, "Give me a Heineken and a plate of nachos." The bartender enters the order into the point-of-sale system.

What's the lesson?

Listen to your front-line employees—in fact, make them your customer research team. I have seen and heard this time and again. Employees deal with unhappy customers, then roll their eyes, knowing full well about all the problems the customers are encountering and also believing that management either knows already or doesn't care. There's no reason for this! At a minimum, you should always listen to your customer-facing employees, internalize the feedback and act on it. They hear and see it all. Next best prize: ask them questions. Better yet: get them to actively solicit customer feedback.

INTERNAL DATA

There are a number of tactics you can use to collect more data from inside your organization. Having an open-door policy is one. Doing regular employee lunches or breakfasts or in-office roundtables is another. Management by walking around is a third. There are others as well.

Skip-Level Meetings

I will discuss the best way to approach "skip-level" meetings later. Here, I want to reiterate how valuable they are as tools for gathering data. The employees you speak with who *don't* report directly to you will give you insights into details that probably aren't on their managers' radars. More important, this is an extremely valuable way to confirm whether your managers and their teams are aligned—if you hear radically different things from your reports and *their* reports, you have a problem that needs to be addressed right away.

Subbing

Another way to collect data from your organization is to actively substitute for your team members when they are out. Usually, when someone on your team goes on vacation, it's easiest to just let things run for that week or two. The people who report to you know you're around if they need something but you don't take over actively working with them, right?

I learned the value of *not* doing this when our first wave of employees started taking their seven-year sabbaticals. Six weeks is too long for autopilot. So, I actively sub in for team members on sabbatical. Sit in their offices. Have weekly meetings with their staff as a group and 1:1. Work with them on their goals. Attend meetings that I'm not normally invited to.

The insight I get into things in specific areas of the business is great. I learn more about the ins and outs of everyone's work, more about the team dynamic and more about how the team works with other groups in the company. Most importantly, I'm learning more about how my staff members and I interact and how I can manage that interaction better in the future. I'm making or suggesting some small changes here and there on the margin.

You don't need to wait until someone takes a leave of absence or a lengthy sabbatical to try this technique out. You can use any vacation someone on your team takes as an excuse to get closer to the front lines. You will be amazed at how much you learn.

Productive Eavesdropping

A while back, we did some pretty extensive renovations of our office. For better or for worse, we did this work without moving out. We basically crammed everyone into one half of the office while the contractors were working on the other half; when that work was done, we all crammed into the finished half.

One of the interesting side effects of this project is that I shared my office with Anita Absey, our head of sales. It was the first time I shared an office in quite a while, at least since the first year of the company's life when we all sat in one big room together. The two of us got in a lot more time together than we usually do. As much as we tried to block out the sound coming from across the room, there was plenty of inadvertent eavesdropping in both directions.

For my part, I enjoyed it. I had more insight into the sales organization. I got much more of a window into what Anita works on than usual. We had a lot of quick back-and-forths. When we had our weekly check-ins, they were half their normal length, since we had already covered much of the topics in our casual conversation.

There are some companies that have a "no office" policy for everyone. While there are challenges to that kind of office layout (I definitely have many confidential or private conversations throughout the day and spend a lot of time on phone calls or Skype), I am considering making that change here now. I recently visited the office of my friend Jon Zabusky, CEO of Seamless, and he has a no office policy, including a Leadership Table where his entire senior management team sat shoulder to shoulder all day, with plenty of private conference space nearby as needed. However you institutionalize productive eavesdropping, it's a great way to collect data from your team.

The bigger you get, the more important it is that you get good at collecting data, from wherever you can collect it. Even if you're the kind of decision maker who acts on intuition, intuition works best when it's informed by knowledge and experience.

CHAPTER TWENTY-FOUR

MANAGING IN TOUGH TIMES

If you lead your company long enough, you will lead it through some difficult stretches. Sometimes, they will be caused by a downturn in the economy. Other times, they will be caused by the business itself—either as a result of competitors, industry context, or execution. Managing in tough times is much harder than managing in good times. It's also more important not just for getting through the tough time but for reshaping the company for the future.

MANAGING IN AN ECONOMIC DOWNTURN

One of the benefits of running a company for more than a decade is that you start seeing some of the same macro trends more than once. For me, that means having lived and led through both the 2000 recession and the 2008 meltdown. The two recessions hit the Internet economy quite differently. The first one was devastating for Internet companies, since the Internet wasn't mature yet as either an advertising or commerce vehicle and much of the money fueling the growth of the sector was stock market money in a bubble. The second was, in some ways, productive for Internet companies, as the more mature sector was able to steal dollars from traditional sectors in the name of efficiency.

That said, leading and managing through both downturns was quite challenging and revealing. Your people are nervous. They're concerned about their bank accounts and their jobs. As CEO, you have to be even more present, more transparent and more communicative than usual. You have to set the right tone on expenses with your own decisions. The troops need to know that you care about them and that you have a steady hand on the wheel.

Some of the things I have learned about managing in a downturn are timeless.

Hope Is Not a Strategy— But It's Not a Bad Tactic

Your business is not immune to economic downturns. It will do what everyone else's will: struggle to hit its numbers, struggle to collect bills, lose customers. There is no reason to hope you will be different. If in fact your business is the one in a million that is immune—or, better, countercyclical—you will know it and can act accordingly. It's better to hunker down and prepare for the worst, even as you hope for the best. Assume that there will be a long road to recovery. Rarely is there a strong "V-shaped" bounce back from a true downturn. Plan for a long (four to eight quarter) time to return to normalcy.

If you have a real business, you need to be it for the long haul. Keep pursuing opportunities. Keep investing in the future. Don't pare back your vision and ambitions. Just make more conservative investments, insist on shorter payback windows, and adjust expectations about time frames.

Remember, as difficult as it is to ratchet down, sometimes ratcheting back up is even harder and you don't want to put yourself in a position where critical functions need to be rebuilt from scratch when things get better. Starving HR, for example, only means that when it's time to hire again, no one is there to do that work. Starving IT just means that nothing works—when you're ready to hire again, your employees have solved 5 problems in 50 different ways that need to be corralled. Starving training and development means that your individual contributors will feel like their years of hard work aren't appreciated when you have to bring in a new layer of management because they haven't had the feedback and coaching to get that promoted themselves.

You have to get your company through the downturn but you also have to keep your eye on the future. Hope may not be a strategy but it can be a useful background tactic.

Look for Nickels and Dimes under the Sofa

In the fall of 2008, we were on a crusade against extraneous expenses. We kept hacking away at the bigger and more obvious items. Fewer consultants. Turn that offsite meeting into an onsite meeting. Reduce the number of new hires. Then we realized that we needed a new target on our income statement to reduce expenses further: the line item known as "Other G&A" (i.e., "General and Administrative Expenses"), which different companies call things such as "General Office," or simply "Other." It's a relatively inconspicuous line on the income statement but it's inherently problematic *not* because it encompasses a huge amount of expenses but rather because it inherently doesn't have an owner and rarely has a budget.

As we dug into the gory details of "Other G&A," our team came to a realization: it's not that we buy too many pens, per se. It's that the absence of someone being in charge of that line item means that no one manages it to a budget—or even just manages it to some kind of reasonability test.

Little things add up to big things in the end. Whether it's duplication of expenses, too much FedEx, forgotten recurring items, or the storage locker that we forgot about years ago, you will spot little ways to save money left and right. Sneak those items into "Other G&A," and nobody will take responsibility for managing them responsibly.

Making Tough Financial Decisions

It's almost inevitable that during your tenure as CEO, you will have to make some tough calls to reduce expenses—the toughest of all, of course, being the need to lay off some of your staff. These decisions suck and it's easy to view them through the lens of math: pick the biggest areas of cost savings, implement them, and don't worry about the little things. That's a mistake. Sometimes it's the smaller things that attract attention and breed cynicism when left in place.

Even if you're not an extravagant company, there is almost always room to save. When your priorities in a downturn become protecting everyone's job, everyone's salary, and health benefits, you start realizing that extraneous items don't always count for a lot. Sending 5 people to a big trade show can have a comparable impact to sending 10. You don't have to be the vendor who picks up the tab at the end of the night. You don't need to pay for half the company to have cell phones to retain top talent.

When the economic downturn hit in late 2008, we scrambled to reduce our expenses in every way possible besides cutting heads so that we (hopefully) wouldn't have to do layoffs. One of the things we cut was Pilates class in our Colorado office, an expense that couldn't have cost more than $2,000/year. Practically speaking, it didn't make a difference to our budget one way or another. Even for a company obsessed with its employees and their well-being, this felt like something that had to go in an era where we're cutting back. (Picture your employees rolling their eyes at a sushi buffet lunch, saying, "We should have given this up so Sally could have kept her job.") Your symbolic action here tells the rest of your employee population that it's time to buckle down and fly straight. They will.

Never Waste a Good Crisis

As Barack Obama's first chief of staff, Rahm Emanuel, said when Obama took office in 2009, right after the financial meltdown started, you should "never waste a good crisis." If you can lead your organization to get more done with less when times are tough, that means you have improved the collective ability of your organization to prioritize, execute, win, and beat the odds. Your job as a leader is to figure out how to make those things stick when times get better.

Holding your organization's collective nerve in a crisis can change a lot of things about your organization for the better and there's no need to reverse course on those things just because we can. Here's one example, one of many we had from the 2008–2009 period: When we cut our travel budget by 50 percent, everyone on the team looked at us like we were crazy and said there was no way we'd be able to make budget. Guess what? We *beat* the slashed budget by almost a third, without complaint! Why should we triple it going forward to get back to where we were?

ARTICULATE THE PROBLEM

I have always thought that the ability to stare down adversity in business is a critical part of being a mature professional.

How you manage the emotions of your organization when times are tough is key. Just as leadership counts extra in an economic downturn when people are afraid for their jobs, leadership counts extra when your business faces its own challenges. People may not be scared or insecure but they are suddenly aware that there is more scrutiny on their performance. When things are going well, everyone benefits and it's easy to overlook problem areas in the business. When things aren't going well, everyone is in a bad mood and it's easy to blame everyone and everything.

A while back, we were having some specific challenges in the business that were *really* hard to diagnose. It was like peeling the proverbial onion: every time we thought we had the answer to what was going on, we realized all we had was another symptom, not a root cause. We're a pretty analytical bunch, so we kept looking for more and more data to give us answers. We kept coming up with, well, not all that much—besides a lot of handwringing.

It wasn't until I went into a bit of a cave (i.e., took half a day's quiet time to myself) and started writing things down for myself that I started to get some clarity around the problem and potential solutions. I literally opened up my computer and started writing—and writing and writing. At first, the thoughts were random. Then they started taking on some organization. Eventually, I moved from descriptions of the problem to patterns, to reasons, to thoughts about solutions.

What really put me on a track to solutions (as opposed to just understanding the problem better) was starting to *talk* through the problems and potential solutions. It didn't take more than a couple of conversations with trusted colleagues/advisers before I realized how dumb half of my thoughts were, both about the problems and the solutions, which helped narrow down and consolidate my options considerably.

Even better than solving the problems, or at least a driver of being able to solve them, is feeling more in control of a tough situation. That's probably the best thing I have learned over the years about the value of articulating problems and solutions. For a leader, there is no worse feeling than being out of control—and no better feeling than the opposite. Some level of control or confidence is required to get through tough times.

I suppose this concept is not all that different from any 12-step program. First, admit you have a problem. Then you can go on to solve it. The point I am trying to make is more than that: it's not just admitting you have a problem. It's actually diving in deep to the potential causes of the problem and writing them down and, better yet, speaking them out loud a few times. That puts you on the road to solving those problems.

That's the best way to lead the organization out of the rough patch. Once your business gets big enough, you have to realize that you're not alone in having highs and lows any more. While it's nice to have company in that, whiplash can be destructive to a broader team, so you have to manage it carefully when it happens to others. Identify the problem clearly, isolate its drivers and restructure yourself for success in the future, whether that means changing people, structure, or strategy.

Management Moment

Delegate Decisions to Domain Experts

Companies succeed when the decision makers understand the substance of the issue and when those same people make decisions, plan for execution, execute, and follow up. If you're not the best person to make a particular decision in your organization, either because you aren't close enough to the issue or aren't going to be involved in its ultimate execution, then don't make the decision. Delegate that decision to someone else. You don't have to look too far to see a lot of examples of how the absence of domain expertise, has led to spectacular failures, from Enron to Wall Street's meltdown. With a little humility, these are avoidable errors. Identify your experts and delegate relevant decisions to them.

CHAPTER TWENTY-FIVE

MEETING ROUTINES

Without question, board meetings and team offsites are some of the most productive and enjoyable experiences of my professional life. As far as meetings go, they represent an extremely small slice of what can be a very big problem. CEOs go to dozens of meetings a week. It's important to keep them valuable and productive and to avoid "death by meeting."

LENCIONI'S MEETING FRAMEWORK

As I mentioned earlier, Patrick Lencioni is one of my favorite business writers and we now use his framework for mission, vision and values from *The Advantage* at Return Path. He's also written a series of business fables, all of which include valuable lessons that are easy to understand and easy to communicate. His books include *The Three Signs of a Miserable Job* (on how to create meaning for people in their day to day work when they're not doing something intrinsically meaningful like curing a disease or feeding the homeless), *The Five Temptations of a CEO* (a summary of five leadership traps every CEO has to avoid), *The Four Obsessions of an Extraordinary Executive* (the flipside of *The Five Temptations*, focusing on positive traits)—and *Death by Meeting*.

Death by Meeting isn't about attending too many meetings, which is what *I've* always called "death by meeting." It's about staff meetings that bore you to death. With a great story featuring characters named Casey and Will (my two oldest kids' names, which had me chuckling the whole time), Lencioni describes a framework for splitting up your staff meetings into four different

TABLE 25.1 Patrick Lencioni's Meeting Framework from *Death by Meeting*

Meeting Type	Time Required	Purpose/Format	Notes
Daily check-in	5–10 minutes	Share daily schedules and activities	Don't sit down Keep it administrative Don't cancel even when some people can't be there
Weekly tactical	45–90 minutes	Review weekly activities and metrics and resolve tactical obstacles and issues	Don't set agenda until after initial reporting Postpone strategic discussions
Monthly strategic (or ad hoc strategic)	2–4 hours	Discuss, analyze, brainstorm, and decide on critical issues affecting long-term success	Limit to one or two topics Prepare and do research Engage in good conflict
Quarterly offsite review	1–2 days	Review strategy, competitive landscape, industry trends, key personnel, team development	Get out of office Focus on work; limit social activities Don't overstructure or overburden the schedule

Source: © The Table Group, http://www.tablegroup.com/books/dbm/death_by_meeting.pdf

types of meetings: the daily stand-up, the weekly tactical, the monthly strategic, and the quarterly offsite (see Table 25.1).

There's definitely something to the framework. Over the years, we have done all four types of meetings, though we have never had all four in our rotation at once (that felt like overkill). At a minimum, I think that any two get the job done much better than a single-format recurring meeting. As long as you figure out how to separate status updates from more strategic conversations, you're directionally in good shape. If you vary the time, place and format enough to be interesting—but not enough to be disruptive—you will keep people (including yourself!) from being bored to death.

Run Great Meetings

Meetings are a company's most expensive endeavor. (Just calculate the cost in salary of everyone sitting in a senior staff meeting for an hour or two!) Run good meetings yourself and don't enable bad behavior and you' will be a model for senior staff members who run their own meetings.

There are a few rules every meeting needs to follow, regardless of format:

- *Have an agenda*. What are you going to discuss? What kind of contribution do you expect from each stakeholder? What kind of decision do you need to come to at the end?
- *Start and end on time*. There's no excuse for tardiness. (That includes any sort of audiovisual setup—don't force people to watch you set up a projector for 15 minutes. Get there early and make sure it's set up in time.) End times are just as important: if meetings always run long, they will always start late as people scramble to make it on time.
- *Clearly lay out next steps*. A meeting should lead to future action. What is it? Make sure everybody is agreeable before the meeting ends and follow up with written confirmation.

Otherwise, make sure your meetings are as short as possible, as actionable and as interesting as possible. Don't hold a meeting when an email or five-minute recorded message will suffice. Don't hold a weekly standing meeting when it can be biweekly. Cancel meetings if there's nothing to cover. End them early if you can't fill the time productively. Vary the tempo of your meetings to match their purpose—the same staff group can have a weekly with one agenda, a monthly with a different agenda and a quarterly with a different agenda.

SKIP-LEVEL MEETINGS

I was talking to a CEO the other day who believes that it is "wrong" (literally, his word) to meet one-on-one with people in the organization who don't report to him. I've heard from other CEOs in the past that they're casual or informal or sporadic about this practice but I've never heard someone articulate that they actively stayed away from it. The CEO in question felt that these meetings, which I call skip-level meetings, undermine managers.

I couldn't disagree more. I've done skip-level meetings for years and have found them to be an indispensable part of my management and leadership routine. If your culture is set up such that you as the CEO can't interact directly and regularly with people in your organization—other than the five to eight people who report to you—you are missing out on great opportunities to learn from and have an impact on those around you.

That said, there is an art to doing these meetings right. My five rules for doing skip-level meetings are:

1. *Make them predictable.* Have them on a regular schedule, whatever that is. The schedule doesn't have to be uniform across all these meetings. I have some skip-levels that I do monthly, some quarterly, some once a year, some "whenever I'm in town."
2. *Use a consistent format.* I always have a few questions I ask people in these meetings—things about their key initiatives, their people, their roadblocks, what I can do to help, what their point of view is about the company direction and performance, and how they are feeling about their role and growth. I also expect that people will come with questions or topics for me. If I have more meaty ad hoc topics, I will let the person know ahead of time.
3. *Vary the location.* When I have regular skip-levels with a given person, I try to do the occasional one over a meal or drink to make it a little more social. For remote check-ins, I now always use Skype or videophone.
4. *Do group meetings.* Sometimes, group skip-levels are fun and enlightening, either with a full team or a cross-section of skip-levels from other teams. Watching people relate to each other gives you a really different view into team dynamics.
5. *Close the loop.* I almost always check in with the person's manager *before and after* a skip-level. Before, I ask what the issues are and if there is anything I should push on or ask. After, I report back on the meeting, especially if there are things the person and I discussed that are out of scope for the person's job or goals, so there are no surprises.

Doing skip-levels often and well empowers people in the company. Managers who feel disempowered by them aren't managers you necessarily want in your business, unless you really run a command-and-control shop.

Return Path Senior Director of Global Corporate Communications Tami Monahan Forman Presents A Cheat Sheet for CEO Communication

Speaking—at meetings, over email, on the phone—isn't enough for CEOs. It's also crucial that you be heard. Tami Forman, Return Path's Senior Director of Global Corporate Communications, offers some advice about how to assure that what gets said is what gets heard.

One of a CEO's most important functions is communication. Internally, you are communicating with your executive staff, your employees and your board. Externally, you are communicating with clients, prospects, the press, analysts (industry and, in some cases, financial), and other influencers on your business.

Need to get better right now? Try this CEO communication cheat sheet:

- *Know thyself.* I believe there are two kinds of CEOs: those who can tell their story well and those who can't. Your first job is to figure out which one you are. If you're the second kind, get help.
- *Hire a head of communications whom you can trust.* The relationship between a CEO and the head of communications is really important to the success of the business. If you don't trust that person to give you good advice, it will be much harder for you to work with him or her to convey a tight, cogent message, both internally and externally.
- *Remember that you are working in a fishbowl.* Everyone is watching you. For CEOs like Matt who works in glass offices, this is literally true. It's metaphorically true for all CEOs. Everything you do and say carries weight.
- *Pay attention to non-verbal messages.* It's not just what you say or what you write that sends a message. Your behavior is being observed and your employees make assumptions based on that behavior. For example, sending emails while you are supposed to be on vacation suggests to people that they will also be expected to stay plugged in while off. If that's the message you want to send—and it might be if yours is a fast-paced, high-growth business where "always on" is the rule—that is fine. If it's not, think twice.
- *Repeat yourself—a lot.* Communicate with your team about the big goals for the company and teach them how to communicate with their teams. Send an email; have a meeting; send another email; print it out on a piece of cardstock for people to hang on their bulletin boards. If the message is critically important to the business, you can't say it too many times.
- *Keep it simple.* We live in the age of information overload. Everyone you are trying to communicate with—the press, your employees, even your

spouse—is being bombarded with messages from every angle. Work at figuring out how to boil you key messages down as succinctly as you can. What's the takeaway? How few words can you use to convey that takeaway?

- *Don't bullshit.* We are living in an age of transparency. People know when you are lying or even when you're just "spinning." So the advantage gained by lying is basically zero—no one will believe you anyway. Being honest about challenges and obstacles actually has two important benefits. First, it helps people to trust you and trust the company. Second, it helps your employees help the company. They can't fix what they don't know is broken. (By the way, this advice is triply true for media relations. Trying to snow a reporter is bound to come back and bite you.)
- *Don't rely too heavily on email.* In modern organizations, a lot of information gets disseminated by email or other written media. That's fine but remember that different people learn in different ways. Using a variety of communication methods—including live meetings, audio recordings and videos—can help the messages sink in deeper. Also, different media convey messages in different ways. During the 2008 financial crisis, I encouraged Matt to make an audio recording of an update on the state of the business instead of sending our employees another email. He got a lot of positive feedback, including one employee who commented that hearing the confidence in Matt's voice made him feel better. You can't make that same impact with an email.

If you are a naturally good communicator, consider yourself blessed. You have a big advantage over people who have to work to develop this skill. If you aren't, don't despair. Communication is a skill that can be learned. Not everyone can be Hemingway or Steve Jobs. Anyone can learn to write and speak well.

Tami Monahan Forman, Senior Director
Global Corporate Communications at Return Path

RUNNING A PRODUCTIVE OFFSITE

My senior team has four offsites per year. I love them. They are, along with my board meetings, my favorite times of the year at work. Here's my formula for those meetings:

- *Why.* There are a few purposes to our offsites. One is that our senior team is geographically distributed across four offices at the executive level and six or seven at the broader management team level. So these are the only times of the year that we are all actually in the same place. Even if we *were* all in one place, we'd still do them. The main purpose of the offsite is to pull out of our day-to-day duties and tackle strategic issues that require more uninterrupted time. The secondary purpose is to continue to build and develop both personal relationships and team dynamics. It's critically important to build and sustain deep relationships across the executive team. We need this time in order to be a coordinated, cohesive, high-trust, aligned leadership team for the company. As the company has expanded (particularly to diverse geographies), our senior team development has become increasingly critical.

- *Who.* Every offsite includes what we call our Executive Committee. Ours is mostly composed of my direct reports, though that group also includes a couple of other senior people who don't report directly to me but who run significant parts of the company (seven to eight people total). For two of the four offsites, we also invite the broader leadership team, which is for the most part all of the people reporting to the Executive Committee (another 20 people). That's new; in the earlier days, it was just my staff and maybe one or two other people as needed for specific topics
- *Where.* Offsites aren't always offsite for us. We vary location to make geography work for people. We try to contain costs across all of them. Every year, probably two of them are actually in one of our offices or at an inexpensive nearby hotel. The other two are at somewhat nicer places, usually one at a conference-oriented hotel and then one at a more fun, resort kind of place. Even when we are in one of our offices, we really treat it like an offsite—no other meetings and so on—and we make sure we are out together at dinner every night.
- *When.* Four times per year, at roughly equal intervals. We used to do them right before board meetings as partial prep for those meetings but that got too crowded. Now, we do them between board meetings. The only timing that's critical is the end-of-year session, which is all about budgeting and planning for the following year. Our general formula when it's the smaller group is two days and at least one dinner. When it's the larger group, it's three days and at least two dinners. For longer meetings, we try build a few hours of fun activity into the schedule so it's not all work.
- *What.* Our offsites are extremely rigorous. We put our heads together to wrestle with and sometimes solve tough business problems, from

how we're running the company to what's happening with our culture, to strategic problems with our products, services and operations. The agenda for these offsites varies widely but the format is consistent. I open every offsite with some remarks and overall themes—a mini-state-of-the-union. Then we do some kind of "check-in" exercise either about what people want to get out of the offsite or something more fun like an envisioning exercise, something on a whiteboard or with Post-its, and the like. We always try to spend half a day on team and individual development. Each of us reads our key development plan items from our most recent individual 360 and does a self-assessment, then the rest of the team piles on with other data and opinions, so we keep each other honest and keep the feedback flowing. Then we have a team development plan check-in that's the same but about how the team is interacting. We always have one or two major topics to discuss coming in and each of those has an owner and materials or a discussion paper sent out a few days ahead of time. Then we usually have a laundry list of smaller items—ranging from dumb/tactical to intellectually challenging—that we work in between topics or over meals. (Every meal has an agenda!) There's also time at breaks for subgroup meetings and ad hoc conversations. We do try to come up for air but the together time is so valuable that we squeeze every drop out of it. (Some of our best "meetings" over the years have happened side by side on elliptical trainers in the hotel gym at 6 A.M.) We usually have a closing "recap" exercise as well.

- *How.* Lots of our time together is just the team, but we usually have our long-time executive coach facilitate the development plan section of the meeting.

Management Moment

Be an Active Listener

When I was a little kid, I remember my cousin David asking my Grandpa Bill why, at some extended family gathering, he spent the whole time listening to some friend or distant relative yammer away rather than talk more himself. Grandpa's response: "I already know what I have to say—what I didn't know was what he had to say."

Grandpa's words still ring true. As we have adapted them in our core values at Return Path, "you have two ears and one mouth for a reason." Just being present and not multitasking in meetings as a leader is important but it isn't enough. It's always better to ask questions, listen to conversations and shape them around the edges—rather than shutting down the conversation by diving in with the answer at the onset of a debate.

CHAPTER TWENTY-SIX

DRIVING ALIGNMENT

During the 2012 presidential campaign, Mitt Romney got a lot of flak when he said, "Companies are people, too." It was probably (well, certainly) the wrong thing in the context of a presidential election but it can be a useful analogy—especially when discussing alignment. When a major issue comes up at your company, is everybody at the table trying to serve the same "person's" interests? Or is one person serving the engineering team, another person serving the sales team, one board member serving the VC fund, another serving the early-stage angel investors—and another serving the CEOs? Or is everybody serving the *company's* interests? If they're not, your team is misaligned—"nobody" else's interests are nearly as important as those of the company.

FIVE KEYS TO STARTUP ALIGNMENT

You can't align everybody behind your company's interests if you can't clearly define and communicate those interests. Doing so requires five steps:

1. *Define the mission.* Be clear to everyone about where you're going and how you're going to get there (in keeping with your values).
2. *Set annual priorities, goals and targets.* Turn the broader mission into something more concrete with prioritized goals and unambiguous success metrics, as described in the prior chapter.
3. *Encourage bottom-up planning.* You and your executive team need to set the major strategic goals for the company but every member

of your team should be able to design their own path to contribution. Just be sure that you or their managers check in with them to ensure that they remain in sync with the company's goals.

4. *Facilitate the transparent flow of information and rigorous debate.* To help people calibrate the success—or insufficiency—of their efforts, be transparent about how the organization is doing along the way. Your organization will make better decisions when everyone has what they need to have tough conversations and then make well-informed decisions.
5. *Ensure that compensation supports alignment (or at least doesn't fight it).* As selfless as you want your employees to be, they will always prioritize their interests over the company. If those interests are aligned—especially when it comes to compensation—this reality of human nature simply won't be a problem.

I've discussed each of those steps in some detail earlier in this book. Taken in sequence, they're the formula for alignment.

Fig Wasp 879, Revisited

Leadership takes on a different role when the company is aligned. Think back to our example of the 900+ varieties of fig wasp as described by Richard Dawkins. You think fig wasps have a CEO? Or a division president who reports to the CEO that oversees both fig wasps and fig trees, making sure they all cross-pollenate before the end of the quarter? Nope! As a CEO, you may be the most important person in the organization sometimes, or in some ways. I can easily construct the argument that you're the least important person in the shop as well. If you do your job and create an organization where everyone knows the mission, the agenda, the goal, the values, the Big Hairy Audacious Goal (or whatever you want to call it)—without it needing to be spelled out every day—you have done a large swath of your job and can spend more time focusing on building your organization, training your people, building key customer and partner relationships, and looking forward several quarters or years out to start plotting out your next moves as a company.

ALIGNING INDIVIDUAL INCENTIVES WITH GLOBAL GOALS

It's always great to hear people say that they'd do their jobs even if they weren't paid to—but the reality of post-lottery-jackpot job retention rates suggests otherwise. You and every member of your team work for pay. (Though, as I explain the next section, money isn't enough if there isn't purpose behind it.) That's the most global incentive you have to offer.

When I described startup compensation in Chapter 12, I went into a lot more detail about how that compensation can be divided among cash, bonuses and equity. All of that advice can be applied on a case-by-case basis. What about using compensation to align your entire team behind the company's best interests?

At Return Path, our top 30 to 40 executives are on the same incentive plan. Marketers aren't rewarded for hitting marketing milestones while engineers are rewarded for hitting product milestones and back-office personnel are rewarded for keeping the infrastructure humming. Everybody is rewarded when *the company* hits its milestones.

The results of this system are extraordinary:

- *Department goals are in alignment with overall company goals.* "Hitting product goals" shouldn't matter unless those goals serve the overall health of your company. When every member of your executive team—including your CTO—is rewarded for the latter, it's much easier to set goals as a company. There are no competing priorities: the only priority is serving the annual goals.
- *Individual success metrics are in alignment with overall company success metrics.* The one place where all companies probably have alignment between corporate and departmental goals is in sales: the success metrics that your sales team uses can't be that far off from your overall goals for the company. With a unified incentive plan, you can bring every department into the same degree of alignment. Imagine your general counsel asking for *less* extraneous legal review in order to cut costs!
- *Resource allocation serves the company, rather than individual silos.* If a department with its own compensation plan hits its (unique)

metrics early, members of that team have no incentive to pitch in elsewhere; their bonuses are secure. If everyone's incentive depends on the entire company's performance—get ready to watch product leads offering to share developers, unprompted.

This approach can only be taken so far: I can't imagine an incentive system that doesn't reward *salespeople* for individual performance! While nobody complains when things go well, it is a challenge when things go poorly—*everybody* gets dinged if the company doesn't meet its goals, no matter how well they or their departments performed. It's a tough pill to swallow but it's also a lifesaving bit of medication. If your company misses its goals, nobody should have occasion to celebrate.

Sometimes, Things Are Messy

Many people who run companies have highly organized and methodical personality types—that's probably how they got where they are in life! If you work long enough to espouse the virtues of fairness and equality with the way you manage and treat people, it became second nature to want things to be somewhat consistent across an organization.

The longer I've been a startup CEO and the larger my company has gotten, the more I realize that some things aren't meant to fit in a neat box. Sometimes, inconsistency is not only healthy but critical for a business to flourish.

It's taken me a while to embrace messiness in our business. I fully acknowledge that I am one of the more hyperorganized people around, which means this hasn't come naturally to me. The messiness has been very productive for us. I think it's come from the combination of two things: we are a results-oriented culture, not a process-driven culture and we give managers a lot of latitude in how they run their teams.

Let me give a few examples that I've observed over the past few years.

- Our sales team and our engineering team use pretty different methodologies from each other and from the rest of the company in how they set individual goals, monitor progress against them and compensate people on results.
- The structure of our sales and service and channel organizations in Europe are very different from our emerging ones in Latin America

and Asia/Australia. Even within Europe, they can vary greatly from country to country.

- Although we have never been a company that places emphasis on job titles, our teams and leadership levels have become even more inconsistent over the years: sometimes a manager or director has a bigger span of control or more impact on the business than a VP does; sometimes individual contributors have more influence over a broad section of groups than a manager does; and so on.

I'm certainly not saying that striving for some level of consistency in an organization is a bad goal—just that it's probably not an absolute goal. Sometimes, embracing messiness makes a lot of sense. Or perhaps phrased more actionably, as long as they follow high-level guidelines and values, allowing individual managers to use their own judgment and creativity in setting up teams and processes can be an incredibly productive and rewarding way of maximizing success across an enterprise.

Management Moment

Create "Stop Doing" Lists

Challenge everyone on your team to make a "stop doing" list, which forces people to critically evaluate all their ordinary processes and tasks and meetings and understand which ones are outdated—and therefore a waste of time. This causes people to do some extra work in the short term but a lot less wasted work in the long term.

CHAPTER TWENTY-SEVEN

HAVE YOU LEARNED YOUR LESSON?

Everything is a potential opportunity to learn a lesson and apply it to your business: from the story of fig wasps in a popular evolutionary biology text (see Chapter 9), to an anecdote about dancing, drawing five-year-olds (see Chapter 11). Important as those are, you still have to formalize procedures for learning valuable lessons from the outside (benchmarking) and from within (postmortems, or after-action reviews). As always, you can be haphazard, or you can follow a few simple best practices, like the ones I outline below.

THE VALUE (AND LIMITATIONS) OF BENCHMARKING

In the past few years, my team and I have executed a ton of external benchmarking projects—comparing our processes and performance to those of our competitors or partners. Each of these projects has different leaders inside Return Path doing both systematic and ad hoc phone calls and meetings with peer companies (and companies we aspire to be like) to understand how we compare to them in terms of specific metrics, practices and structures. It's some combination of the former management consultant in me rearing its head and me just trying to make sure that we stay ahead of the curve as we rapidly scale our business.

Why go through exercises like these? One answer is that you don't want to reinvent the wheel. If a noncompetitive, comparable company has solved a problem or done some good, creative thinking, then I say "plagiarize with pride"—especially if you're sharing your best practices with them. The reality of scaling a business is that things change when you go from 50 to 100 people, or 150 to 300, or 300 to 1,000. Unless you and your entire executive team have "been there, done that" at all levels—or unless you are constantly replacing execs—there's not exactly an instruction manual for the work you have to do.

A second, equally valuable, answer is that benchmarking can uncover both problems and opportunities that you didn't know you had (or at least validate theories about problems and opportunities that you suspect you have). Learning that comparable companies convert 50 percent better on their marketing funnel than you do, or that they systematically raise prices 5 to 7 percent per year regardless of new feature introduction (I'm just making these examples up) can help you steer the ship in ways you might not have thought you needed to.

What are the limitations of benchmarking? As our CTO Andy Sautins, said to me the other day, sometimes no one else has the answer, either. We do run into this regularly: a tough technical problem where literally no one else does it well, like disaster recovery, or in dealing with channel conflict problems, or trying to streamline our commission plans. Sometimes, a particular circumstance you face is actually unique. That's not true most of the time (everyone has to have a disaster recovery plan) but creative entrepreneurs breed inventive business models and sometimes those just run into situations that others aren't familiar with.

Sometimes you find out that you are actually best in class at a particular function! In those cases, one could just chalk up the exercise to a waste of time but I still think there is learning to be had from studying others. If there are other companies that are also best in class, I always encourage group brainstorming among the top peers about how to push the envelope further and be even better. This can even take the form of a regular peer group meeting/forum.

On the whole, I find benchmarking a good management practice and a particularly good use of time. Like everything, it's situational and you have to understand what you're looking for when you start your questioning. You also have to be prepared to find nothing and go back to your own drawing board. Good entrepreneurs have to be great at both inventing and, as I noted earlier, plagiarizing.

Learning from Extremes

Earlier in the book, I mentioned that the either/or between *meden agan* (Greek for "everything in moderation") and *Oder gor oder gornisht* (Yiddish for "all or nothing") is a bit of a false dichotomy. There is obvious value to taking a moderate approach and there's a lot to be learned from going to extremes. Here, I want to point out how extremes can be great places to learn and develop a good sense of what "normal" or "moderate" really is. Let me give three examples:

- We were having a buy-versus-build conversation at work a few years ago as we were considering an acquisition. Some people in the room had an emotional bias toward buy, others toward build. So we framed the debate this way: "Would you acquire the company for $1 instead of building the technology?" (Yes!) "Would you buy it for $10 million?" (No!) Taking the conversation to the extremes allowed us to frame the question in a rational way: where is the price where buy and build are in equilibrium?
- In a moment of workplace solidarity, my colleague Andrea Ponchione and I completed a five-day juice fast a few weeks back. I came away with two really interesting learnings that I got only from being extreme for a few days:
  - I like fruits and veggies (and veggie juices) a lot and don't consume enough of them.
  - I sleep *much* better at night on a relatively empty stomach.
- As I mentioned in Chapter 10, I overhauled my "operating system" at work to stop interviewing all candidates for all jobs when we got too big a few years ago. What finally convinced me to do it was something one of my colleagues asked me, which was, "Will you be able to keep these activities up when we have 500 employees?" (No) "So what is the difference if you stop now and save time versus stopping in 6 months?"

In every case, thinking about extremes gave my team and me perspective on the full spectrum.

THE ART OF THE POSTMORTEM

It has a bunch of names: the after-action review, the critical incident review, the plain old postmortem. Whatever you call it, it's crucial to institutionalize best practices and learnings after critical incidents. They're productive, and they can be cathartic if something has gone wrong.

The origins of the postmortem are with the military, which routinely uses this kind of process to debrief people on the front lines. Its management application is essential to any high-performing, learning organization.

Here are my best practices for postmortems:

- *Timing.* The postmortem should be held after the incident has passed, usually for several weeks, so that members of the group have time to gather perspective on what happened, but not so far out that they forget what happened and why. Set the stage for a postmortem while in crisis (note publicly that you will do one) and encourage team members to record thoughts along the way for maximum impact.
- *Length.* The postmortem session has to be at least 90 minutes, maybe as much as 3 hours, to get everything out on the table.
- *Agenda format.* Our postmortems include the following section:
  - Common understanding of what happened and why
  - My role
  - What worked well
  - What could have been done better
  - What are my most important learnings
- *Participants.* Err on the side of including too many people. Invite people who would learn from observing, even if they weren't on the crisis response team.
- *Use an outside facilitator.* This is a *must* when the participants are largely senior people. We often use my executive coach, Marc Maltz from Triad Consulting. (See his contribution to Part Five.) You could also use a senior HR person from inside the organization, as long as that person or his or her "client organizations" didn't really have much to do with the incident.
- *Your role as leader.* Set the tone by opening and closing the meeting and thanking the leaders of the response team. Ask questions as needed but be careful not to dominate the conversation.
- *Publish notes.* We publish our notes from our postmortems not just to the team but to the entire organization, with some kind of digestible executive summary and next actions.

When done well, these kinds of meetings not only surface good learnings, they also help an organization maintain momentum on a project that is no longer in crisis mode and therefore at risk of fading into the twilight before all its work is done.

I should also note that postmortems usually connote that something went wrong. You should also do them at other times as well. Sometimes there are great learnings about successful product launches or successful recoveries of a key account, for example. We also periodically pull up in the middle of a large project and do what we call a "midmortem" to make sure we capture learnings as we go and give ourselves ammunition to course correct.

Sometimes, There Is No Lesson to Be Learned

We once had a very unusual employee situation at Return Path. A brand new senior executive we brought into the company to be our first-ever senior head of HR and organization development resigned very abruptly after only two weeks on the job, citing a complete change of heart about her career direction and moving on to a government position in economic and community development. Unfortunately, the person resigned by cell phone, gave no notice and provided no assistance with transition. What a disappointment—especially coming from an HR professional!

After getting over my disbelief/irritation/rage (not easy, not a small amount), after communicating this difficult message to the company and after sending a thoughtful-yet-cathartic note to the person, I sat down to think a little bit about how I could have prevented or at least spotted the situation in advance.

We interviewed the person thoroughly: 10 people internally conducted interviews and I interviewed the person for almost four hours myself, conducting one of the most rigorous interviews I've ever conducted given how critical this position was to our organization. I also checked five references on the person, all of which were sterling. I had an executive coach with whom I work interview the person. Everything checked out; the person's attitude and enthusiasm about the position couldn't have been better.

My conclusion on the lesson learned here? "Sometimes, there is no lesson to be learned." There may be ancillary lessons around handling the situation once it became apparent but I think the core lesson I'd hope to get out of this—that we could have done something different in the interview process or orientation or first few weeks to prevent or at least spot this ahead of time—appeared to be nonexistent.

Management Moment

Connect the Dots

"Connecting the dots" means helping others network internally, or helping others connect their work to the work of others, or helping others connect their work to the mission of the company—or even to the outside world.

As a business leader, you are in a really good position to help connect the dots in a growing organization because you spend time with people across different functions and teams and offices. That gives you a pretty unique view across the organization. It makes you particularly well suited to perform this unique and vital task.

CHAPTER TWENTY-EIGHT

GOING GLOBAL

In Chapter 15, I discussed the challenges of managing remote offices and employees and the advantages of keeping your team in one place for as long as possible. Now, I have to qualify that: it's just as important to be close to your customers as it is to be close to your colleagues. Once you develop an international presence, or even a major customer base in a particular location, you should start thinking about having a local presence. Just be sure to do it right.

SHOULD YOUR BUSINESS GO GLOBAL?

Not every business needs to global. If you're a business-to-consumer (B2C) company, it may not get you anything: customers don't expect much in the way of personal contact with employees from Facebook, Twitter, or Evernote. You may need some level of in-language customer support but that can be done from anywhere.

It's very important if you're in a business-to-business (B2B) company. In fact, it's almost a truism of sales: Germans like to buy from Germans. The French like to buy from the French. Canadians like to buy from Canadians; French Canadians like to buy from French Canadians and Americans like to buy from Americans! Put your salespeople where the customers are. (One exception to this rule is that customers of freemium software products don't expect a significant amount of interaction with the companies they buy from.)

HOW TO ESTABLISH A GLOBAL PRESENCE

The simplest way to establish a global presence is through M&A, which I discuss in detail in the next chapter. Buy your biggest resellers (who are already somewhat aligned with your company) or buy local competitors (who are already doing largely what you're doing). This pattern is so common that plenty of foreign entrepreneurs have built businesses out of starting knock-off local competitors to U.S. companies, on the assumption that the company they're copying will acquire them. If they did a decent job of it, why not? While international expansion through M&A can be expensive, it comes with revenue, customers, local operations, and local leaders.

Sometimes, neither of those options is available: you have customers (or potential customers) in a new market but no resellers or competitors there. Given how difficult it is to start a local office absolutely from scratch, some CEOs are tempted to buy tangential companies and repurpose them. The assumption is that the infrastructure is there—developers, algorithm experts, manufacturers, what have you—and repurposing is simpler than hiring a team from scratch. I would never understate the extent of the hiring challenge (see Chapter 10) but retraining isn't any easier and is often impossible, like teaching a cat to bark. The similarities you're looking for may be the wrong ones: a Java developer is a Java developer but maybe it's more important to have a developer who knows your industry, even if they're specialists in .NET. Or vice versa. You won't know until you have pulled the trigger—and bad acquisitions are very expensive mistakes.

When there isn't an appropriate M&A opportunity, the best approach is probably the (seemingly) hardest approach: starting the global office on your own by hiring from the ground up.

OVERCOMING THE CHALLENGES OF GOING GLOBAL

Our first two new countries, France and the UK, were really tough to launch. We had really limited brand recognition abroad and we had no network to tap into either for hiring or checking references. As a result, we ended up turning over our first two country managers within a year or two, which really set us back. Early employees in those two countries also had to deal with a very "do it yourself" environment—everything from office space to phone systems, to computer setup, to health benefits. We have gotten the routine down now and we are much bigger and better known outside the United

States, so we were able to launch newer markets like Brazil and Australia a lot more smoothly, with more infrastructure and back-office know-how.

These are the two main challenges to going global and some things you can do to overcome them:

1. *If you can't buy something, it's like starting a new company.* This isn't just true of the obvious challenges of running a company: gaining market traction, finding the right talent. When you're in a new context, all sorts of things that you largely take for granted in the United States—or pass off to your lawyer or accountant—become major headaches: local regulations, payroll, labor practices, tax structure. In some countries, this is difficult enough that you want to avoid them as long as possible. My short list is Japan, China, Russia, and Belgium, though there are days where running an operation in Brazil feels equally cumbersome and even France and Germany have their own issues.
2. *Hiring is hard; long-distance hiring is much harder.* Most of the tools you have to overcome the hiring challenge at home aren't available abroad. You have no local network to draw on. You're not in that location long enough to take meetings that "get people on the bus." Your reputation, as good as it is at home, probably hasn't traveled to Ecuador or Australia. Checking references when there's a language barrier can be nearly impossible. There's no choice but doing this the hard way: spend a lot of time at your new office and make every effort to have a senior member of your team move there full time—if only temporarily. Remote offices in different states are challenging enough; that challenge is magnified many times over in different countries.

BEST PRACTICES FOR MANAGING INTERNATIONAL OFFICES AND EMPLOYEES

Once you decide to open (or explore the possibility of opening) an international office, there are a few things you can do to make it happen as smoothly as possible:

- *Send executives from headquarters to establish the presence and hire the first people.* I have a confession: we have never been able to pull this off at Return Path. With every international office we have opened—in

Europe, Asia and so on—we have tried to find a local executive who could move to the new location, set up shop and operate the office, if only temporarily. It's never worked out for us but we're going to keep trying. The companies I know that *have* done this swear by it.

- *Set clear expectations with new hires.* Whether or not you do this, make sure you make it abundantly clear to the first several employees you're hiring in a new country that they need to be comfortable wearing multiple hats and dealing with some messiness for a long time.
- *Be smart about local laws and business customs.* Each country has its own everything, from its tax code to its employment laws, to its typical start times and lunch breaks. Don't assume that because you're an American company, everyone else will play by your rules (though by and large, you should be able to insist on English as your official business language for internal communications). Find an expert—they're out there—to help you establish everything from local payroll to client contracts. Be especially wary of local business customs. Showing up at a meeting without a gift or a tie when your counterparts have those is a minor infraction and easily forgiven. A major infraction can get you in trouble with the federal government; make sure you study up on the Foreign Corrupt Practices Act (FCPA).
- *Phase in remote offices gradually.* Don't be hasty when opening a new physical office. You might find after a few months that the team or sales opportunity you were trying to accommodate isn't going to pay off and you don't want to be stuck with tons of infrastructure and a 10-year lease. Start by letting people work from home. When you get to the point where two to three people would come into an office every day, get a short-term rental in a managed office or co-working space. Get your own office only when you have between 10 and 15 team members in the new location. By that point, it's pretty clear that you will be there for the long haul.
- *Find a cultural translator.* One of the main reasons you will be opening new offices is to serve new cultures. You can't do that without someone who knows the ins and outs of the location you're expanding to and can communicate them clearly to the rest of your team. Even if it's someone who reports only to you, it's important not to feel out of touch with an entire office.
- *Do more frequent check-ins.* If you check in with local employees once a week, check in with remote employees at least twice. A quick phone call to see how things are going is a good use of travel time. Remember, at your home office, formal check-ins are probably

supplemented with ad hoc meetings. That's not the case with remote employees, so it's important to be more vigilant.

- *Use video extensively.* Skype is good. Serious videoconferencing setups for conference rooms are great. Desktop videophones rule. Use all of them. Too much important information is lost over email or on the phone.
- *Use a consistent set of collaboration tools.* To reduce friction among your various teams, it's important to choose a single set of collaboration tools and stick with them. If you don't, your employees will waste thousands of hours on the mechanics of collaboration, rather than just collaborating.
- *Beware diverging cultures.* It's not just important to have a strong company culture; it's important to have just one. Don't allow multiple offices to devolve into "us versus them" scenarios. Travel to your offices on a regular basis and rotate people through them as much as possible. This helps create human connectivity and foster a unified company culture. Please note that many of these best practices also apply if you acquire a company abroad—like exporting an executive and doing more frequent check-ins. Unless the company you acquire is quite large, you will want to do more, not less, to integrate them into your organization than you would if they were local.

Startup CEOs want to change the world and this often entails the challenge of expanding your reach into new parts of it. It's difficult, frustrating and, often, very costly. If you want your brand to have global reach, you will need a global team.

Management Moment

Know What Data to Trust

I've always relied on direct interactions with junior staff and personal observation in order to get a feel for what's going on. As we have gotten larger, I worry that I don't get completely candid feedback from deep in the organization. I've started hearing things like, "Of course, you heard that—you're the CEO. People will tell you what they think you want to hear." Ugh.

How do you trust the feedback you're getting? You may be a good judge of character and good at reading between the lines. As personal connections to you are necessarily fewer and farther between as the organization grows, you need to realize that some people may feel uncomfortable being totally open with you—or, worse, that some people may have specific agendas they're pushing.

Your job is to be sure that people understand that you *do* want to hear their voices—but only if they're constructive, and not self-serving.

CHAPTER TWENTY-NINE

THE ROLE OF M&A

"Mergers and Acquisitions" may seem more appropriate as the title for an MBA course than a chapter in this book. "Startup M&A" isn't the oxymoron it sounds like. It's one of the most important tools in every startup CEO's strategic arsenal, as is its flip side: divestiture.

USING ACQUISITIONS AS A TOOL IN YOUR STRATEGIC ARSENAL

Many entrepreneurs are afraid to do acquisitions. It's usually a combination of being daunted by the task—and it *is* daunting—and fear of introducing something that was not invented here. At Return Path, we're at 10 acquisitions and counting. Not all of them have worked but a couple of them have been transformational, and most have been relatively small and good tuck-ins.

Every merger is unique but I have found that you can usually place them into one of four categories:

1. *Buying technology*. Many strategic plans involve the expansion of a company's capabilities by creating a new product. The classic question you have to ask is: "Is it cheaper to buy it or build it?" If you answer the former, it could make sense to buy a small company in order to acquire technology that they have already built or simply to buy the rights to that item of technology. (Once you have it, of course, it's your job to *sell* it.)
2. *Buying teams*. Even if you decide to "build" rather than "buy," you may need to hire an entire team to execute on your latest project.

Buy an entire team (a strategy that's recently been dubbed both "doing an HR deal" and "acqui-hiring") and a single acquisition could take the place of months of recruiting.

3. *Diversifying your business lines.* Buying teams or technology are special cases of M&A. The classic scenario involves buying an entire company and there are two possible reasons for doing so. The first is to diversify into a business you're not currently in. The challenge is to find a new line of business that complements your core business and plays off your current strengths. Anything else simply leads to dissipation and a lack of focus.
4. *Expanding your market share.* Finally, you might decide to purchase a direct competitor in order to expand your market share. If you're locked in an internecine battle with a competitor for years at a time, this option could benefit both parties by creating that one, great company that neither was able to build on their own.

THE MECHANICS OF FINANCING AND CLOSING ACQUISITIONS

The mechanics of M&A are complex enough to merit an entire book. (Those books have been written; when you're ready to pull the trigger, read them.) It's still worth reviewing the broad strokes.

When you're public, acquisitions are easy: you use stock, maybe a little cash. When you're small and private, it's a lot harder. Startup acquisitions are usually a mix of stock, cash and—to keep key employees engaged through an integration period and to optimize business results of the acquired business—earn-out.

Stock

For the acquiring company, the best option is to pay with common, private stock. It's also the hardest option to sell, because it trades one illiquid security where the insiders have control for another one where they do not. You may be able to convince an acquisition target to take your common stock on the basis of your company's track record and reputation and numbers; you may be able to do the same by talking about upside. The company being acquired may want hard cash and you almost certainly want to part with as little as possible unless you have a lot of it relative to the price of the deal—and unless you'd rather not inherit the acquired company's shareholders.

There are two options that could help make a mostly stock deal work when the acquisition target isn't loving the idea of your common stock. If you have a real preference stack, finance the deal with a mix of common and preferred stock, ratcheting up the preferred stock as you take cash off the table. This at least blunts the criticism that the new shareholders are second-class citizens, especially if some of them are venture capital firms that currently hold preferred stock in your acquisition target. For big enough deals, you can also offer observer rights or a full seat on your board.

Cash

Cash is king and you should protect yours as carefully as a chess grandmaster defending his title. The founder of the company you're acquiring knows that as well as you do, so you will have to offer *something* tangible. Too little and you could lose the deal. Too much and there's not enough incentive for future performance.

Earn-Out

Fixed shares and fixed dollar amounts are indisputable. Once the deal is signed, there's nothing more to discuss. Earn-outs for future performance are messier but they are sometimes required to bridge the "bid/ask" gap in a negotiation. Done well, they mean that you pay more for the deal but only if it's working out. Done poorly, they can lead to bad feelings—or even legal battles—down the road.

There are ways to mitigate this risk. First and foremost, an earn-out's criteria have to be as clear and quantitative as possible. Second, those criteria have to be things that will remain in the control of the acquired company for the length of the earn-out; asking an entrepreneur to agree to an earn-out based on sales, for example, when *your* sales force will be doing all of the selling, doesn't make sense. Finally, an earn-out can't be too high a percentage of the deal. The preponderance will have to be cash and stock. Otherwise, the process of judging performance should be shared by both parties. In one of our largest deals at Return Path, each side appointed representatives who met quarterly to agree on performance metrics, adjustments, and so on.

We also designated a third representative in advance who was available to adjudicate any disagreements. We never had to use him.

Whatever mechanism you put in place, trust plays a huge role here. If it's not there, this acquisition might not be a good idea.

THE FLIP SIDE OF M&A: DIVESTITURE

When Return Path turned six years old in 2005, we had gone from being a startup focused on our initial ECOA business to the world's smallest conglomerate, with *five* lines of business: in addition to change of address, we were market leaders in email delivery assurance (a market we created), email-based market research (a tiny market when we started) and email list management and list rental (both huge markets when we founded the company). Some of this diversification was the result of mergers and acquisitions; a lot was the result of internal growth and development.

Five years later, we were back down to a single line of business. It just wasn't the one we started with.

A divestiture has as much potential to transform your business as M&A—and it's just as complex. In fact, there's some additional complexity. If your businesses are entangled—sharing internal resources like HR, IT, and finance—pulling apart the threads can be a hard, messy process. (As we will see in a moment, that's also one of the best reasons to divest an underperforming business.) Business complexity is something any startup CEO should feel comfortable with. Admitting failure is harder.

A divestiture might be cause for celebration: your team created an exciting new product or service with good market potential, then they did it again (look at Occipital selling off Red Laser to eBay). You want to keep your company focused, so you sell one of those businesses off, allowing you to focus internal resources—and giving you a decent infusion of cash (or a potentially valuable equity stake). Nothing complicated about that.

More often, a divestiture is an unpleasant event. Either a merger or acquisition didn't work out or a business-line you have invested considerable time and resources into isn't performing. In other words: you failed. Not comprehensively, not terminally. You failed. Admit it. Suck it up. Move on. Don't and you will slow your business down.

Startups have limited resources and an underperforming unit is a drag on those resources. It's not paying its way, forcing your profitable businesses to fund its existence. Sell it. Stop diverting resources from successful business units to prop up a dud. Use those resources to fuel real growth.

There are external benefits to divestiture as well. It's hard to position a company that's doing a dozen things at once. Recruits, potential investors and industry analysts like the clarity that comes from focus. It makes it easier to hire talent, communicate your message and raise money. As your CMO will be happy to remind you, customers like it, too.

Executing a divestiture is the flip side of acquiring a company, of course, and it's no simpler. You need to first find the right buyer or sets of buyers and negotiate a deal. If the division you're selling is big enough and the range of buyers is wide enough, you might want to use a banker to help. You will have to deal with the receiving end of the "stock, cash or earn-out" question. I learned one really important lesson from our divestiture of Authentic Response, a market research business that we started trying to sell in 2007: the more you can do the hard work ahead of time of untangling the line you're selling from the rest of your business, the better. Otherwise, no buyer will believe your pro-forma financials and they won't necessarily want a long-term operating agreement between your two companies.

ODDS AND ENDS

In either kind of transaction, both parties should have fantastic lawyers—and they should agree in advance on how to use them. With any deal this complex, their tendency will be to run amok and do too much, slowing the process down to a crawl. The best thing you can do is have a detailed term sheet for the lawyers to work from.

Due diligence is also something that requires a level of agreement up front to set expectations properly. How deep will you go? How buttoned up do you expect things to be? If you're acquiring a small company, the resources that you're likely to put on a deal will be much greater than that of your target. You need to make sure you get what you need, while respecting that you might have a CEO on the other side of the table fulfilling every diligence request on his or her own.

M&A Integration Plans

Executing a merger or acquisition is a huge undertaking. When you successfully pull it off, it's time to take on another: *integrating* the acquisition into your company. Not every acquisition succeeds—and a failed acquisition is a very costly mistake. Considering the following details won't *assure* a successful merger or acquisition but they will improve your chances considerably:

- *People*. Above all else, a merger or acquisition is the combination of two teams. Often, this involves a number of hard decisions. At worst, you will have to let redundant employees go; at best, you will be able to reassign them. Whatever you have to do, treat every member of your new, combined team as a human being rather than a line item.
- *Product development*. One of the most common reasons for M&A is to acquire a new product line or development team. Now that you have it, it's time to make good on the promise behind the acquisition and execute. This might involve shutting down one of your own products or reassigning developers to avoid redundancy. Handle this transition delicately or your developers might start working against one another in separate silos, rather than working together toward a new, unified team.
- *Product management*. Your products won't be integrated overnight and you need to maintain both products in the meantime. Moreover, you need to do this while consolidating your technical teams. It's a tricky challenge: working toward a unified team, while experts on both sides maintain legacy products and prepare customers for whatever transition is forthcoming.
- *IT systems*. Ideally, the process of integrating IT systems should begin before an acquisition is complete. If you're a Windows shop acquiring a company that operates on Notes and Domino, they should begin migrating their systems as soon as possible. Integrating similar systems is hard enough; doing it while managing a migration is much harder.
- *Finance*. In part, this is a subset of integrating your IT systems: accounts payable, bookkeeping, payroll—all of it needs to be combined. There are also a number of details around bank accounts and tax entities; your chief financial officer should be able to manage those.
- *Sales*. Every lead in your combined pipelines should be made to feel that this acquisition represents as much of an opportunity for them as it does for you. If they hear mixed signals from account managers who aren't communicating, they will assume the opposite.

- *Marketing.* How are you going to present your combined company? Will you be maintaining two separate brand identities or replacing one with the other? Don't let ego play any role here: if you acquired a more prominent brand, the company could benefit greatly by flying their banner rather than yours.

The items above are in no particular order, with one exception. People come first, here as always. If both teams are aligned as to the goals of your merger, the rest is just details.

INTEGRATION (AND SEPARATION)

No chapter on M&A would be complete without talking a little bit about the human side of buying companies and selling a division. This can be one of the most difficult and disruptive elements of a deal.

If you're acquiring another company, the first people-oriented thing to do is due diligence on the culture of the company you're acquiring. Ignore this at your own peril! Companies that have sick cultures—or cultures that are just radically different from your own—may be incredibly hard to integrate. Even if you love the company's products or technology, make sure you will be able to port the people to your company's operating system or at least acknowledge that if you can't, you will either have to run the business very separately or risk losing most of the people in the business.

Ahead of closing, spend as much time as you can with the other management team to work through the majority of the transitional and postclosing issues: how to work with the new team members and what the shared priorities and goals are. Not only is this helpful in terms of giving you a better sense of how—and whether or not—things will work out culturally but you start building new muscles early on. You also start on the process of integrating the two businesses, which can be a significant undertaking. We have always done merger integration as a joint project, with a leader from our company and a leader on the other side and a massively public project plan that covers every last detail.

There are different models for how radical and forceful you should be about integrating an acquired company. The answer is "it depends," meaning specifically that it depends whether the two businesses are going to be closely integrated or not, especially from a customer-facing perspective.

At a minimum, we have always insisted that acquired company employees become full-fledged members of our team, with all the same benefits, policies and information flow as everyone else in the organization. In some cases, we have eliminated the acquired company brand, email addresses and offices; in other cases, we have kept those things. The trick to getting this balance right is to discuss it openly—if you have an unmovable position, state it up front so everyone understands it. If you are open to discussion about specifics, then have the discussion and recognize that you need to engage in some give and take. You never know—a company you acquire may have some way of doing something that's better than your company, so you can do some level of backwards integration as well!

As a private company, we have always been very transparent with our employees about when we're considering an acquisition and we continue to keep employees posted about deals in progress. This is somewhat risky and you may run into a situation where the target company doesn't want you to do so (that's data as well on that company's culture) but we have always found that it maximizes excitement and buy-in internally.

If you're selling a division of your company, the issues are parallel but less significant. You want to do some financial diligence on the buyer if they're paying you in illiquid stock. If you have people leaving your organization to go to the buyer, you want to make sure they're going to a good place or at least recognize that they're not and figure out how you want to make them whole via some kind of retention bonus. You will want to do as much work as possible to disentangle the operations of the departing business unit—things like accounting, systems and Salesforce.com or other CRM implementations are all hurdles that can be very messy to separate. This is all a cost of the divestiture; you need to view it as such and surely that's how the buyer will view it. The level of transparency you bring to employees around a divestiture is probably more akin to selling your company than buying a company. It's much trickier and you have to navigate the process carefully. Even highly transparent organizations can founder when employees are uncertain of their future, especially when their future becomes untethered from yours. We were up front with the team at Authentic Response when we started that sale process and we instituted retention bonuses to make sure we kept people engaged. I think we made the right call on it but it was really difficult to get through. That said, it would have been unthinkable for us to just sell off the business and spring it on employees as a *fait accompli*.

Management Moment

Don't Run a Hub-and-Spoke System of Communications

Command-and-control managers often like hoarding information or forcing everything to go through them or surface in staff meetings. There's no need for that! If you're a senior manager, almost everyone on your team should have individual bilateral relationships and regular one-on-one meetings without your being there. The same goes for your board and your staff. They should have individual relationships that don't go through you. If you are a choke point for communication, it's just as bad as being a bottleneck for approvals.

CHAPTER THIRTY

COMPETITION

CEOs in highly competitive spaces often claim that competition is critical and that they welcome it. I'm not convinced. It is much better to carve out a niche that doesn't have a lot of competition but still be disciplined about how you innovate and operate. Return Path doesn't live in a very crowded marketplace but take it from me: even without a competitor in sight, running a startup is stressful enough. If you *do* have competition, there are a few things you can do to win—or, at the very least, keep them from causing you to fail.

PLAYING HARDBALL

Two of the "big classics" I mentioned in Part One were written by George Stalk and Rob Lachenauer: *Hardball* and their follow-up article in the *Harvard Business Review*, "Curveball."

As with most business books, *Hardball* isn't really geared toward small, entrepreneurial companies but most of the principles of competition—and how to win—are timeless. The basic principles, each of which gets a chapter, are on unleashing massive force, exploiting anomalies (perfect for the data junkie within), threatening the competition's profit zones, plagiarizing with pride, breaking compromises, and M&A.

The chapter on breaking compromises is my favorite because it deals with a facet of human nature that I think can be devastating to business: the "that's the way it's always worked" conundrum, otherwise known as "baggage." Why does XYZ happen in our business, illogical as it may seem? Because that's how we have always done it!

We have a mechanism for dealing with the problem of baggage at Return Path, which is meant to be disarming, a bit funny but dead serious at the same time. Anytime anyone spots someone answering a question or a challenge with the "that's the way it works" response, they're strongly encouraged to pull themselves out of the situation and respond with a catchphrase like "baggage alert," or "boy, that duffle bag must be heavy," or "hey, nice knapsack—is that new or have you had it for a while?" While it may be a little embarrassing to the recipient, it's meant to challenge norms and bring about creative thought at all levels of the business.

Breaking compromises has led to Southwest and Jet Blue, to Saturn (the car, not the planet) and to automobile leasing. Just think about what it can do for your company or industry!

PLAYING OFFENSE VERSUS PLAYING DEFENSE

I hate playing defense in business. It doesn't happen all the time. Being behind a competitor in terms of feature development, scrambling to do custom work for a large client or doing an acquisition because you're getting blocked out of an emerging space—whatever it is, it just feels rotten when it comes up. It's someone else dictating your strategy, tactics and resource allocation; it's their agenda, not yours. It's a scramble. When the work is done, it's hard to feel great about it, even if it's required and well done.

The best thing you can do when you're behind is to turn a situation from defense into a combination of defense and offense and change the game a little bit. Playing offense, of course, is what it's all about. Your terms, your timetable, your innovation or opportunity creation, a smile on your face, knowing you're leading the industry, and making *others* course correct or play catch-up.

Here are a few examples:

- *You're about to lose a big customer unless you develop a bunch of custom features ASAP.* Use that work as prototype to a broader deployment of the new features across your product set. (Rumor has it that Groupware was started as a series of custom projects Lotus was doing for one of its big installations of Notes.) "Features" may be specific to tech companies but the principle holds true for any business: don't play catch-up with a competitor's offering unless it's an opportunity to develop a significant part of your business.

- *Your competitor introduces new subfeatures that are of the "arms race" nature (more, more, more!).* Instead of working to get to parity, add new functionality that changes the value proposition of the whole feature set. Google Docs, for instance, doesn't need to match Microsoft Office feature for feature, as its value proposition is about the cloud. Don't engage in an arms race; change the rules of engagement.
- *Your accounting software blows up. You have to redo an internal system. It's a total time sink.* Use the opportunity to shift from a new version of the same, old school package you used to run—with dedicated hardware, database and support costs—to a new, sleek, lightweight, on-demand package that saves you time and money in the long run.

The best defense is, in fact, a good offense.

GOOD AND BAD COMPETITORS

While the ideal competition may be *no* competition, there are good competitors and bad competitors and it's important to respond to them differently.

The best competitors are small guys who keep you honest by punching above their weight. They may not have many customers, much in the way of resources or a recognizable brand but they have an idea that—in your heart of hearts—you know to be really, really good. This is the kind of competition you want: the kind that keeps you up at night because they're outperforming you on your own terms. Respond by out-innovating them. If you're at a later stage and have the resources, consider an acquisition.

The worst competition is the opposite: tons of money, not much thought. When they arrive on the scene early, they can be extremely disruptive—and not in a good way. Overfunded startups that miss the value proposition always fail but they can often take a lot of thoughtful competitors down with them. There are two ways this can happen. First, you might be tempted to compete with them on their terms and ramp up your burn rate accordingly. Pretty soon, you're spending money as recklessly as they are and there isn't any left in the bank. The second possibility is subtler but just as damaging: when investors see a certain kind of idea fail, spectacularly, they're less likely to fund a good idea along the same lines. (Selling pet food online isn't a bad idea but it took a long time for investors to take another shot after Pets.com failed to the tune of some $300 million.) The response? Have the stomach to wait them out.

While some techniques for winning are specific to the type of competition you're facing, most of them are universal. Concede that competitors will sometimes out-think you, so out-behave, out-prepare and out-execute them. (Moments when you have been "out-thought" are also the right times to "plagiarize with pride.") Above all else: don't violate your core values for a short-term advantage. Lose a sale to the competition and you will recover. Lose your soul to the competition and you will have a much harder time getting it back.

CHAPTER THIRTY-ONE

FAILURE

Up until this point, I've focused on setting goals and doing everything you can to achieve them. It's time to acknowledge a timeless truth of startup life: there will be failures. *Lots* of failures. At a startup, failures aren't avoidable aberrations. They're part of the process. As I always tell employees, no one has made more mistakes in the history of the company than I have. And mine are usually the biggest ones.

FAILURE AND THE STARTUP MODEL

Perhaps major organizations with long-tested, repeatable business models can afford to work on the assumption that all failure—or nearly all of it—is avoidable. Follow the rulebook; generate revenue; repeat. If something goes wrong, it's simply because you failed to follow directions.

Nothing could be further from the reality of startup life. Steven Gary Blank puts it in third place on his Customer Development Manifesto for Startups: "Failure Is an Integral Part of the Search for the Business Model." This is exactly true: you're creating a new product in a new market (not following an establishment rulebook) and the creation process will involve a number of false starts. That's certainly been the case at Return Path.

One of the most exciting moments in Return Path's history was when we acquired NetCreations, Inc. in the summer of 2004. In a single shot, we acquired the capability to solve one of the biggest problems marketers and publishers talked to us about: building a customer database. The NetCreations acquisition gave us a great client base, a bunch of revenue, a new team, and a new line of business.

The acquisition instantly gave us scale and put us on the map. But ultimately, it didn't work. It was the first step toward our becoming "the world's smallest conglomerate," and we eventually had to divest the business, among other things.

We acquired NetCreations on the assumption that our customers would purchase a full suite of email services at once. That assumption proved false, and the acquisition failed. The important thing is that we learned our lesson and decided to focus on a single line of business (an insight that's allowed us to increase our revenues almost seven-fold in five years). If we forget that lesson and start diversifying prematurely—*that* would be a real failure.

The corollary to Blank's point about failure and the startup business model is that permission to fail is *critical* in a startup or growth company. If you don't give your team permission to fail, you're not giving them permission to innovate. If they don't innovate—then you will fail for sure. I start every management training session by saying that in the past 13 years I've made more mistakes than everyone else in the company combined. Everyone has permission to try breaking my record.

There is one thing you shouldn't give anyone—including yourself—permission to do: fail in the same way twice. You can make every mistake in the book but you should only make them once, learn from them and avoid them in the future.

FAILURE IS NOT AN ORPHAN

It's never hard to collect candidates to take credit for a success. Whenever something goes right, from a major fundraising deal to a good quarter or a big client win, lots of people will take credit—many of whom don't deserve it. Fred Wilson has said it many times over to me: success has a thousand fathers. The flip side of that, though, is that failure is not an orphan.

Companies that have a culture of blame and denial eventually go down in flames. They are scary places to work. They foster in-fighting between departments and back-stabbing among friends. Most important, companies like that are never able to learn from their mistakes and failures to make sure those things don't happen again.

Finger pointing and looking the other way as things go south have no place in a well-run organization. While companies don't necessarily need to celebrate failures, they can create a culture where failures are treated as learning experiences and where claiming responsibility for a mistake is a sign of maturity and leadership. It starts at the top: if the boss is willing to step up and acknowledge a mistake, do a real postmortem and process the learnings with his or her team without fear of retribution, it sets an example that everyone in the organization can follow.

What separates A companies from B and C companies is the ability to recognize and process failures as well as successes. Far from being an orphan, failure usually has as many real fathers as success.

Silver Tail Systems Founder Laura Mather on Learning from Failure

Most CEOs—overachievers that we are—treat failure as something to be avoided at all costs. Silver Tails System Founder Laura Mather has learned to view them as learning opportunities. Given the inevitably of failures (and lots of them) at every startup, it's a reorientation we should all attempt.

Through the journey of starting my own company, I've learned many lessons, the most poignant of which has been learning the importance of failure.

Before starting a company, I had taken pride in being the expert in my field and consistently producing excellent work. When I started raising money in 2008, it became painfully clear that I wasn't an expert at fundraising. I had a lot to learn.

My method of learning how to raise money and create a business plan was typical of how I learn most things—jump into the deep end and sink or swim. This meant that my partners and I made many, many mistakes throughout the fundraising process. For instance, we didn't understand what a venture capitalist (VC) was expecting around market sizing or that enterprise software sales would have to be for more than $250,000. In the beginning, I thought that each of these mistakes was catastrophic. In fact, early in my career, that's how I viewed *all* mistakes. Through this process, I came to understand that mistakes were opportunities.

I soon changed my modus operandi: once I made a mistake, I would try to correct it as quickly as possible. For example, at the end of one pitch the VC told us that he was looking for a different way to understand our technology. He wanted an analogy that showed him how our technology protected a web site by relating it to something in the real world. On the way back from the meeting, my co-founder and I brainstormed ideas. We realized that our software was similar to security guards in a store. You want to let people into the store so that they can buy things but this means that shoplifters can also get into the store. The security guards are in the store to find people who might be stealing. Our software is similar: it assumes that you must allow people to interact with your web site but you need to monitor for bad actors.

When we got home from the meeting, we drafted two new slides and sent them to the VC. The turnaround time on the new slides was less than five hours.

We sent the slides after 8 P.M. but got an immediate positive response. Leaving that analogy out in the first place wasn't a catastrophe; adding it on the basis of the advice we got significantly improved our presentation.

In the startup world, because you have the luxury of moving very quickly, you are going to make mistakes. That's okay. It's better to make a fast decision and move forward with that than to spend too much time in the decision making process. You just need to be sure you are ready to make adjustments when you realize your decisions are not turning out as anticipated.

The fundraising process taught me the most valuable lesson I learned in my entrepreneurial career: success isn't measured by your lack of stumbles but by the quality of your recoveries.

Laura Mather, Founder, Silver Tail Systems

Management Moment

Lighten Up!

We have a very trusting environment at Return Path, with flexible work-from-home and vacation policies and a general attitude that more autonomy is a good thing for everybody. So you can imagine my team's surprise when I announced a new rule a few years ago: We were going to start monitoring Internet usage in the office, and browsing social media sites would not be tolerated. No Facebook. No MySpace. No Twitter. No exceptions.

April Fool!

Being a startup CEO is serious business, so it's important to be lighthearted whenever possible. The Facebook prank was one way that I tried to do this. I've also dressed up in a full gorilla suit on Halloween and done my best to honor International Talk Like a Pirate Day on September 19. This isn't about "working hard and playing hard." It's about introducing moments of levity in an intense, hard-driving environment. Everybody on your team needs those moments and everybody will appreciate them.

Life's too short to be serious all day long.

Return Path Board Member and Costanoa Venture Capital Founder and Managing Director Greg Sands on How the Role of the CEO in Execution Changes Over Time

Greg Sands is one of the many invaluable members of my incomparable board. Below, he contributes a great—and somewhat surprising—last word on how the CEO's role with respect to execution changes over time.

The role of CEO in a startup changes radically as the company grows and as the focal point of the company changes. These phases overlap so this framework is admittedly a stylized view. Running a company from start up to growth phase through these phases requires completely different skill sets, so in some ways resembles my favorite sport, the triathlon, where you swim, then bike, then run.

CEO as Product Manager: Achieving Product-to-Market Fit

In a startup, the CEO is typically a founder or co-founder. In this case, he or she is often the person who invented the product or at least the one who first spotted the business problem and brought resources together to solve the problem. The first job is all about product, starting with finding Product-to-Market Fit by clearly identifying a problem and finding prospects or customers who will work with you to solve it.

CEO as Lead Sales Representative: The Sales Learning Curve

A start up CEO needs to be able to sell effectively but the key success factor during this phase is to help the company learn how to sell in a scalable way. I chuckle every time I hear someone say, "We have built the product and have a few beta customers, now all we need to do is hire a sales guy." It's much harder and more complicated than that.

The CEO as sales leader has some unusual characteristics that other sales people won't have. She knows the market exceedingly well, may have created the product and often has a founder's natural charisma and leadership. She can adapt on the fly in a face-to-face meeting and make up new features. Carrying the CEO title adds stature and she can commit company resources on the spot. A sales rep or even a new VP of sales is never going to be able to sell the way the CEO does. Hence, understanding and mastering the sales learning curve is a critical next step.

CEO as Leader and Manager: Building a Learning Organization

After core product market fit has been demonstrated and the sales approach is repeatable, the CEO role shifts into another gear. Where previously she had to be focused on product and sales—because the company's survival depended on it—the company has evolved to where she can raise her head a bit and focus on some other areas, such as strategy, culture and hiring. Of course, any good CEO has been doing some of these things all along the way but as she gets into scaling, they are more important than ever.

This only scratches the surface of all the elements of being a great CEO from startup through the scaling phase of the business. If you master product market fit, the sales learning curve and build a learning organization you will be ready for more challenges and open for more growth ahead.

Greg Sands, Founder and Managing Director, Costanoa Venture Capital

PART FOUR

BUILDING AND LEADING A BOARD OF DIRECTORS

You can learn a lot about strategic planning, talent management and financing and execution from working in a company. You may do large pieces of those things every day and you may even lead some of them. One of the very unique aspects of a CEO's job is building and leading a board of directors. Unless you're one of the few non-CEO executives who spends a huge amount of time with your CEO and board, it's hard to practice building and leading a board until you're actually doing it.

This section will walk through the main aspects of managing a board, from recruiting board members to publishing materials for your board to consume, to running board meetings and making decisions, to working with your board on potentially thorny topics like your compensation or even the board's performance.

CHAPTER THIRTY-TWO

THE VALUE OF A GOOD BOARD

I know a number of CEOs who dread their boards of directors. They roll their eyes when they talk about preparing for board meetings or sitting through them. They fear a loss of control. They have an image of boards as a collection of grumpy old men in a smoke-filled, wood-paneled room, banging a gavel, calling for motions and votes and generally following Robert's Rules of Order. The board of your startup doesn't need to be that way. If you build and manage it correctly, it can be an incredibly valuable asset to your business.

WHY HAVE A BOARD?

Why have a board? Well, for starters, most states require you to have one, although you could be the only member. Eventually, if you take on outside investors, you will need to have a board that represents all shareholders, not just you and other founders and employees. (There are also some good technical and legal reasons to have a board and those are covered well in Brad Feld and Mahendra Ramsinghani's forthcoming book, *Startup Boards*.)

Even if you technically don't need a board, there are plenty of good reasons to have one.

Everybody Needs a Boss

We are all accountable to others for our work in one way or another. Unless you're the rare startup CEO who owns 100 percent of their own company and doesn't grant employees any options, you have other shareholders. Creating a board of directors is a good reminder that you have a boss—and that you have to play by the rules and maximize value for all shareholders. Accountability is crucial. Think about it this way: no matter how much you loved your favorite class in college, how many papers would you have written if your professor hadn't assigned them and given them due dates?

The Board as Forcing Function

A board can help you run your organization by creating a cadence of regular, recurring deadlines. Unless you're in a business that has significant external deadlines imposed on it by partners or customers, it can be difficult to pick deadlines for projects, drive your team hard to meet those deadlines and keep those deadlines from slipping. Your team knows that many deadlines are arbitrary. By making a commitment to your board that something will be done by a certain date, you raise the bar and remove much of the arbitrariness from the decision.

You can also use the board as a forcing function for quality. Sure, a CEO of a small company can read someone's scribbled bullet points or a half-baked spreadsheet. However, if you are presenting the same information to your board, you will polish it up, which will force you to think through what you are presenting.

Pattern Matching

Good board members are really strong at pattern matching: seeing a chain of events or metrics about your business, matching it to one or more comparable situations they have seen in the past, then providing advice, context, history, or a connection to another CEO. I've found this to be true in terms of both strategic issues and operational ones. As Mark Twain once said, "History does not repeat itself but it does rhyme."

Forests, Trees

A good board will help you see the forest for the proverbial trees. You're close to your business and in the weeds of the day-to-day. Your board isn't. As a result, board members can sometimes point out things that you completely miss when looking at your operating results, your staff or your own performance. They may be obvious in hindsight but someone has to give you that rearview mirror.

Honest Discussion and Debate

Finally, provoking, listening to and participating in the discussion and debate at a productive board meeting can be one of the most valuable things you do in a given quarter. Sometimes even great and fearless executive teams are wary of disagreeing with a strong CEO. A great board isn't. A healthy board discussion will push and challenge you and your team's assumptions. More than that, individual board members should push and challenge each other.

While the board can have dramatic impact, you never want your team to think the board runs the company's day-to-day operations. Any time you hear an employee say something like "Oh we have to do that because the board told us to," you should gently remind him that you and the management team run the company, not the board.

I know a couple of CEOs who didn't need to have a formal board of directors based on their corporate structure and ownership. They elected to have boards and each one of them considered his board a key asset to the business and felt accountable to the board, even if those boards didn't necessarily have the power to fire the CEO.

As a final note on this topic, some companies have an advisory board instead of a board of directors in the early days but there's no reason you can't have both moving forward. However, advisory boards tend to be much less formal—and much less helpful.

Return Path Board Member and Foundry Group Managing Director Brad Feld on Startup Boards

Brad has been one of my most valuable partners for more than a decade. He was an early investor in Return Path and he's been an active adviser since the day we met. (He was also gracious enough to ask that I write this book for his Startup Revolution series!) Below, he contributes his thoughts on startup boards.

I've had the pleasure of being part of the Return Path board of directors for a dozen years. Having worked with Matt and the board as the company grew from 20 people to over 400 people today has been a powerful experience and has informed much of my thinking about how an effective board works. I expect that if you read *Startup Boards: Reinventing the Board of Directors to Better Support the Entrepreneur*, you will see many of Matt's thoughts here reflected there.

Many CEOs view their board simply as their boss or as a Rolodex or as a necessary evil they have to deal with on a monthly basis. Oftentimes, venture capitalist (VC)-backed company boards consist only of founders and their investors. They end up being *reporting boards*, where the CEO simply updates the board on a periodic basis about the company's performance. They allow investors to ignore the company except for when there's a board meeting, at which point everybody hustles to get up to speed on what happened in the past month.

As a CEO, your board can be a powerful tool with which you build your company. If you don't take advantage of it, you are wasting a precious resource. While you may not have complete control over selecting all of your board members, as some may be linked to your agreements with your investors, you are responsible for setting the tone and tempo of the board. You get to establish the ground rules, engage board members however you think will help the most, hold board members responsible and use the board as strategically as you can.

Every board is different and each board member brings something unique to the table. Take advantage of this, both by building the board with a diverse set of skills and perspectives, as well as engaging the board to maximize the value you get from each board member—and the board as a whole.

Matt has done this skillfully at Return Path over the last dozen years. This section describes how he did it.

Brad Feld, Managing Director, Foundry Group

CHAPTER THIRTY-THREE

BUILDING YOUR BOARD

The first step in having a great board of directors is to carefully and deliberately build the board over time. You're never going to have an awesome board without having amazing board members. Your board can be just as important to you as your executive team and you should spend just as much time and energy building one as the other. I've had about a dozen board members over the years, some better than others.

WHAT MAKES A GREAT BOARD MEMBER?

My top five characteristics of a great director are similar to my top five characteristics of a great executive (except for the last one):

1. *They are prepared and keep commitments.* They show up to all meetings. They show up on time and don't leave early. They do their homework. They are fully present and don't email during meetings.
2. *They speak their minds.* They have no fear of bringing up an uncomfortable topic during a meeting, even if it impacts someone in the room. They do not come up to you after a meeting and tell you what they really think. I had a board member once tell my entire management team that he thought I needed to be better at firing executives more quickly!
3. *They build independent relationships.* They get to know each other and see each other outside of your meetings. They get to know individuals on your management team and talk to them on occasion as well. None of this communication goes through you.
4. *They are resource rich.* I've had some directors who are one-trick or two-trick ponies with their advice. After their third or fourth

meeting, they have nothing new to add. Board members should be able to pull from years of experience and adapt that experience to your situations on a flexible and dynamic basis.

5. *They are strategically engaged but operationally distant.* This may vary by stage of company and the needs of your own team but I find that even board members who are talented operators have a hard time parachuting into any given situation and being effective. Getting their operational help requires a lot of regular engagement on a specific issue or area. They must be strategically engaged and understand the fundamental dynamics and drivers of your business—economics, competition, ecosystem, and the like.

As I said, there's a lot of overlap between great executives and great board members but there are important distinctions as well. You need everybody on your team to keep commitments, but you shouldn't care particularly about your CFO's industry connections and you absolutely don't want your CTO to be operationally distant. The most crucial similarity between the two lists, though, is that they exist: with the exception of certain investor appointments, you should select board members as rigorously as you would any other senior hire.

RECRUITING A BOARD MEMBER

Likewise, my recruiting process for directors is just as rigorous as what we go through when hiring a new senior executive.

1. *Take the process seriously.* Devote as much focus to building your board as to building your executive team—both in terms of your time and in terms of how you think about the overall composition of the board, not just a given board member.
2. *Source broadly.* Get a lot of referrals from disparate sources. Reach really high. Remember that asking someone to join your board is a pretty big honor for them, so that ask becomes a good calling card for you. I've had meetings with some amazing CEOs over the years when I've initiated a cold call around the person being a potential board member. Not all have worked out but almost all of them took the meeting.
3. *Interview many people.* Conduct interviews face to face and conduct multiple interviews with finalists. Also, for finalists, have a few other board members conduct interviews as well.

4. *Check references.* As with hiring, check references thoroughly and from multiple sources in different contexts.
5. *Have finalists attend a board meeting.* Give the prospective board member extra time to read materials and offer your time to answer questions before the meeting or even do a one-on-one meeting in person to prep the candidate. You will get a good firsthand sense of a lot of the preceding top five items this way. You want to see a prospective board member dive into the flow of a conversation in a meeting, even if he or she doesn't know a ton about the material. Someone who is deferential or afraid of saying something dumb or making waves, even during an audition like this, is likely to behave that way once on the board as well.
6. *Have no fear of rejecting potential board members.* Even if you like them, even if they are a stretch and someone you consider to be a business hero or mentor and even after you have already put them on the board—and, yes, even if they're a VC. This is your inner circle. Getting this group right is one of the most important things you can do for your company.

As I mentioned earlier, CEOs should go through the same process vetting a future venture investor who will have a board seat.

COMPENSATING YOUR BOARD

What about compensating your board members? These are your bosses, so deciding what to pay *them* might feel awkward. Nonetheless, this is an issue that will inevitably come up, so it's useful to keep a few guidelines in mind:

- *Venture directors.* This one is easy: venture directors should receive no additional compensation. This is part of their job. If a VC insists on separate option grants or cash compensation, resist. In fact, this is a red flag: high-quality VCs would never ask for additional payment.
- *Management directors.* This one is even simpler: nothing.
- *Independent directors.* This is the one case in which board compensation is appropriate. Until you're a big, public company, independent

> directors should be compensated exclusively via equity. (The rule of thumb is "less than a senior hire but not a ton less.") That equity should vest over their term as a director (usually four years), with "single-trigger" acceleration in the event of an acquisition.
>
> If a director candidate insists on cash compensation, find another candidate. (In some cases they will ask for a consulting deal. Tell them that you'd be happy to consider them as a consultant but that is independent as their role on your board.)

One other item to note: vesting terms for director equity isn't a formality. You *can* fire an underperforming board member and that may very well happen before their term is up. I've seen multiple instances of CEOs or boards firing underperforming VC directors, sometimes by leaning on other partners in that director's firm to take over the board seat, sometimes as part of a broader overhaul of a board at the time of a financing.

You don't always have the ability to fire an underperforming director but even if you don't, you owe it to your board and to your company to give open and honest feedback and strive for continuous improvement of your board. By adding this element of rigor to your board process, you are further driving a culture of accountability, transparency and rigorous debate to the board culture. You'd be surprised how even the most callous or arrogant board members respond to peer feedback saying they're not getting the job done, as long as they respect their peers.

BOARDS AS TEAMS

Having great individuals on your board is only the first step toward having a great board. As with building any team, you want to make sure you field a collection of superb individuals who complement each other nicely in terms of experience and personality. Among the three VCs currently on our board, two have operating experience, one as a founder and one in product management. Among the two industry CEOs, one has more of a business development focus and the other has deep technical expertise. We have a world-class CFO with significant corporate development experience as well. Some directors are excitable and quick to react, others are more reflective; some are aggressive and others are more conservative; some have extremely colorful metaphors, while others are a bit more steeped in traditional pattern recognition. That diversity makes for great conversations.

Fred Wilson has regularly written that "the success of an investment is in inverse proportion to the number of VCs on the board." Though it hasn't been my experience, I see Fred's point. I'd argue that the same statement is true of founders or management as well. Boards help govern the company and watch out for shareholder interests. Boards give outside perspectives and strategic advice to the company's leadership. Boards hire and fire the CEO. More and more every day with large public companies, boards keep management honest. How can these critical functions occur when a board has too many members of the management team on it? They can't. We have had outside directors only, other than me, from Day 1. I'm not advocating that boards meet 100 percent apart from senior management; just that other members of the management team aren't officially directors.

STRUCTURING YOUR BOARD

I regularly get asked the following questions about board structure:

- How big should my board be?
- Do I need any committees and how do those work?
- Should I be chairman or should someone else or what happens if someone else wants to be?

New CEOs especially will often get pressure to handle these issues one way or the other, either by including far too many people on the board of directors or overcomplicating it with multiple committees. The reality is that things can and should be much simpler.

Board Size

The size of your board is directly related to how large and complex your company and shareholder base are. If you are pre–Series A financing, then a board of three is plenty. Once you have raised a Series A, have a five-person board for a long time, until you are starting to think about going public. At that point, increase it to seven people. I'm not sure it matters all that much, as long as you have great directors and a manageable conversation. There are unruly boards of three and high-octane boards of seven. The main thing I'd suggest around your board's size is to:

- Never have more than one representative of management on the board (you).
- Have as many independent (nonmanagement, noninvestor) directors as possible, preferably industry CEOs or large strategic partners/customers.

The value is in the balance and diversity of opinion and experience, not the size.

Note: Although it's not permitted in a handful of states and countries, it's okay to have an even number of directors if you have a good and high-functioning board. We have had long stretches of time over the years with four or six directors. As I always said at those times to our board, "If it comes down to a tie vote about something big and contentious, we have bigger problems."

Board Committees

The topic of board committees is also a relatively easy one for private companies in early stages. Most companies have two: a compensation committee and an audit committee.

- *Compensation committee.* You need a group of directors to figure out how much the company should be paying you and overseeing your decisions on what the company is paying other senior executives.
- *Audit committee.* You need a group of directors to speak directly to your outside auditors to make sure that your income statement and balance sheet are accurate and follow generally accepted accounting principles (GAAP).

Neither committee really needs to meet more than one or two times a year until you get much larger (i.e., approaching $100 million in revenue or about to go public). At that point, you might need a third committee on nominations and governance as well—but that's something I haven't gotten to yet at Return Path.

Note: All committees can be "committees of the whole" in smaller companies.

Chairing the Board

Should you be chairman of your own board? Up until the Enron scandal and the ensuing Sarbanes-Oxley legislation in the early 2000s, almost all CEOs were also chairman of the board. My latest read is that 75 percent of public companies are still that way, although there is a growing movement to separate out the CEO and chairman roles. There may well be good reasons for that with larger, public companies and companies with long and potentially checkered pasts that are rife with governance issues—and it's a very common practice for nonprofits and associations with different stakeholder structures. In closely held, private companies, it probably doesn't matter much either way.

If you're a typical, VC-backed company, you probably have directors who explicitly represent at least 50 percent of your shareholder base on your board, so you're unlikely to run afoul of your largest stakeholders. If your board or a major investor insists on someone else being chairman, you could always push back and suggest appointing a "lead independent director" instead. Either way, not being chairman or having another lead director only means two things:

- You still run the meetings and write all the materials, since you run the business.
- You have one person to consult with on the meeting agenda and possibly the materials ahead of time.

In other words: no big deal either way.

RUNNING A BOARD FEEDBACK PROCESS

Do you evaluate the performance of your board? If not, you should! A lot of CEOs think it's pointless to give board members any feedback, but failure to do so is just as big a miss as failure to give your staff feedback. How else are they going to understand where they're serving you and the company well and where they're not?

Running a board feedback process need not be lengthy or cumbersome. If a board is healthy, it doesn't even have to be run all that often. (There's nothing magic about an annual process. It could easily be every 6 or 8 or even 12 quarters). I developed a simple survey that I run anonymously through Survey Monkey. There are about two dozen questions in these broad areas:

- Issues—is the board working on the right things?
- Culture—does the board work openly and in a rigorous way?
- Structure—does the board have the right number of directors and committees?
- Process—does the board have the right number of meetings, good agendas, good clarity of role?
- Information and resources—are meeting materials good?
- Committee structure and performance.
- Board member evaluations—each board member ranks each board member against a number of criteria.
- Management evaluations—each board member ranks all regularly attending members of the management team against a number of criteria specific to their performance in board meetings

The exact survey we run is available at www.startuprev.com.

The one thing I've never done is ask members of my staff to evaluate the board. That would be more of a 360. Quite frankly, it's a good idea that I'll incorporate in the future.

The report-out and ensuing discussion also don't have to be particularly formal or difficult. I just include our survey's results, with my commentary, as part of our executive session materials for the following board meeting and I moderate a discussion of the results and commentary at the meeting's executive session. If I had a major problem or disconnect in the survey results, I might handle it differently. (For example, I might have the conversation facilitated by another director or by an outside facilitator or coach.) So far, that hasn't been necessary for us.

BUILDING AN ADVISORY BOARD

Many companies have some form of an advisory board. As I mentioned earlier, an advisory board isn't a great substitute for a true board of directors but it can be a useful addition to the company's brain trust.

If you are building an advisory board, the first thing you have to do is figure out what kind of advisory board you want to build. One type of advisory board actually functions as a group. You call regular meetings. You have a single agenda. You want the group to help you problem solve together and you appreciate the dynamic of the conversation among the advisors. A second type of advisory board is a board in name only. In reality, it's just a collection of individual advisers.

Regardless of which type of advisory board you construct, there are a few simple guidelines for running an effective one. These are similar to the guidelines for running a board of directors:

- Clarify the mission, role and expected time required from advisers on paper, both for yourself and for people you ask.
- Figure out the types of people you want on your advisory board up front, as well as a couple candidates for each slot. For example, you may want one financial adviser, one industry adviser, one seasoned CEO to act as a mentor or coach and one technical adviser.
- Aim high. Ask the absolute best person you can get introduced to for each slot. People will be flattered to be asked. Many will say yes. The worst they will do is say no and refer you to others who might be similarly helpful (if you ask for it).
- Be prepared to pay for people's time somehow, likely in small stock option grants.
- Work your advisory board up to the expectation you set for them. Make sure you include them enough in company communications and documents so they are up to speed and can be helpful when you need them. Treat them as much like a board of directors as you can.

At Return Path, we never had a true advisory board but we have had about a dozen advisers over the years, all of whom have received small stock option grants (one or two have even received multiple grants). The people on our advisory board have always taken my calls and been helpful as needed—and more than that have offered proactive advice and information flow regularly.

CHAPTER THIRTY-FOUR

BOARD MEETING MATERIALS

Preparing well for a board meeting is an incredibly important part of the job of running a board—whether you're officially the chairman or not. Like any group or team meeting, the better the preparation, the more effectively you can use the meeting time. Unlike other groups or teams, your board meets only a few times per year. The advance preparation is even more important to reorient directors to the details and context of your business and its current state.

Remember, the individuals on the board are not first and foremost members of your board, like you are. They have day jobs. VC directors can sit on a dozen boards at once. I think when Brad Feld first joined our board, he was on over 30 other boards!

THE BOARD BOOK

The Board Book, a combination agenda and comprehensive report, is the document that will organize and direct your meetings. My formula for a good Board Book is pretty straightforward and it tees up a good conversation at the board meeting. One of my long-time directors, Scott Weiss, once cautioned that "the board will consume whatever you put in front of it." So you have to be incredibly careful about both what you put into the book and how you put it in the book.

- *Use a consistent format for the Board Book for all board meetings.* It's okay to change the format once in a while (annually or less often) but board members come to think of the Board Book like a newspaper or magazine they read regularly. They know where the sports section is. They know where to find their horoscope.

- *Publish the Board Book in a single PDF document.* Everything. Gather your cover memo, all spreadsheets, reports, memos, and presentations in one place, then combine them into a single PDF in an order that makes sense to read from front to back. Then, when it's all compiled into a single PDF, number the pages in the PDF. Even if some of the original documents are numbered themselves, it's a good practice to have a single bold numbering scheme for the whole document. We wrote a simple Adobe Acrobat macro to accomplish this (available at www.startuprevolution.com). Sometimes, I send separate documents in the following cases: third-party documents like audits or valuations; signature pages, which are easier to print out and fax or scan if they're separate; or confidential memos that are only intended for directors, not observers or management. All core meeting materials are in one document. An emerging trend, which is a logical extension of this, is to put this whole document up on a collaborative workspace like Google Docs so that board members can comment on it and ask questions between receiving the materials and the meeting and the management team can comment online. This reduces the amount of "noise" in the board meeting and allows you to focus that time better, which I'll talk about more in the next chapter.

- *Send out the Board Book no later than the Friday afternoon prior to the board meeting.* If your board meeting is on a Monday, maybe go for Thursday afternoon. I've found that it's less important to give directors a set number of days to prepare for a meeting than it is to give them a weekend plus a business day. Also, having a consistent distribution time, like a consistent format, helps train board members to plan their prep time.

Sample Return Path Board Book

Here's the typical structure of our Board Books, which might be a helpful guidepost in general for how to structure your advance reading materials (see the next chapter for how time allocation works across the various topic areas in an actual board meeting):

1. Cover memo:
   a. Cover note that frames the entire meeting, highlighting critical discussion topics as well as events since the last meeting.

   b. Meeting logistics: time, dial-in, address, driving directions.
   c. Agenda.
2. Official business:
   a. Short cover note running through the issues for discussion and approval.
   b. Series of relevant documents, which could include:
      i. Prior meeting minutes for approval
      ii. Other resolutions for approval
      iii. Stock option grants
      iv. Outside valuations, audits
      v. Financing update
      vi. Other transaction update
      vii. Legal update
3. Retrospective:
   a. Short cover note recapping the prior reporting period since the last meeting, again highlighting the things you want to discuss in the meeting.
   b. All historical reporting and scorecards, well organized and easy to follow.
4. On my mind:
   a. Short cover note that lists the three to five issues that are most on your mind (or your executive team's collective mind), with a graphic that shows the issues that were on your mind *last* meeting and which ones map forward to *this* meeting.
   b. Very short memos on each of the three to five issues written by the owner of the issue on your team. The memos need to be succinct and also tee up the specific discussion or outcome you'd like to achieve during the meeting.
5. Executive session: Separate memo optional, if useful for you to tee up confidential issues.
6. Closed session—no materials.

THE VALUE OF PREPARING FOR BOARD MEETINGS

Beyond being an important part of managing a board, taking the time to prepare a great set of materials for your board is up to half the value in having a board and having board meetings.

While board meetings are exhausting for a CEO—you are "on" for hours on end—the most exhausting part is probably the preparation for the meetings.

Our Board Books average 100 pages—and that's for a regular meeting, not an offsite or annual planning meeting. The preparation can take days of intense work: meetings, spreadsheets, documents, occasionally even some soul searching. By the time the meeting starts, my team and I are fully prepared for it. Before the meetings have even started, we have already gotten a huge percentage of the benefit out of the process.

Pulling materials together is one thing but figuring out how to craft the overall story is something entirely different. That's where the rubber meets the road and where good executives are able to step back. Remember what the core drivers and critical success factors are; separate the laundry list of tactics from the kernel that includes strategy, development of competitive advantage and value creation; and then articulate it quickly, crisply and convincingly.

CHAPTER THIRTY-FIVE

RUNNING EFFECTIVE BOARD MEETINGS

The objective of board meetings should always be to have great conversations that help you and your executive team think clearly about the issues in front of you, as well as making sure your directors have a clear and transparent view of the state of the business. Great conversations come from a team dynamic that encourages productive conflict. Many boardrooms are so ego-laden that people just talk over each other. Our group doesn't function that way. We are engaged and we are politely in each other's faces during meetings. No one is afraid to voice an opinion and we listen to each other. There's no surefire formula for achieving this level of engagement but there are a few guidelines you can follow.

SCHEDULING BOARD MEETINGS

Schedule board meetings far in advance and stick to that schedule so you make sure you have as close to 100 percent attendance at every meeting as possible. Make sure that you or your executive assistant knows each board member's general schedule and travel requirements and whether they manage their own calendar or have their own executive assistant. Set your board meeting schedule for the year in the early fall, which is typically when people are mapping out most of their year's major activities. If you know that one of your board members has to travel for your meetings, work with the CEOs of the other companies to coordinate meeting dates. Vary the location of meetings if you have directors in multiple geographies so travel is a shared sacrifice.

In the startup stage of the business, we ran monthly meetings for an hour, mostly call-in. In the revenue stage, we moved to six to eight meetings per year, two hours in length, maybe two a year as longer form and in-person. As a growth-stage company, we run quarterly meetings. They're all in person, meaning every director is expected to travel to every meeting. We probably lose one director a couple times a year to a call-in or a no-show for some unavoidable conflict but for the most part, everyone is present. We leave four hours for every meeting; it's almost impossible to get everything done in less time than that and sometimes we need longer.

Many years (not every year but as needed) we have also held a board meeting offsite, which is a meeting that runs across 24 hours, usually an afternoon, a dinner and a morning. It is geared toward recapping the prior year and planning out the next year together. It's extra exhausting to do these meetings and I'm sure it's extra exhausting to attend them but they're well worth it. The intensity of the sessions, discussion and even social time in between meetings is great for everyone to get on the same page and remember what's working, what's not and what the world around us looks like as we dive into the deep end for another year.

BUILDING A FORWARD-LOOKING AGENDA

The second step in having great board meetings is to set an agenda that will prompt the discussion that you want to have. As I mentioned in the prior chapter, having a consistent format for the advance reading materials that mirrors the meeting is the key. Keying off our format for Board Books from the prior chapter, our time allocation of the topic areas to be covered during board meetings, assuming a four-hour meeting, is the following:

1. Welcomes and framing (5 minutes).
2. Official Business (no more than 15 minutes unless something big is going on).
3. Retrospective (45 minutes):
    a. Target a short discussion on highlighted issues.
    b. Leave some time for Q&A.
4. On my mind (2 hours):
    a. You can spend this entire time on one topic, more than one or all, as needed.

    b. Format for discussions can vary—this is a good opportunity for breakout sessions, for example.
5. Executive session (30 minutes): This is your time with directors only, no observers or members of the management team (even if they are board members).
6. Closed session (30 minutes): This is director-only time, without you or anyone else from the management team.

This agenda format focuses your meeting on the future, not the past. In the early years of the business, our board meetings were probably 75 percent "looking backward" and 25 percent "looking forward." They were reporting meetings—reports which were largely in the hands of board members before the meetings anyway. They were dull as anything. They were redundant: all of our board members were capable of processing historical information on their own. Today, our meetings are probably 10 percent "looking backward" and 90 percent "looking forward"—and much more interesting as a result.

IN-MEETING MATERIALS

We also focus on creating a more engaging dialogue during the meeting by separating out background reading from presentation materials. In our early days, we used to do a huge PowerPoint deck as both a handout the week before the meeting and as the in-meeting deck. That didn't work well to create an engaging meeting.

There's nothing more mind-numbing than a board meeting where the advance reading materials are lengthy PowerPoint presentations, then the meeting itself is a series of team members standing up and going through the same slides, one by painful one, bullet by excruciating bullet—that were sent out ahead of time.

Then we separated the two things so people weren't bored by the PowerPoint—because the PowerPoint was new! We started making the decks fun and engaging and colorful as opposed to simple text and bullet slides. That was a step in the right direction but the preparation consumed twice as much time for the management team and we certainly didn't get twice the value from it.

Now we send out a great set of comprehensive reading materials and reports ahead of the meeting and then we have a completely PowerPoint-free meeting. No slides on the wall. This changes the paradigm away from a presentation—the whole concept of "management presenting to the board"—to an actual discussion. Everyone—management and board—is highly engaged. No checking email. No yawns. Nobody nodding off.

PROTOCOL

Attending a board meeting is a real privilege as well as a great learning experience for anyone in the company. Regardless of your meeting format and duration, you need to insist on good meeting behavior from your directors—and, of course, you and your executive team need to role-model it yourselves.

This is your meeting, even if the board is your boss. If a board member is flouting your requests, try to get the whole board to agree on ground rules for meetings so you have additional support in policing offenders.

Attendance and Seating

Miss Manners-y as it might sound, you have to manage meeting attendance and even seating very carefully. I've always thought about meeting attendees in four categories:

- *Core executives* are the people who are working on the things the board cares most about. They attend every meeting. In our case, that's been our CFO, head of sales, co-founder, and head of product. These people are expected to speak regularly, facilitate specific discussions and be quite familiar with and have relationships with board members.
- *Other executives* need to cycle through board meetings once or twice per year so they have enough exposure to the board and vice versa, even though they may not be leading any particular topic (though that's a good idea if the timing works). It's important to communicate to them that just because they're not in every single meeting doesn't mean that their role isn't important; it's just a part of the business that the board doesn't focus on.
- *Others at the company* are invited to join each meeting strictly as an observer. This can be a form of reward or development but it's a great opportunity to give your high-performer/high-potential group a little more oxygen.

- *Board observers.* Over time, you may have to agree to give someone board observer status in connection with a financing. You should be as parsimonious as possible in adding official observers, as more people around the table can have a dilutive effect on meeting dynamics.

I have only one rule for seating during board meetings. Directors have to sit at one end of the table together. Everyone else can fill in the rest of the table or side seating. This may sound silly but it drives much better conversation among board members if they feel like they're at a smaller table.

Device-Free Meetings

We have all been in meetings where everyone is on a laptop or tablet or smartphone the whole meeting, no one makes any eye contact with the speaker or facilitator and it's hard to get a pulse out of the group as a result. Demand a no-device policy for meetings. If a director insists on using one to take notes, it's okay to request that they do so on paper. Even if they are actually taking notes instead of multitasking, you never know if they're really taking notes or sneaking a peek at email. Make sure to let board members know that if they have to take a call or respond to something, it's okay to do so or you can even schedule a break around it, rather than trying to wedge that activity into the meeting room and meeting time.

EXECUTIVE AND CLOSED SESSIONS

Executive and closed sessions are in some ways the most important parts of board meetings. We always have an executive session (board members only), then a closed session (board members only, without CEO or other management directors) for at least a few minutes at the end of every meeting. Even if there's nothing specific to discuss, it's a good practice to have these sessions for two reasons.

First, if there is something specific to discuss, those who leave the room won't feel like "something is up" since the sessions are a regular occurrence.

Second, you never know what happens to a conversation when the group dynamics change. Even if there is no agenda, no memo, no formal topics, a simple "How do you think that meeting went?" or "What's keeping you up at night that you didn't write about in this Board Book?" can yield a really rich conversation in a smaller group setting.

Our board doesn't hold back much, if anything at all, but the executive session is a good time for us to connect 100 percent freely about management issues as well as elements of business strategy and performance that might be better hashed out without others present.

As for the closed session, it doesn't matter if you're on the board or, more likely, if you're chairman of the board. This time allows the other directors an even greater degree of freedom to discuss the business or your performance without worrying about saying something in front of you—and without hearing your opinion or any defensive (even if unintentional) reaction. Just make sure that another director always closes the loop with you after closed session to tell you what happened or give you any additional feedback or direction that may have come out of it. It's probably best to appoint someone to be regularly in charge of this so there's no question about it.

Return Path SVP of Sales and Service Anita Absey on Staff/Board Interactions

Some CEOs keep their boards locked down: all interactions to or from the board pass through them and board members are discouraged from fraternizing with the employees. At Return Path, every member of our executive team has personal relationships with our board. Return Path's Head of Sales, Anita Absey, describes the benefits of this approach.

Some of the best insights I have received as a sales leader have come from open, engaged discussions between the board and my colleagues on the senior management team. I'm not talking about operational details or the day-to-day running of the business but the strategic guidance and perspective derived from their diverse experiences and outlooks. Additionally, the opportunity to listen to board members discuss our company and get the benefit of their viewpoints is invaluable.

This kind of constructive dialogue is a gift and the ability to have honest, open interaction without fear of retribution has to be based on the underlying values and culture of the organization. If transparency and feedback are highly prized, then the management team is free to engage with the board and its individual members to the benefit of the organization as a whole.

In preparation for board meetings, our executive team compiles the information required to inform the board of where we are, where we might be stuck and where we want to go as a business in the next quarter, the next year and in the years to come. The board members then get a few days to review the materials, so that the ensuing meeting is completely discussion based rather than presentation based.

The board provides a skeptical view when necessary and challenges our assumptions to be sure that we have considered all outcomes of our intended plans of action—without telling us what to do. That is an inspiring and really helpful way to get us to exercise more critical thinking and adopt a thorough, "external" view of our ideas. I was once told, for example, that my proposed solution to a thorny sales channel conflict was "like taking a sledgehammer to a mosquito." Well, you can be sure that I'm more critical and precise in my approach to problem solving. I try to always have a very precise plan of execution, one that allows us to be nimble and flexible based on changing circumstances.

In addition to the face-to-face board meetings, we have a two-day offsite at least once a year, which gives us plenty of working time and personal time to interact with our board. As corny as it may sound, the times spent bowling, participating in a group cooking class and skiing help to build trust and deepen engagement.

Over the years, I have also relied on our board members to help me network with sales leaders in other organizations in order to get an understanding of how they have approached challenges like global expansion, sales operations infrastructure and compensation planning. The insight and shared experience both validates ideas and offers fresh perspectives on challenges.

A board that is on the journey with you, engaged with the company and the management team, is a cornerstone of company success.

Anita Absey, SVP of Sales and Service, Return Path

CHAPTER THIRTY-SIX

NON-BOARD MEETING TIME

Time with members of your board other than the few hours in actual board meetings is as important to get right as time in board meetings. I'd categorize the time you need to spend with directors in three buckets: ad hoc, pre-meeting, and social.

AD HOC MEETINGS

You have one-on-one meetings with people who report to you. You almost certainly vary them between phone, in-office and out-of-office. Why should your board be any different? Ad hoc meetings are just that—unscheduled (not recurring), opportunistic, sometimes social. I try to meet with each of my directors a couple of times per year without having a specific reason to do so.

For ones who are local to me, dropping by their office or scheduling a quick breakfast or drink is easy. For out-of-towners, I let their executive assistants know that I'd like them to tell me when they're traveling to New York and to save me a slot; or I make a point of seeing them when I'm in their city.

These meetings are good opportunities to establish and solidify direct and personal relationships with each member of your board. The more you know about them and what's going on in their lives, the more you can get out of them in meetings and the more you can help them make useful connections for you. If you don't think of board members as your boss—if you think of them as your strategic inner circle—how great is it to be able to sit with each of them periodically to talk about things going on in your head that you can't share with anyone else?

PRE-MEETINGS

Sometimes, you will have a tough issue coming up at your next board meeting. You are unsure about whether to fire a co-founder. You are worried your largest customer is about to bail. You just discovered that one of your top coders might have stolen code from his former employer and used it in your code base.

Rip off the bandage and call your board members one at a time. Give them a heads up about what they're about to see or hear. Tell them what your initial instinct is about the topic. Let them hear your emotions about it.

Whatever it is, board meetings—and Board Books—are not the place for surprises. Get the surprise out of the way; let your directors digest the news; let them read about it dispassionately in your Board Book. Then have the discussion when cooler heads (usually yours) prevail.

Again, you should make recourse to pre-meetings only when you really need to prep board members for an extraordinary situation. Don't get into a regular rhythm of having "the meeting before the meeting," just as you don't want to get into the habit of having "the meeting after the meeting." In most cases, the give-and-take should happen in the open. Use your judgment to determine if you're facing a special case.

SOCIAL OUTINGS

As I mentioned, a high-functioning board isn't materially different from any other high-functioning team. The group needs to have a clear charter or set of responsibilities, clear lines of communication and open dialogue. As with any team, making sure that the people on a board know how to connect with each other as individuals is critical to building good relationships and having good communication—both inside and outside of board meetings.

We have always done a dinner either before or after every in-person board meeting to drive this behavior. They take different forms: sometimes they are board-only; sometimes board and senior management; sometimes just dinner; sometimes an event as well as dinner, like bowling (the lowest common denominator of sporting activities) or a group cooking class. Whatever form the social time takes—and it doesn't have to be expensive at all—I've found it to be an incredibly valuable part of team building for the board over the years.

You'd never go a whole year without having a team lunch or dinner or outing. Treat your board the same way!

CHAPTER THIRTY-SEVEN

DECISION MAKING AND THE BOARD

Your board's job is to help you and your team make important decisions. It's *not* their job to make those decisions for you. The key is to lead conversations in a way that will produce forthright and actionable advice—*especially* when there's strong disagreement among your board members.

THE BUCK STOPS—WHERE?

I made a dumb comment once at a board meeting that got me thinking.

We came into this particular meeting with, in addition to lots of the regular updating and reporting, one specific strategic topic we wanted guidance on from the board about. It was something that had been nagging the management team for a while without an obvious solution. We had a great conversation about the topic with the board and got very clear guidance as to their perspective on what we should do. I agreed with most of it, albeit with a couple of modifications. More than anything else, I was happy for the note of clarity on an issue with which we'd been struggling internally.

My dumb comment: "That's pretty clear direction. We will go do that." Whereupon Greg Sands, one of our board members, politely reminded me that it's not the board's job to make decisions and make things happen, only to give advice and counsel. I shouldn't take their words as gospel and assume they will work.

Good point.

The board is your boss. (You are on your board but so are two or four or six other people.) While there are some items where the board does have the final say, the overwhelming majority of your actions and the actions within the company are really up to you and your team. You can seek guidance when you feel you need it but that guidance doesn't come with a guarantee that it will work operationally—nor does it give you the ability to look the other way if things don't work out in the end.

MAKING DIFFICULT DECISIONS IN CONCERT

Sometimes boards do have to make tough decisions. How do you go about steering those conversations?

The first thing I'd like to point out is that for about half of our 13-year existence, our board has had an even number of people on it. Not for any particular reason. Sometimes it just worked out that way. (There are jurisdictions where you can't legally do that.) It's also interesting that one out of two people who have heard that from me over the years (including other CEOs) have responded immediately by asking something like "What do you do if there's a tie?" If there's a tie, we have bigger problems.

Not all boards are the same. Some are very political, by which I mean not all directors have aligned interests. This may be more likely to occur in later-stage companies, when the cost bases of different investors' shareholdings are radically different and the topic of exits—or even down-round financings—comes up. However, there is still a way to rally a board to regular unanimity when a thorny or even just an important strategic issue, comes up. My formula for doing that is simple:

1. *Lay out the facts dispassionately*. Write your memo or position paper. Do a full set of pros and cons. Costs and benefits. Payback analysis. What-must-be-true fishbone chart. Whatever format it takes, go for "just the facts, ma'am," and have someone disinterested like your significant other or parent or communications person read it before it goes to the board to make sure all bias is flagged and removed.
2. *Have a strong point of view*. Even if you're not the chairman of your board, you run the show. The board wants to hear that you care about something and why. Otherwise, there's a vacuum that they could step into, which isn't good. In the end, your board is *highly* unlikely to dramatically overrule you if you have a strong and well-founded opinion on something.

3. *Do your homework and lay your groundwork.* Make sure you understand each board member's bias coming into the conversation. Talk to each person individually, even if you feel like you and they are likely to be in agreement. When you're in agreement, you can ask the board member to be supportive but still express their point of view. When you're not in agreement, at least get the other board member to acknowledge his or her frame of reference so that if it comes up during the meeting, you have license to call it out. When in doubt, sell ahead of time.
4. *Let the discussion happen naturally.* Whatever the State of Delaware tells you, this is why you have a board in the first place. Ask provocative questions. Step back and listen to the debate. Jump in and quietly steer when you need to. One of three things will happen: the board will agree with you and you can move forward; the board will not agree with you, in which case you can call the conversation to a halt and declare that you need more time to work on the topic; or the board will shape your opinion of the issue in a way that's productive for you and the company in the end.

While my company has had a long history, with many decisions along the way that turned out to be bad ones, we have never had a moment where the board looked at me and said, "*You* made a bad call here." I don't think that's because I've been overly political and good at working the board. It's certainly not for lack of opinionated and independent directors. I think it's because every time we have had a fork in the road, we have looked at it together and figured out which way to go based on the facts.

MANAGING CONFLICT WITH YOUR BOARD

Our board is an unusually good one, so I don't have a lot of experience managing conflict on the board. Over the years, though, I've had two difficult situations come up that I can draw on to paint at least a vague picture of how to handle things with the board at tense moments.

The first one is how to handle a poor performance review from a board. I had one of those about two years into running the company and there was a moment where I really thought, "uh oh, my job is at risk." All you can do in these situations is dive into the feedback. Ask for clarity on it. Don't be defensive, even if you disagree with the feedback. Involve or start working with an executive coach and give the board some visibility into that process and a direct connection with the coach. Work hard at the feedback and press for another review off cycle if you feel you have course-corrected.

A second difficult situation that can come up is around managing conflict between directors whose interests are not aligned around a financing. In my case, I had a down round where one institutional investor refused to participate and the other investors wanted to wipe that investor out—which would have wiped out all common shareholders and management as collateral damage. The other investors offered to grant new equity to management after the wipeout but that left other common shareholders out (and it also would have completely started management's vesting clock from scratch).

Our company's outside counsel helped point me in the direction of a solution by reminding me that board members have a broad fiduciary duty to the company and *all* its shareholders. They aren't just representatives of their own shareholdings. So I brought 10 Return Path baseball hats into the meeting, five black and five white. I literally made everyone in the room wear one hat when commenting as a shareholder and the other color hat when commenting as a director. That simple gesture helped everyone come to terms with the challenge of the situation and it led to a much happier end result.

Brad Feld on Firing a CEO

Sometimes, the conflict between a CEO and his or her board get close to being unmanageable. Brad Feld describes the unfortunate situations when CEOs are on the verge of being fired.

When we make an investment at Foundry Group, we hope that the CEO at the time we invest will be the CEO for the duration of the company. Some venture capitalists (VCs) take this view; others take the view that the CEO is easily replaceable. As a CEO, it's important that you understand the philosophy of your investors before you take money from them. Fortunately, it's easily discoverable these days: often, all you need to do is ask.

In my case, I have a deeply held belief that my role is to support the CEO any way she needs help—until I don't. I view it as a binary switch: I am 100 percent in, completely committed and will play however the particular CEO wants me to. If for some reason the switch flips—which it does sometimes—it's my responsibility to deal with it.

My first move is to have a calm conversation with the CEO and express my feelings. I use as much data as I can to explain why I am no longer supportive of the CEO. I suggest several specific things that need to change for me to get back to a happy place and be supportive again. Even if there are other investors in the company, I have a private conversation with the CEO first. At this point, it's a problem *I'm* having—not necessarily one the other investors or the board as a whole is having—and I want to take one shot at repairing the situation.

If the CEO responds positively and constructively, I'll start a rhythm of talking directly to the CEO on a weekly basis about what's going on in the company. Rather than be in response mode, I go into proactive mode: I'm clear about what I'm expecting, what I'm doing and what I hope the CEO is doing. During this cycle, I've found that things either get better fast or they gradually degrade.

If they get better fast, I flip the switch back to "happy" and go back into "What do you need from me?" mode. I'll stay here indefinitely, unless the switch flips again. If it flips again, I think hard about whether this is a temporary situation, in which case I try again or a permanent situation, at which point it's time to fire the CEO.

During this time, I solicit additional feedback and perspective from the other investors, founders and management team. I try not to bias the discussion but I'm extra tuned to what others are thinking and feeling about the CEO's performance. Sometimes, this takes on a life of its own; a small amount of stimulus often generates a huge amount of negative feedback on the CEO. Other times, it confirms that I'm having an issue but one that's isolated and fixable.

I never make a unilateral decision to fire a CEO; I don't believe this is appropriate. If I get to a point where I think the CEO needs to be replaced, I'll be direct about it with the other board members. I listen for feedback carefully, am willing to try different approaches and am open to changing my mind, even at this point.

On infrequent occasions, it does turn out that the right decision is to fire the CEO. I like to do this the *Men in Black* way. I invite the CEO to a meal at a restaurant. I do not say what is going to happen in advance. Once we sit down, I begin with the punch line—usually some version of "The board has decided to fire you. I'm happy to talk about it as much as you want and answer any questions but the decision has been made. Before the end of the meal, I'd like to talk in depth about a transition plan." While I don't have the magic Neuralyzer from MIB that erases memories at the end of the conversation, I try to leave things on a positive, constructive note with a clear path forward.

Brad Feld, Managing Director, Foundry Group

CHAPTER THIRTY-EIGHT

WORKING WITH THE BOARD ON YOUR COMPENSATION AND REVIEW

In Corporate America and certainly in the land of startups, the board's biggest, weightiest, and most important responsibility is probably hiring, firing or compensating the CEO. In this chapter, I'll focus on compensation, which really means performance management and compensation.

THE CEO'S PERFORMANCE REVIEW

As I mentioned in Chapter 11, some kind of formal performance management process on you as the CEO is critical. It will help you understand the impact you're having on your organization, your strengths, your weaknesses, and your road map to being a better CEO.

You're not the only customer for your performance review. The board is an equally important customer. How can they properly figure out your compensation and guide you as your boss if they're not contributing to and reviewing your performance appraisal each year?

The three most important things about your performance appraisal are that you:

1. *Have one.* This is where 90 percent of CEOs fall down. Even though your board, as your boss, should do this, you are the leader of your board—regardless of whether you are chairman. Lead them in this process as you would anything else
2. *Publicly acknowledge the results of your appraisal.* This is Step 1 toward internalizing the feedback and making public commitments about acting on it, which leads to Step 3.
3. *Act on it!* Feedback is a waste of everyone's time if you don't learn from it and drive self-improvement, whatever your mechanism is for that (see Part Five on self-management for more on this topic).

There are many ways you could run this process. You could run an open 360 process with your staff and your board together with a professional facilitator, as I described earlier on. You could run a closed and anonymous survey that is administered by your human resources head or by an appointed board member. Alternatively, you could do something in between with a facilitator (preferably your coach) and an open discussion among board members with no staff present. Again: *how* you structure this is less important than making sure *that you do it.*

YOUR COMPENSATION

I talked extensively about compensation earlier, so I'll focus here on your interactions with your board about compensation, both yours and others.

The three components of CEO pay are the same as the three components of executive pay: base pay, incentive compensation and equity. While it can be awkward to talk about your own compensation and while CEOs who are young and single sometimes like to ignore cash compensation, it's critical to spend real time on compensation for yourself and your executive team each year so that everyone on the team, including you, is compensated fairly. You need to guide your board meticulously and dispassionately through this process at least once a year. Ideally, you have a compensation committee to do this work with you. If you don't, you should!

I bring all three elements of compensation together in a single document once each year. (You can find the template we use at Return Path on

www.startuprev.com.) Base pay is simple: award raises or redline pay based on individual performance, company performance and benchmarking against previous years.

Incentive pay and equity are more complex.

Incentive Pay

In terms of plan design, you and your team need to be thoughtful about incentive compensations plans and payout every year. You need to pitch; the compensation committee needs to catch. Build your proposed plan based on what you think the most important objectives are for the company to build shareholder value each year. Answer this question for yourself: "If we did all of this, would we be totally excited at the end of the year?" If the answer is yes, you have a good plan, regardless of the specific metrics. It could be entirely based on revenue or revenue growth. It could be entirely based on EBITDA, operating profit, a combination of the two, or neither. Whatever you do, make the plan as simple and quantitative as possible (even if it's a series of black-and-white qualitative goals, each worth a percentage of the overall plan).

Another guidepost could be uncapped, which, particularly when your metrics are revenue and profit, makes a lot of sense. If you achieve revenue or profit metrics that clearly build a ton of shareholder value beyond plan, you should participate in that success.

Payout is much easier, particularly if the plan is simple and quantitative. At the end of the year, you report back to the Compensation Committee what the percentage attainment was. If you want to have a conversation about increasing the number or decreasing it based on other factors, you can do that but you should have a *very* good reason. You should 100 percent make sure that you accrue the bonus payments on your monthly income statements over the course of the year (based on a reasonable projection of the year's likely outcome from each point in time).

As a side note, for the past several years, we have had 30 to 40 members of the company's leadership team participate in exactly the same incentive compensation plan (with sales leaders participating at 50 percent of their target, with the other 50 percent as commission against their territory). This can be a key part of driving alignment on your leadership team. Per the prior paragraph, you can always request that your Compensation Committee give you some discretionary powers over individual bonuses if you feel that a few individuals deserve more than base plan attainment based on their individual work during the year.

Equity

I've heard of very, very few examples of startup or even growth-stage companies where CEOs have less than a 5 percent stake in the business and are earning less than 0.25 percent per year—and those are usually more mature companies with crowded cap tables and a more certain financial outcome.

Early in the company's life, the optimal form of equity for you (i.e., before the IRS determines it's valuable) will likely be Restricted Stock, which doesn't cost much of anything to buy and will certainly leave you with optimal tax treatment of any gains. You can make something called an 83B election with the IRS when you get the stock. This is much less common to give to other employees, though I've never been sure why.

In addition to working with you to determine your own equity stake, every board expects to set up an option pool. Experienced venture capitalists and outside directors will have a general sense of what's reasonable and fair. Your option pool will have to be resized or refreshed regularly, especially if you're adding lots of staff in rapid succession and raising multiple rounds of financing. After making high-level decisions about the size of your option pool, your board should give you quite a bit of discretion in distributing equity to your employees.

EXPENSES

Although not nearly as important as performance management or compensation, your expenses are also a point of relevance for your board. For about nine years, no one approved my expenses. About four years ago, I decided it would be a good idea for our CFO to start approving them. Then there was some scandal at some big company that caught my eye in the *Wall Street Journal* about a CEO abusing his expenses. I decided it was time to ratchet up the CEO expense policy.

For the past couple of years, my executive assistant, Andrea and I have aggregated all of my expenses for the full year. And I mean all of them. Everything that goes through a regular expense report and everything that doesn't, like car services that are directly billed or things that get billed to the corporate card. We pull out things that aren't personal, like Pizza Friday for the office or extra fans during the heat wave. Then we categorize all expense items, analyze them on a per-night or per-trip or per-person basis as appropriate, footnote extraordinary items and compare them to the prior year's

number for the same line item. The template I use for this can be found at www.startuprev.com. Then we send them to the board, cc'ing my CFO, controller and our outside auditor in case anyone on the board has any questions. We also ask our auditor to comment specifically during the annual audit as to whether my expenses are appropriate and in the range of what they would expect based on what they see at other companies.

As usual, transparency rules. If you have nothing to hide, share it all. As more CEO scandals erupt, you might as well get ahead of the curve with your board.

CHAPTER THIRTY-NINE

SERVING ON OTHER BOARDS

One of the best things you can do as a CEO and board member of your own company is to serve on another company's board of directors. There's nothing like a real-life counterpoint to make you take a step back and think about how to build and run an effective board. Find something—another startup, a nonprofit, your high school or college alumni association—to join as a board member. Watch and learn how other leaders lead and how other boards present materials, run meetings and discuss thorny issues. You might have the bandwidth to do one or two of these but probably not more.

THE BASICS OF SERVING ON OTHER BOARDS

First prize is to serve on the board of directors of a company that looks generally like yours, though probably smaller or earlier stage. Second prize is to serve on another noncorporate organization's board of directors or board of trustees. Third prize, though still quite relevant, is to serve on another organization's advisory board.

You can add a lot to another board and organization based on your experience, which is unique and powerful. The best advice I can give you is that you should do two things as you sit on another board.

Be the board member that you want on your own board. Be honest and direct. Be constructive but don't hold back. Do your homework, come prepared for meetings and pay attention.

Don't hesitate to vet the organization and board before you join it and don't hesitate to quit if you can't have an impact and aren't learning anything from the experience.

Your time is incredibly scarce and valuable—and if it's not well spent, there's no reason to be polite and stick with something where no one is getting real value.

If you are asked to serve on an outside board of directors or even an advisory board, make sure you are interested in the subject matter of the company or that you have a good reason to want to spend time with the entrepreneur or the other board members for other reasons. Don't be afraid to say no if these conditions aren't met. It's your time—no reason to be too altruistic.

Clarify your time commitment up front and try to get some form of compensation for your effort, whether a modest option grant (size totally depends on the time commitment) or or the ability to invest in the company.

Be sure to let your own board know. Ask for permission if the business you're advising is at all related to your company and get the permission in writing for your own HR file (yes, you have one of those, too, as your company grows!).

Finally, follow through on your commitment to the entrepreneur and resign from the board if you can't.

Return Path Board Member and Postini and Authentic8 Co-founder Scott Petry on Serving on Other Boards

Two-time entrepreneur Scott Petry applies everything he learned from his first company Postini (acquired by Google in 2007), to his current work as co-founder of Authentic8. Better yet, he can apply everything he's learned from the numerous boards he's served on. The key is choosing the right boards and applying the right level of commitment to them.

Having another operating executive on your board can bring a meaningful alternate perspective to a group often dominated by financial investors. As a CEO, the other side of the coin might be even more beneficial: sitting on outside boards gives you a perspective that is not available elsewhere. Where else would you be able to see such a melting pot of personality and perspective, to be exposed to so many situations and to be part of collaborative problem solving?

Each company that I'm involved with is different and thus exposes me to a wide range of situations, challenges and solutions. Moreover, seeing how other teams deal with their board has helped me both as a board member and as a CEO working with others.

Growing companies face a common set of scalability issues: product, market, scaling, fundraising, and so on. Each company also has its own unique challenges. These can be market driven, cultural, financial, technical—whatever. As a board member, you get a front-row seat as management works through these issues. Even if they aren't problems your business may face, you can learn a lot by seeing teams acknowledge and respond to challenges.

As with any communal activity, boards are heavily influenced by personality. As a board member, you're exposed to personalities working in concert and working through conflict. While almost universally uncomfortable, working through conflict can provide the most meaningful lessons. I've seen situations where management and the board might as well be speaking different languages; I've seen strong personalities try to shove their position down others' throats; and I've seen meeker personalities follow the passive-aggressive script to the letter. Regardless of the situation, boards ultimately need to unify and act.

Being involved with different boards has given me a more general perspective as well. I've learned that not every board member's ego is calibrated equivalently and not every member has the same expectations of the company. Certainly, each board member wants the company to succeed but each measures success differently. Some board members may be looking to return funds to their LPs. Others might focus on high-visibility company metrics as a way to buttress their own or their firm's reputation. Others might be participating as a way to keep connected to bright people or solve hard problems through innovative means. Individual motivations are all over the map. That variance in objective can be the source of frustration and conflict between board members and management—and a source of learning for other CEOs. Where else could you see these situations play out in real time? Where else could you participate in resolving them?

As a CEO, I take what I learn in other boards and apply the lessons to myself. Am I really hearing what the board is saying? Am I communicating to the board in a way to ensure that I'm being heard? Are we focusing on what is most important? Given what I know about the motivations of the members, is another approach in order? Have I seen this situation before and how would another CEO have handled it?

Participating in outside boards gives the CEO a perspective that is not available elsewhere. It's like a front-row seat in a graduate lab class on entrepreneurship. You're exposed to the best and the worst of group dynamics. You can dramatically improve your skills by applying these lessons to the way you work with your board.

Scott Petry, Co-founder, Postini and Authentic8

SUBSTANCE OR STYLE?

I had an interesting conversation the other day with a friend who sits on a couple of boards, as do I. We ended up in a conversation about some challenges one of his boards is having with their CEO and the question to some extent boiled down to this: a board is responsible for hiring/firing the CEO and for being the guardians of shareholder value but what does a board do when it doesn't like the CEO's style?

The biggest challenge I've had over the years sitting on other boards is trying to figure out the line of proper governance between being a director and being a CEO. My natural instinct is to speak up, to define and solve problems. That's not necessarily the right role for an outside director who is there to help guide management (and, sure, ultimately hire and fire management).

There are lots of different kinds of CEOs and corporate cultures. Some are command-and-control, others are more open, flat and transparent. I like to think I and Return Path are the latter and of course my bias is that that kind of culture leads to a more successful company. I've worked in environments that are the former and while less fun and more stressful, they can also produce very successful outcomes for shareholders and for employees as well.

So what do you do as a board member if you don't like the way a CEO operates, even if the company is doing well? Here are some specific questions, which probably fall on a spectrum:

- Is it grounds for removal if you think the company could be doing better with a different style leader at the helm? Probably not.
- Is it fair to expect a leader to change his or her style just because the board doesn't like it? Less certain but also probably not.
- Is it fair to give a warning or threaten removal if the CEO's style begins to impact performance, say, by driving out key employees or stifling innovation? Probably.
- Is it fair to give feedback and coaching? Absolutely.

I find myself very conflicted on the topic. I certainly wouldn't want to work in an organization again that had what I consider to be a negative, pace-setting environment but is it the board's role to shape the culture of a company? Is that just style, or is it substance?

Union Square Ventures Managing Director Fred Wilson on How Managing Startup Boards of Directors Change over Time

Fred has been a Return Path investor and adviser since the beginning and his blog, A VC, *was one of the things that inspired me to start blogging in 2004. In more than three decades as a VC, Fred has watched dozens of boards evolve from Series A to exit.*

Every company should have a board of directors. At the start it can simply be a one-person board consisting of the founder. It should not stay that way for long: if you're your own board, you won't get any of the benefits that come from having a board. These benefits include but are not limited to advice, counsel, relationships, experience, and accountability.

The shareholders elect the board of directors. There is usually a nominating entity that puts directors up for election by the shareholders. If the founder controls the company, then he or she is usually that nominating entity.

I am a fan of a three-person board early on in a company's life. I generally recommend that founders put themselves on the board along with two other people they trust and respect. The election of directors in this scenario is simply a matter of the controlling shareholder voting them in.

This situation changes a bit when investors get involved. If the founder retains control, then the situation does not have to change. The founder can still nominate and elect the directors he or she wants on the board. However, investors can and will negotiate for a board seat in some situations. This is less common for angel investors and more common for venture capital investors.

The way investors negotiate for a board seat is usually via something called a shareholders' agreement. This is an agreement between all the shareholders of the company. It contains a bunch of provisions but one of the provisions can be an agreement that the shareholders of the company will vote for a representative of a certain investor in the election of the board of directors. The representative can even be named specifically. For many of the boards I am on, this is how my seat is elected. For venture capital investments, this is a very typical provision.

Adding an investor director does not mean that the founder loses control of the board. It can remain a three-person board with one investor director and two founder directors. Or the board can be expanded to five and the investors can take one or two seats and the founder can control the rest. These two situations are common scenarios when the founders control the company.

As a company moves from founder control to investor control, the notion of an independent director crops up. An independent director is a director who does not represent either the founder or the investors. I am a big fan of independent directors and like to see them on the boards I am on. Boards that are full of vested interests are not good boards. The more independent-minded the board becomes, the better it usually is.

When the founder loses control of the company (usually by selling a majority of the stock to investors), it does not mean the investors should control the board. In fact, I would argue that an investor-controlled board is the worst possible situation. Investors usually have a narrow set of interests that involve how much money they are going to make (or lose) on their investment. It is the rare investor who takes a broader and more holistic view of the company. So while investor directors are a necessary evil in many companies, they should not dominate or control the board. The founder should control the board in a company he or she controls and independent directors should control a board where the founder does not control the company.

When and if a company goes public, the shareholders' agreement will terminate and public company governance standards will dictate how a board is selected and elected. There will most likely be a committee of the board that is called the nominating committee. That committee will select a slate of directors that will be put up for election by all the shareholders of the company at the annual meeting. Most public company boards have staggered board terms such that a subset of the board is elected every year. Three-year and four-year terms are most common.

It is possible for the shareholders to put up an alternative slate. In theory, this approach could be used in both private and public companies but in reality it is almost entirely limited to public companies. This will be perceived as a hostile move by most companies and they will fight the alternative slate of directors. This "alternative slate" approach is most commonly taken by "activist investors" who take a meaningful minority stake in a public company and agitate for changes in the board, management and strategic direction of the company. It can also be used in a hostile takeover effort. It is rare for an alternative slate to take control of a company but it is fairly common for a new director or two to get elected in this way.

Boards should evolve. Boards should recruit new members on a regular basis. Board members should have term limits. I like the four-year term. I've been on boards for much longer. I'm in my thirteenth year on one board and my eleventh on another. These are not ideal situations but they involve companies I invested in while I was with my prior venture capital firm and I have a responsibility to my partners and the founders to see these situations through.

A much better example is Twitter, where I was the first outside director, taking a board seat when Twitter was formed in the spinout from Obvious and USV made its initial investment. Over time, Twitter added several investor directors and then started adding independent directors. By last fall, Twitter had the opportunity to create a board with two founders, a CEO, three independent directors and one investor director. As a shareholder, that sounded like the right mix to me and I voluntarily stepped down along with my friend Bijan, who had led the second round of investment.

The point of the Twitter story is that boards evolve. In the first year, it was me and two founders and a founding team member. In the second year, it was me and Bijan, two founders and a founding team member. In the third year, it was three investors, two founders and two senior team members. In the fourth year, it was three investors, two founders, a CEO and three independents. Now it is one investor, two founders, a CEO and three independents. Many of these changes in the Twitter board happened at the time of financings. That is typical of a venture-backed company.

In summary, the shareholders elect the board. That is the essential truth in every company. How they elect the directors can be very different from company to company. For public companies, it is largely the same for all. In private companies, you get what you negotiate for, so negotiate the board provisions carefully. They are important.

Most important, build a great board. They are not that common. You owe it to your company to do that for it.

Fred Wilson, Managing Director, Union Square Ventures

PART FIVE

MANAGING YOURSELF SO YOU CAN MANAGE OTHERS

Self-management is a combination of self-awareness and self-regulation. Self-awareness means understanding what you're doing and the impact it has on those around you. Getting that down leads directly to self-regulation or the ability to control your actions and not have them control you. Why are those important skills to have as a CEO? Both of them open the door to your being not just an effective manager but an empathic one—the key to being an influential one. Sure, you could theoretically coerce people into doing what you want. Let's face it: that's not much fun and great people don't like to be coerced for a living.

Self-management means realizing that you are in a fishbowl. You are always on display. You set the tone at your company. You are a role model in everything you do, from how you dress to how you talk on the phone, to the way you treat others, to when you show up to work, to how you act at work. You can't let people see you sweat too much—especially as you get bigger. You can't burn yourself out, even if you feel like you're working 24/7. You can't come out of your office after bad news and say "we're dead!" You have to be very intentional about how you "show up" at work.

That's what this final section of the book is all about.

In this section, I cover nuts-and-bolts topics such as creating your own operating system and how to work with an executive assistant, an executive coach and a peer group (the support system makes all the difference in the world!). I also talk about more personal topics like staying fresh and healthy and integrating family life and work life. The last section of the book is on taking stock—how I reflect on my job as CEO periodically and make sure I still want to be doing it.

CHAPTER FORTY

CREATING A PERSONAL OPERATING SYSTEM

Without question, your time is your scarcest resource. There is only one of you in your company—and you can't hire a second you. Figuring out how to get the most out of your day is a critical skill. Figuring out how to optimize your team is an incredibly important part of managing yourself.

In this chapter, I'll discuss managing your agenda, managing your calendar and managing your time. Think of these three sections in descending order of abstraction. Managing your agenda means understanding generally what you're supposed to be doing. Managing your calendar means making time for those things. Managing your time means being as productive as possible at those things as well as doing all of the important (or unimportant) distractions that invariably come up in your day.

While I'm going to talk about a few different tools for managing my time throughout this chapter, I generally refer to all of these tools together as my Operating System. Just as your company has an Operating System, you should have one, too.

Where Does Your Operating System Live?

I keep my Operating System in Excel but you can use any system you want: I know CEOs who keep their Operating Systems in Outlook, Google Drive, Evernote, and a range of other tools. There's no magic to any particular tool as long as you can access your Operating System 24/7 on whatever device you happen to have at any point in time. Whatever and wherever your Operating System is, you have to absolutely live in it and look at it multiple times per day. I typically keep it open all the time on my dual-monitor display.

MANAGING YOUR AGENDA

Having a really tight Operating System starts with having a really tight agenda. *Your agenda is your job description, overlaid with a sense of current priorities.* (If you're struggling with the overall picture of your job description, this book should have been a good starting point for you!)

Here are some questions I keep in the Agenda tab of my Operating System document:

- *Strategy.* Are we doing enough here to build sustainable competitive advantage?
- *Plan.* Do we have the right plan in place to scale revenues and profits?
- *Market.* Am I spending enough time with clients, resellers and partners?
- *People.* Do we have the right people? Are we investing enough in development?
- *Culture.* Is this an awesome place to work? Are we staying nimble enough?
- *Execution.* Are we executing on our plan? If not, why not?
- *Financing.* Is there enough cash in the bank? For how long?
- *Board.* Do we have the right directors? Am I using them enough?
- *Me.* Am I doing enough to learn and grow as a leader?
- *Current.* What's most important, right now?

In my To Do tab, I input the answers to all of those questions—especially "What's most important, right now?"—and turn them into tasks and projects. Each item on the To Do tab has a due date for its next step. That column is color-coded around its deadline (red = "Today/Past," yellow = "Upcoming in the Next Week," white = "Further Out in the Future"). The column is sortable by topic area as well as due date. Again, this spreadsheet is up on my second monitor all day long, so any time there is a spare moment, I can review it and start working on the critical upcoming items.

Once a month, I go back, review the Agenda tab, make sure it's current, then review the To Do tab to make sure it flows from the Agenda tab.

Since my agenda is, in some respects, the company's agenda—and since I follow David Allen's principles in *Getting Things Done* of having all of this stuff listed in one place—my Excel document has a series of other tabs in it as well:

- *Delegated.* This tab tracks all tasks I assign to others on my team, with next steps and due dates (color-coded, as in the To Do tab).

It's an easy mechanism for following up and making sure things are getting done on time.

- *Company scorecard*. This tab lists the company's scorecard and stated goals for the year or the quarter, so I can easily check on this as I'm assigning tasks to myself or others.
- *Development plans*. This tab lists my and my direct reports' development plans so they're also handy for one-on-one and staff meetings. A development plan doesn't do anyone any good unless it's being actively reviewed and worked on.
- *Networking*. This tab lists everyone I need to meet, internally (skip-levels) and externally. It has specific columns for location, so my assistant and I can schedule meetings in a given city when I travel there, as well as desired frequency of meeting, with the simple logic that turns a "schedule" flag red when it's time to set something up.
- *Thoughts*. This is a catch-all tab that lets me write stuff down as it appears in my head. I review it every month or quarter when I reset my agenda.

All-in, tight management of your agenda, with whatever system you use, is a critical starting point for managing your time.

An Essential Time Management Resource

Although my Operating System has evolved a lot over the years and has had a lot of influences contribute to its structure and purpose, probably the largest influence on it has been David Allen's seminal work on personal productivity, *Getting Things Done*. If you're a CEO and you haven't read this book, read it now!

MANAGING YOUR CALENDAR

With your overall agenda set, you can now start planning out your calendar in weeks, months, quarters and even a full year. Here are some of the key building-block elements to my calendar and how I think about them in relation to each other and to the rest of my Operating System (note that these track pretty closely with some of the main elements of the Company Operating System that I described in Chapter 17):

- *Board meetings*. These have to get locked in early and tend to be anchor points for other things going on at the company.
- *Staff meetings*. Whatever your meeting routine is, mark off the big staff meetings—like quarterly offsites or all-day meetings—early. We usually schedule offsites sometime about a month prior to a board meeting to make sure we're hitting execution points and surfacing issues we need to discuss with the board.
- *All-hands meetings*. It's good to mark these off so other people can schedule around them. At Return Path, they typically follow board meetings by a week or so, since we use board materials to prepare for them.
- *Company events*. Summer party? Holiday party? Community Service week? Whatever the events, you will want to schedule around these as well.
- *Staff 1:1s*. I usually set these as recurring appointments in my calendar, though not all staff members have the same length of meeting or frequency.
- *Blocking off work time*. I know some people who block off a handful of hours in the middle of the day each day or once a week for work time, so that their calendar doesn't fill up and they can use the slot to catch up on their own work. I assume it can work but I've never been a fan of this for a CEO because time in the middle of the day is prime time for others to need access to me. My "work time" tends to be before 9 and after 5.
- *Industry events*. These dates are usually known well in advance and almost always involve travel.
- *External things*. If you're on outside boards or have a CEO forum or something like that, you will want to note all of those dates in advance.
- *Vacations*. Critical to plan these out early, even if there's no natural forcing function like kids' school calendars to align to. If you don't map them out and keep the dates clear, you will never take time off.

MANAGING YOUR TIME

Having the major building blocks of your calendar set for a year or a quarter means you're likely to avoid scheduling conflicts with your most important meetings. That's a good start. Once you have all of that set, you can start to manage your time more effectively.

I have historically been very open with my calendar. For most of my career, people who want to meet with me, both internally and externally (with the exception of random vendor solicitation) generally have gotten to meet with me. Some of this is generosity but I'm also a compulsive networker and have always made time proactively to meet with people just to meet them; learn more about different pockets of the industry or finance; meet other entrepreneurs and find out what they're up to or help them; and connect more broadly from there. I've also routinely been on multiple boards at the same time, as I've found that's a very helpful part of my management routine.

As the company has gotten larger and more geographically spread out—and as my kids have arrived, accompanied by a house with a longer commute—I've taken to being more judicious with my time. I could probably do an even better job at it but I've started taking control much more of the minutes in my day. As anyone on my team will tell you who pops into my office, sends me an instant message or calls me, my initial response is always, "just a second," as I insist on finishing whatever quick task or thought I'm working on before engaging with the person. I'm increasingly reducing meeting times from 60 minutes to 30 or from 30 to 15. I'm also more frequently responding to requests on my time with things like "can you send an email for starters?" so I can respond asynchronously. I have to respond to requests for meetings with the occasional "no, that's just something I don't have time for now."

My executive assistant (see the following chapter) has been playing a larger role in helping me structure things so that I have blocks of free time during the day and I make sure I "schedule" time to work on major things that I know will take up a lot of time.

FEEDBACK LOOPS

One tool I've developed over the years to serve as a feedback loop or check on my Operating System is a simple time allocation model.

First, I am religious about keeping an accurate calendar—including travel time between meetings or on planes—and I go back and clean up meetings after they have happened to make the calendar an accurate reflection of what transpired after the fact. At the end of each quarter, my assistant downloads the prior three months' worth of meetings and we categorize them to see where my time went. Then, we make changes to the upcoming quarter's calendar to match targets based on my agenda. For what it's worth, my categories have changed over time but they have always been pretty high level. Currently, they are "Free," "Travel," "Internal," "Board," "Client/

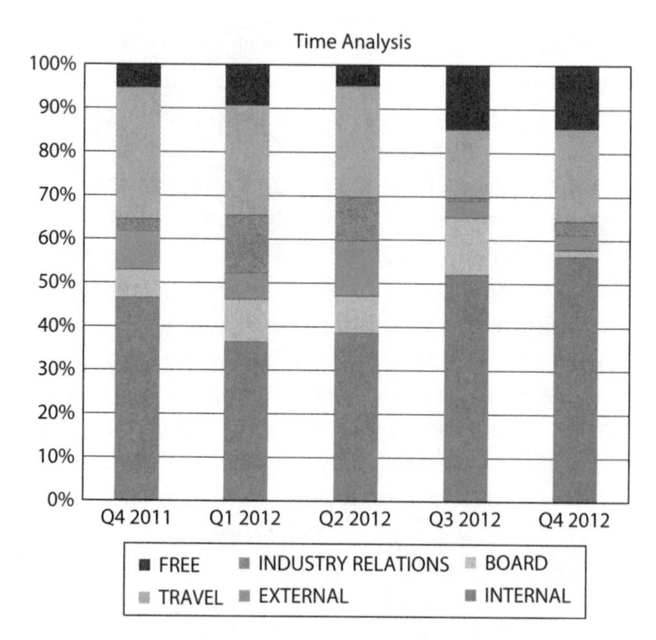

FIGURE 40.1 Sample Quarter-over-Quarter Time Analysis

External," and "Non-work" (by which I mean outside business activities like serving on other boards). See Figure 40.1 for a sample of this time analysis.

Looking at the buckets in isolation in a given quarter isn't so useful but looking at the trends over time and comparing them to where I tell myself I want to be spending my time has been really helpful in keeping me proactive and on track. I routinely generate conclusions like "Wow! I need to cut back on travel!" or "I wasn't in-market enough last quarter." The kinds of shifts you can make are to be proactive instead of so reactive; to cut meetings, shrink them or group them when appropriate internally; to use videoconferencing instead of travel where possible—and to be just a little more selfish and guarded with your time.

Management Moment

Don't Be a Bottleneck

You don't have to be an Inbox-Zero nut (though feel free if you'd like!) but you do need to make sure you don't have people in the company chronically waiting on you before they can take their next actions. Otherwise, you lose all the leverage you have in hiring a team. Don't let approvals or requests pile up. I worked for a guy once who constantly had a line of people at his door waiting for his comments or approvals on things. This was in the days of the paper inbox and people were constantly going into his office, finding the thing they'd left for him in his inbox and moving it to the top of the pile in the hope that he'd get to it sooner so they could continue their work.

As you have a larger and larger team, your job is much less about getting good work done than it is enabling others to get good work done. If you're a bottleneck, you're not doing your job.

CHAPTER FORTY-ONE

WORKING WITH AN EXECUTIVE ASSISTANT

If creating a personal Operating System is the first step to good self-management and time management, the second step is learning how to find and work with an executive assistant.

Other CEOs regularly ask me what value an executive assistant provides, particularly in an era where almost everything can be done in self-service, lightweight ways. It's tempting for CEOs of startups and even companies that are just out of the startup phase, to want to do it all themselves, either because they feel like that they don't need help on small tasks or that it's important to send the message that nothing is beneath them.

I'll say it again: time is your scarcest resource and as the leader of an organization, anything you can do to create more of it is worthwhile. A good assistant does just that—literally creates time for you by offloading hundreds of small things from your plate that sure, you could do but now you don't have to. A great executive assistant can create three to four hours per day for you. That's a *lot* of time that you can put either back into work or into the rest of your life.

FINDING AN EXECUTIVE ASSISTANT

There are generally two different models of finding a great executive assistant. One is to find a super-smart, entry-level person whom you can convince to do the job for 12 to 18 months with the promise that they will be promoted if they do a great job. A second school of thought is to find a career executive assistant, someone who has been there and done that job for other CEOs of larger companies. I've seen both of these models work and I used to use the first model myself. Then about eight years ago, I ended up frustrated that I had a string of very good assistants who kept getting bored and itching to get promoted out of the role and I was constantly starting over with the next one and the next one. At that point, I found another model that works—sort of a hybrid of the two—which is finding a smart person who is past entry level, who hasn't necessarily worked in an office job before (they might have a background in retail or hospitality) and who thinks the job is interesting in and of itself. You have to be prepared to continue to add responsibilities to the person's role and pay more for it every year to make this model work. Not having to train a new assistant every year is incredibly valuable.

No matter what model you follow, of course, you have to have someone who is incredibly well organized (no dropped balls!), great at multitasking, friendly and personable, a solid communicator and, perhaps most important, not gossipy. My long-time assistant, Andrea Ponchione, excels in every respect.

WHAT AN EXECUTIVE ASSISTANT DOES

I'd classify a great assistant as a bit of an alter ego—one definition of which is "second self"—literally an extension of you as CEO. That means the person is not just doing things *for you* but acting *as you*. Think about the transitive property here. Everything you do as CEO is (in theory) to propel the whole company forward. So everything your alter ego does is the same. A great assistant isn't just your administrative assistant. A great assistant is an overall enabler of company success and productivity. You do have to invest a lot of time in getting someone up to speed in this role for them to be effective and you have to pay well for performance but a great assistant can literally double your productivity as CEO.

Andrea was kind enough to provide me with a bulleted list of her job description, which I've annotated with my comments on how I take advantage of that part of her role.

Update and maintain calendar, schedule meetings and greet visitors	My calendar is like a game of Sudoku. I can and do schedule my own things but Andrea handles a lot of it. She also has access to all my staff's calendars, so she can just move things around to optimize for all of us. Finally, she and I review my calendar carefully, to make sure I'm spending my time where I want to spend it.
Answer and screen direct phone line	The bigger we get, the more vendors call me. I can't possibly take another call from a wealth management person or a real estate broker. Screening is key for this!
Plan and coordinate company-wide meetings and events	This is an extension of managing my calendar and accessing other executives' calendars—and a pretty key centralized function.
Plan and coordinate senior team offsites	As part of my desire as CEO to "act like you're the host of a big party," I like this to be planned flawlessly. I do a lot of that work myself but I need a partner to drive it.
Collect and maintain confidential data	Every assistant I've ever had starts by swearing an oath around confidentiality.
Prepare materials for board meetings and senior team meetings	Building Board Books is time consuming and great to offload. My executive team and I put together the table of contents, then everyone pours materials in to Andrea and—Poof!—we have a Board Book. For staff meetings, she manages the standing agenda, changes to it and the flow of information and materials so everyone has what they need when they need it to make these meetings productive from start to finish. In our case, Andrea is part of our senior team and joins all of our meetings so she is completely up to speed on what's going on in the company. This really enables her to add value to our work. She's not just a passive participant—she's contributed great ideas over the years!
Coordinate and book travel (domestic and international)	Painful and time consuming, not because Expedia is hard to use but because there is a lot of complexity and change to manage and coordinate for certain trips. While it takes a while to get an assistant up to speed on how you like to travel or how you think about travel, this is ultimately a big time saver.
Prepare expense reports	You *can* do it but it's easier not to.
Manage staff gifts and anniversary presents for all employees	This is a big one for me. I call every employee on their anniversary and send them a gift. Once a month, a stack of things to sign magically appears on my desk and then gets distributed.
Manage investor database	I assume someday we will have a system for this. For now, IR is a function that Andrea coordinates for my CFO and me.

Assist CEO and senior team with projects as needed	The person in this role is really valuable in helping to organize, research or execute major projects of any kind. Good use of time.
Prepare quarterly time analysis	This is a big one for me. Every quarter, Andrea downloads my calendar and classifies all of my time, then produces an analysis showing me where I'm spending time; my classifications are internal, external, non-RP, free, travel, board/investor. This really helps us plan out the next quarter so I'm intentional about where I put my hours and then it helps her manage my calendar and balance incoming requests. (For more details, see the "Feedback Loops" section in the previous chapter.)
Help with communications	This wasn't on Andrea's list but I'm adding it. She ends up drafting some things for me (sometimes as small as an email, sometimes—with a lot more guidance—as large as a presentation), which is very helpful. (It's always easier to edit something than create it.) I also ask Andrea to read any emails I send to "ALL" ahead of time, to make sure they make sense from someone's perspective other than my own.

EA Extraordinaire Andrea Ponchione on Working with an Executive Assistant

As I'm writing this book, Andrea, who has worked with me for almost eight years now, is on maternity leave and I'm reminded of just how valuable a great and long-term executive assistant really is! Here, my irreplaceable EA discusses how CEOs can get the most from their assistants.

There are two problems to solve for when thinking about an executive assistant (EA). The first is hiring a great one. (A less-than-great EA can actually *slow down* your productivity.) The second is to empower your assistant to be an extension of yourself. This takes practice but when you get it right, it will make all the difference.

There are several characteristics to look for when hiring an assistant. To start, a great EA must love what they do. Clearly, this should be true of any hire, but it's especially true when hiring an EA due to the rigors of working closely with an executive. Your EA will struggle if the fit is wrong and this struggle will bubble up to you. Generally, the more a person cares about their job and enjoys the work, the higher quality work they will produce. In the case of an EA, this could not be truer.

Just as important, the EA must be comfortable with ambiguity and have a talent for adapting in response to change. A CEO's schedule can and does change from day to day. What is more, each day is typically crammed with meetings, deadlines and the like. Appointments, conferences and travel arise unexpectedly and in ways that seem nearly impossible to negotiate with existing commitments. It is essential that the EA adeptly handle the last-minute hiccup and seamlessly go with the flow to make everything work. If it's not obvious already, any EA who aspires to a rigid schedule is likely to have a tough go of it.

Once you have hired a great EA, do everything you can to extract all the benefits of having them at your side. The first key tactic is for you as a CEO to set aside time for your assistant. Despite the challenges of a busy schedule, setting a consistent and recurring time to make sure you both are on the same page is essential. In doing this, your assistant will learn your working style and expectations. It will also serve as a conduit to build a good rapport between the two of you. You will be working closely with this person, so it's important that you have a good relationship.

That said, you never want to assume that your assistant can read your mind. (Although if she is really good, she might be able to!) Communication is important. Be clear about tasks and deadlines and communicate them thoroughly. You will be your assistant's mentor in many ways. She will learn directly from you and use that education immediately.

Andrea Ponchione, Executive Assistant, Return Path

CHAPTER FORTY-TWO

WORKING WITH A COACH

When a member of our board first suggested I work with a coach, I thought it would be a good idea for one reason: to learn how to get people to stop suggesting I work with a coach. A decade later, my coach, Marc Maltz, is one of my most valuable assets and advisers.

CEO coaches come in lots of shapes and sizes. Some are almost therapists, while others are retired CEOs themselves. Some are quiet and lead you to conclusions on your own and some are more in your face. You have to find one that's a good fit with your style, your pace of work and your ability to pay. It's one investment that I wouldn't shortchange as you try to grow your business and your career—even if you have done it all three times before.

THE VALUE OF EXECUTIVE COACHES

We started Return Path in December 1999. Within 10 months, the company hadn't had time to turn into much of anything at all when the great Internet bust happened. We kept grinding forward in 2000 and 2001 and the end of that year had us going through a painful 50/50 merger with our only direct competitor and recapitalizing the company. We were still alive, even kicking but things were not going well.

When one of our board members, Fred Wilson, sat down with me to give me feedback that I could be doing a better job in a few specific ways and perhaps I might benefit from working with a CEO coach, my immediate thought was, "Clearly, the one part of my job that I'm not great at is managing my board, otherwise Fred would know how brilliant I am! Maybe the coach can help me with that."

Fred introduced me to Marc Maltz from Triad Consulting, who had done some coaching work for other CEOs in his portfolio. I half-heartedly agreed to take an initial meeting and told Marc that I wanted help learning how to manage my board. He politely smiled and said he'd be happy to help with that but that perhaps we could start working together with him doing a 360 evaluation of me; maybe that process would highlight another thing or two to work on besides managing a board.

I grudgingly agreed. I didn't think I had a lot to learn. My upward reviews from my team were really strong, so they clearly liked me. I'd raised money successfully three times, built a strong strategic partnership with the top large player in our industry and convinced a competitor to join forces with us. For Pete's sake, I was the CEO! Didn't that mean I was the boss?

Ah, the arrogance of youth.

Ultimately, I overcame my initial resistance to working with a coach because (1) he was right that I had another thing or two to work on, and (2) he allowed me to come to that conclusion on my own—though he certainly served up the right data to make that conclusion a bit more obvious than it had previously been.

I had to wait for a board member to insist that I work with an executive coach. I urge you to take the initiative here and engage one of your own volition. You absolutely will not regret it.

AREAS WHERE AN EXECUTIVE COACH CAN HELP

I've worked with my coach in many, many different capacities over the years. Here are some examples of the work that he's done with me and my team:

- *Coaching me.* A good coach helps you review the critical incidents of your day-to-day job by helping you develop the muscles around self-awareness and self-regulation so that you can get to empathy and, ultimately, influence.
- *Coaching individuals on my team and my team as a team.* My coach has done that same work with others on my executive team as well, helping them raise their game. Equally important is the work he's done with our whole senior team *as* a team. Marc shows up at each of our quarterly offsites for at least a day to help facilitate the "development" section of the meeting where we look critically at how we're doing and what we need to do differently going forward.
- *Learning from instruments and other frameworks.* Good coaches, even ones who aren't trained as industrial psychologists, know how to

administer some key instruments to help you understand different aspects of your personality and management style. Some of the things we have used over the years include the Myers-Briggs Type Indicator, the Thomas-Kilmann Conflict Mode Instrument, the Hay Group management style survey, the Action-Design framework for having difficult conversations, and the Signature Themes from Now, Discover Your Strengths. These instruments are only mildly interesting in and of themselves. (It's great that I'm an "ESTJ." Now what?) The real power in the instruments comes in understanding how to regulate those characteristics and how they match up against the personalities and styles of those around you. That's what a good coach will help you do.

- *Critical meeting facilitation.* A good coach can help you facilitate critical meetings, like postmortems or even just a tough executive team meeting you may have a hard time chairing because you're also contributing heavily to its content.
- *360 review process.* A specific subset of meeting facilitation is running live 360 reviews.
- *Organization design.* Most CEO coaches, whether or not they have formal training in organizational design, will be good at helping you think through it. If they have been around long enough, they will have seen lots of different models and will be able to help you understand the puts and takes of, say, hiring a COO, or having marketing report to sales.

The impact of all this work is impossible to quantify other than to say that, more than a decade later, Marc is still one of my and the company's most trusted outside advisers. In fact, I give him credit as one of a few reasons we're still in business!

Triad Consulting Executive Coach Marc Maltz on Working with a CEO Coach

If my long-time coach, Marc Maltz, has taught me anything, it's that I don't have all the answers. Here is his perspective on the value of working with an executive coach.

"A gem is not polished without rubbing, nor a man perfected without trials."

—Chinese Proverb

The biggest risk for a CEO is to lose sight of the boundary between yourself and the role you fill. The role of a CEO coach is to help you navigate this often-turbulent terrain between self and role.

When you are the CEO, everyone seems to want a piece of you. You must decide who gets your attention, especially when there isn't enough to go around. It's not just about prioritizing—as CEO you need to leverage insight about yourself to effectively navigate the organization and the world in which your organization operates, including customers, key stakeholders and the board. No matter how prepared you think you are, as CEO you will be tested.

You are CEO because you command expertise in the organization's work and have convinced others that driving success will have your constant attention. You probably didn't anticipate the need to be a master of organizational dynamics, of individual and group psychology or in how these play out across the many disciplines that make up your organization.

Becoming the CEO is your commitment to being tested in every possible way. Your coach is your confidante, someone with whom you can think through intimate details of your role, yourself and your work.

You should engage a coach to:

- Learn about yourself.
- Learn about your part in how you engage with others.
- Better manage yourself with individuals and groups.
- Learn about what you may not know about your organization.
- Think about how to develop your board, team(s) and organization.
- Master your role.

Having a coach isn't enough. You need the *right* coach. Here are some questions to consider when engaging a coach:

- Does the coach understand your thinking? Are they able to help stretch or challenge your thought process?
- Does the coach recognize the values that drive your choices? Are they able to help you see the implications of the values you hold most dear?
- Do you feel a connection with the coach and his or her method of working?
- Most coaches like to do some fact finding about you when starting—are you comfortable allowing the coach to talk to an array of people around you, including the board, your direct reports and others inside and outside of your organization?

Perhaps the primary purpose of a coach is to help you develop a new level of organizational empathy and learn to learn *as a CEO*. Being open to discovery, whether it is about yourself or your organization, is critical in the journey of developing as a CEO, regardless of age or experience. Maintaining an eye on the future of the business, while navigating the many stressors that exist throughout an organization, is a lonely task. The coach is the one person there to help you productively engage your world and advance your organization, your people and yourself.

Marc Maltz, Triad Consulting

CHAPTER FORTY-THREE

THE IMPORTANCE OF PEER GROUPS

It's often said that being a CEO is the loneliest job in the world. Fred Wilson describes it elegantly in a blog post from 2005:

> I often look at a founder or a CEO, see the tired eyes, an anxious twitch in the cheek or a missing beat in their step and think to myself or say out loud to others—he's got the weight of the company on his shoulders.
>
> Being the founder and/or CEO is heavy duty. To use another cliché, it's lonely at the top. . . . Most people, regardless of how well prepared they are for the role, will find being the leader to be a thankless role at times.
>
> Everyone inside the company is looking to you for answers, leadership, direction and on top of that, they want it with a smile and a pat on the back.
>
> Try doing all that on a day when you find out that the numbers were awful the past month, that your CTO is leaving to do another startup and your lead investor is giving you a hard time.
>
> Frankly, it's a thankless task most of the time. Because who do they report to? A board, not a person. A board is a lot less likely to provide day to day management and support. Groups don't do that, people do. Unfortunately, a board is a group, not a person.

A great coach can help with this. So can a great board, acting as a group or as individuals. Quite frankly, so can a great management team or even an informal "kitchen cabinet" inside an organization. With all of those, something is missing. Even the most empathic boards or coaches, even ones who have been CEOs before, aren't in that job at that moment. There's no substitute for discussing your challenges with active CEOs.

THE GANG OF SIX

I've found that having a peer group of CEOs has been an invaluable asset. There are lots of different ways of finding, joining or starting a CEO group. The most common ones are the Young President's Organization (YPO) and its even younger sibling, the Young Entrepreneur's Organization (YEO). There are others out there like the CEO Forum and Caitlin Cookman. I haven't joined any of those for one reason or another, so I've made my own. (It must be the entrepreneur in me.)

My group consists of the CEOs of six companies based in New York. The companies all have a number of things in common: size (at least 100 people), stage (revenue or growth, not pure startup), private, independent, VC-backed and somehow touching the Internet, though noncompetitive. All of us have worked, in one way or another, with the same CEO coach over time, so he joins our meetings and facilitates the discussion. We meet about six times per year at one of our offices for four hours at the end of the day, usually with a snack and wine or beer. In our first few meetings, we made sure that a couple of us gave our standard investor presentation to the group so that we all started to learn the ins and outs of each other's businesses from the start.

Our meetings are relatively informal. Everyone is extremely good about showing up—we calendar the dates well in advance—so there's a high degree of continuity in the group. Sometimes one of us will email a topic out to the group ahead of time, maybe with some advanced reading. We keep things 95 percent business—though sometimes the personal leaks in a little bit. We start meetings by "checking in" and taking turns running through things going on at our companies. We try to do this part with a 10-minute rule and a timer to keep the conversation moving and we note the topics that require a longer conversation as we go so that we can come back to them once we're done checking in. In the longer form part of the meeting, we help each other solve problems. We challenge each other, sometimes quite aggressively. We laugh a lot together. We understand what each other are going through. There's usually enough empathy in the room to power a small city.

There are lots of different ways to create groups like this and lots of use cases for them as well. My current group is the third one I've had in my career as a CEO, though it's the longest running and most high functioning of them. The others were even less structured dinner groups that didn't have an owner or leader or real commitment to attend 100 percent of the time. As a result, they decreased in utility over time and ultimately disbanded. Some of the more professional groups cost real money to join and have even more rigid structures, time commitments and formal presentations. As with most things like this, it's less important what kind of peer group you form or join than it is that you form or join one.

PROBLEM SOLVING IN TANDEM

The kinds of topics that a peer group can tackle together are extremely varied. My group usually ends up focusing on things that are challenges unique to the CEO job: managing a board or investors or a financing; hiring and firing executives; setting/changing strategy; organizational and cultural challenges; and, in a couple of cases, selling companies. Sometimes we just share best practices on things that are maybe less weighty. It occurs to me that my CEO forum is kind of like a live version of this book—and in fact the members of the group are all represented among the different outside contributors here.

Once, one member of my CEO forum had an offer to sell his company and he was really struggling with whether or not to take the offer. The terms were, in his mind, "good, not great." This is exactly the kind of issue it can be quite difficult to talk through with a management team or a board, many of whom will have their own emotions, hopes, dreams—and balance sheets—to think through. The rest of our group helped this CEO focus on what was right for the business and what was right for him personally.

The value you will get from a group like this is hard to quantify but easy to articulate. To come back to Fred's comment, having the weight of the company on your shoulders is not an easy thing to bear. Having a group of identically situated people to lean on makes it much easier.

CHAPTER FORTY-FOUR

STAYING FRESH

Staying fresh has always been about three related things: staying mentally fresh for work; staying healthy; and making sure I have enough time for myself that's not about work. All of this plays into what Stephen Covey calls "Sharpening the Saw," in his books *The 7 Habits of Highly Effective People* and *The 8th Habit*—both worth reading.

MANAGING THE HIGHS AND LOWS

I was reminded recently of one of my favorite entrepreneur sayings: What drives me nuts isn't the inevitable presence of highs and lows of running a new company; it's when they happen at the same time.

It's one thing to get used to the roller coaster ride of running a startup. That's part of the fun and the challenge of it all. There are great moments when everything's working beautifully. Your strategy is proving to be spot-on. Your team is executing brilliantly. Your biggest client renews and gives you a testimonial. Then there are the dark moments of despair. You're running out of cash. The new product release is behind schedule. A competitor steals a top client. No one lives for the lows but you at least grow to anticipate them and realize that "this, too, shall pass."

The thing I can never get used to is when those highs and lows occur simultaneously. It just seems unfair. Let me enjoy the good news—whatever it is—for at least a day or two before clocking me with something terrible! But perhaps that's just another, even more poignant part of the humbling process that comes with running a startup.

The best way to handle the stresses of the highs and lows is to keep yourself fresh! One analogy I tend to use around the topic of keeping myself fresh is about running shoes. I usually get new running shoes every three to six months, depending on how much mileage I'm logging. I find the same thing every time: I may not realize I'm uncomfortable running in the old shoes but the minute I put the new ones on, I realize just how far the old ones had deteriorated and just how much better life is in the new ones. Same model shoe—just a fresh pair. I run faster, stronger and happier.

I often find that small tweaks to renew and refresh existing processes, relationships, thought patterns and work product make an enormous difference in the energy I bring to work and in the quality of the work I do. Recently, for example, I had two such events.

First, I did my periodic overhaul of my Operating System. I changed some categories and formatting, rethought some items, cleaned out dead ones, added some new ones. *Voila*! I went from semi-ignoring the system to running my priorities by it once again. I've had my most productive week in a long time.

Second, I completely rethought the dynamics of my relationship with someone on the team. It had grown stale. Check-in meetings weren't interesting or productive any more, just perfunctory. We sat down and crafted a new way of working together, a new list of topics we were going to tackle together that added more value to the organization. It was like a breath of fresh air.

These were minor tweaks, not major overhauls. And yet, they were as valuable—and refreshing—as a new pair of running shoes.

STAYING MENTALLY FRESH

I keep myself mentally fresh for work by maintaining a basic level of self-discipline. Having my act together in small ways makes me feel like I have my act together in all ways. It's a little like the "Broken Windows" theory of policing formulated by George L. Kelling and James Q. Wilson in the early 1980s: if you crack down on graffiti and broken windows, you stop more violent crime, in part because the same people commit small and large crimes and in part because you create a more orderly society in visible, if sometimes a bit small and symbolic, ways.

At Your Company

These are some of the ways I apply the "Broken Windows" theory to my own life and work as a CEO:

- *Have a clean inbox at the end of the day*. This also comes from David Allen's theory of workplace productivity and it works. A clean mind is free to think, dream and solve problems. The quickest path to keeping it clean is not having a pile of little things to deal with in front of it, taking up space.

- *Show up on time.* It may sound dumb but people who are chronically late to meetings are chronically behind. The day is spent rushing around, cutting conversations short—in other words, unhappy and unproductive. The discipline of ending meetings on time with enough buffer to travel so you can start it on time—and not waste the time of the other people in the meeting—is important.
- *Dress for success.* We live in a casual world, especially in our industry. Sure, I sometimes wear jeans or a Hawaiian shirt to work—even shorts if it's a particularly hot day. No matter what I wear, I make sure to look neat and professional, not sloppy. The discipline of "dressing up" carries productivity a long way. Want to really test this out at the edges? Try wearing a suit or tie or dress shoes that click when you walk one day to work. You feel different and you sound different.
- *Follow rules of spelling, grammar, and punctuation.* Writing, whether for external or internal consumption, is still writing. I'm not sure when everyone became e. e. cummings and decided that it's okay to forget the basic rules of spelling, grammar, and punctuation. Make sure your emails and even your instant messages follow the rules. You look smarter when you do. Maybe—maybe—go with abbreviations on Twitter or SMS. I wouldn't normally consider a lot of those formal business communications.

I could go on and on but I think you get the idea. A little self-discipline goes a long way at work—and in life!

Out and About

Besides working on self-discipline, I also try to keep mentally fresh by exercising my work brain in nonwork ways. Let me give you a couple of examples of that.

First, I like to spend time mentoring other entrepreneurs. I do this occasionally in formal ways via programs like TechStars or SeedCamp but I've done this informally for probably a dozen different entrepreneurs over the years. Even the occasional networking breakfast with a new CEO who knows people in common with me counts. While I hope my time spent with other entrepreneurs is useful for them, they're also useful for me. They help me generate good, specific ideas for my own business. I think I come away from every single meeting I have with any entrepreneur with at least one new to do for myself and my team at Return Path. There's nothing quite like seeing how another company or entrepreneur operates to spur on good thinking. Second, these meetings help me to crystallize my own thoughts and ideas. Much like writing my blog and this book, problem/solution sessions with other entrepreneurs force me to condense a cloud of ideas down to a simple sentence or paragraph.

Second, I try to focus my extracurricular time on helping organizations with the challenges that I'm most used to working in and around professionally. Earlier in my career, that meant I was helping organizations understand and use technology or online marketing and communication more effectively. One of these organizations was the golf course where I play and the other was my cousins' new wine store. Through both experiences, I had to define business requirements, work with vendors from selection through contract and then work with the vendor and the organization on deployment and process change. Both bits of work were directly useful for me to take lessons back and apply them to our processes and work with clients at Return Path, because I was suddenly The Client as opposed to my usual role as The Vendor. The learnings from the other side of the table are incredibly valuable and kept me mentally fresh.

PetCareRx CEO (and Amateur Positive Psychologist) Jonathan Shapiro on Ensuring Your Own Happiness

Jonathan Shapiro, three-time CEO of Lillian Vernon, MediaWhiz and now PetCareRX, is currently getting his master's degree in positive psychology—on the side! Here, he offers some great advice about staying fresh and happy on the job.

Entrepreneurship is a noble endeavor. Entrepreneurs are society's creators and they put their financial and emotional lives on the line for the creative process. While noble, entrepreneurship is hard. Even when they succeed, all new businesses will have to overcome numerous challenges. Having decided to jump into this noble arena, the key to staying fresh and energized is enjoying the journey.

Research can help make your travels most rewarding. Over the past decade, world renowned researchers like Martin Seligman, Chris Peterson, Barbara Fredrickson, and Sonja Lyubomirsky have led an explosion in the scientific understanding of what leads to human flourishing. This science makes it clear that our well-being and emotional energy depend not only on achievement but also on good relationships, engagement, positive affect (i.e., a little fun), and meaning. Following this science suggests a few travel tips to help you along your entrepreneurial expedition.

1. *Make time for friends and family and work with people you like, trust and admire*. Because it is often lonely at the top, this network, that will applaud your progress and bolster your spirits during the tough times, is essential. Schedule time with your most important friends and family.
2. *Be fully engaged in bringing your ideas to life*. Measure progress not only by the ultimate goal but by the battles along the way. Throw yourself fully into the effort, knowing that some you will win and some you will lose. When faced with a setback, make it a learning moment. On missing the first 2,000 times to find a workable filament, Edison famously remarked, "I never failed even once; it just happened to be a 2,000-step process."
3. *Have some fun along the way*. You will also have successes as you build your business. Proactively hunt for wins, big and small (e.g., the next sale, software deployment, capital raise or satisfied customer) and honor them. Celebrating these will keep your team and you energized.
4. *Add meaning to your endeavor by making it about more than money*. Be sure you can describe how your business will make your clients or customers and potentially the world better off. Research makes it clear that individuals who find their work meaningful beyond financial rewards report higher job satisfaction, higher job performance, less job stress and longer tenure. This includes the CEO!

While not a psychologist or social scientist, perhaps Teddy Roosevelt said it best.

> It is not the critic who counts: not the man who points out how the strong man stumbles or where the doer of deeds could have done better. **The credit belongs to the man who is actually in the arena,** whose face is marred by dust and sweat and blood, who strives valiantly, who errs and comes up short again and again, because there is no effort without error or shortcoming but who knows the great enthusiasms, the great devotions, who spends himself for a worthy cause; who, at the best, knows, in the end, the triumph of high achievement and who, at the worst, if he fails, at least he fails while daring greatly, so that his place shall never be with those cold and timid souls who knew neither victory

nor defeat. *(Author's note: I had selected this quote for the epigram to the book before seeing Jonathan's contribution—it's so good that it's worth printing twice in the same book.)*

If you have jumped into the entrepreneurial arena, you are "daring greatly" to serve a "worthy cause"—the creation of something new. Remember to enjoy the journey, travel with friends, learn along the way, celebrate the wins and make your business about something great.

Jonathan Shapiro, CEO, PetCareRx

STAYING HEALTHY

I had breakfast with a relatively new CEO the other day who said one of the things he was struggling with was being tired and feeling overworked. I told him that one of the things I make sure I do, come hell or high water, is to exercise at least three times per week and usually four or five times. He said he used to be a serious athlete but that he had stopped exercising when he started the business and asked me how I could afford those three hours per week to exercise. I asked him how he could afford *not* to spend that time!

There's a virtual cycle that comes from being in shape. You have more energy. You think more clearly. You eat more healthfully and drink less. You sleep much better at night. Of course, the opposite is also true: there's a vicious circle of being out of shape. You don't sleep as well, so you are more dependent on caffeine. You're not as focused during the workday. You probably eat and drink more, later at night. All of which leads to not sleeping well another night—and then the cycle repeats.

I try to think of the three hours of exercise every week as an investment in my own productivity. Here's my quick and dirty math on my "investment" of three hours per week of working out:

- Minutes spent exercising: 180.
- Work minutes during the week, assuming a 60-hour week: 3,600.
- Loss factor: 15 percent for travel time and other structurally nonproductive time.
- Net number of work minutes during the week: 3,060.
- Required productivity improvement to "balance" the 180 minutes of exercise: 6 percent.

Is there anyone out there that doesn't think you're 6 percent more productive when you're in shape? I'm not even factoring in the side benefit of (most likely) waking up earlier in the morning and getting a jump on your day as part of regular exercise. Or the fact that people who exercise need less sleep.

All that said, regular exercise doesn't just impact your productivity and give you more energy; it helps keep you healthy. Obviously, there is more to staying healthy than just exercise but it's a good start!

Union Square Hospitality Founder and CEO Danny Meyer on Balancing Body, Mind, Heart, and Spirit

Danny Meyer is one the most successful restaurateurs in the world and someone I've had the pleasure of knowing a bit over the years. In a field famously dominated by hotheads and egomaniacs, he's found a way to strike that elusive "work-life" balance—or, rather, to move past it toward something that's actually achievable.

Like every CEO, I started failing at "balancing work and home" long before I became a CEO. If I had to assign a start date to that particular failure, it would probably be 1985: at the age of 27, after a few months as an assistant manager at Pesca in Manhattan and a few more months of culinary training in Italy and Bordeaux, I decided to open my first restaurant, Union Square Cafe. The response was universal: "You're nuts!"

They might have been right. Restaurants are a complex business and I didn't know anything about that business when I opened my first one. I just had a hunch: the key was treating customers right. In 1992, my hunch was validated when Union Square Cafe won the James Beard Award for Outstanding Service. The naysayers were wrong about my first restaurant, so I gave them something else to naysay about: a second restaurant. To further complicate matters, my wife, Audrey and I had just had our first child. It didn't take long for the chorus to start again: "You're nuts!"

Perhaps, but I kept going. Within a few years, I had four restaurants and three kids. When I get to four restaurants and four kids, Audrey informed me that there weren't going to be any more kids. There were still going to be more restaurants. There was going to be something else. In 2005, around the time I opened The Modern, I decided to take on a new challenge: writing a book. A business book. I knew what everybody would say, so I didn't tell anybody. Not my family. Not my staff. I wrote the book in secret, on flights and on the subway. *Setting the Table* was another success—but it was time to admit that I *had* gone nuts.

For two decades, I'd been trying to achieve that elusive "work/home balance." I never could. There was never enough of me to go around. I wasn't fully present at home because I was anxious about work and I expected my staff to read my mind when I was anxious about not spending more time at home. Finally, I found a new path. Balance *is* important but "work" and "home" are the wrong categories.

What you *must* keep in balance are your "body," "mind," "heart," and "spirit." If those are out of balance, no startup CEO—nobody at all, for that matter—can achieve their maximum potential. More important, you can cater to all four at work *and* at home.

Today, I can be fully present for my staff when I'm at the office, for my customers when I'm at one of the restaurants and for my family when I'm at home. I can run alongside Riverside Drive with my wife, shut off my thoughts after a difficult day and serve body, mind, heart, and spirit at once. Neglect them and all you can do is try to buy your way out. Eventually, the cost will be too high.

Danny Meyer, Founder and CEO, Union Square Hospitality

Exercise is a perfect segue to "me time": time that you're not spending working or actively thinking about work. It's impossible to not have work running in the background at some level. My concept of "me time" has been pretty straightforward over the years, though it has gotten more difficult, along with the rest of my time management, as my company and my family have gotten larger. These things aren't necessarily right for everyone but I do my best to:

- *Keep weekends to myself and my family (with at least a few minutes exclusively for myself).* That doesn't mean I never, ever do any work on weekends. Most weekends, most of the time, I either don't do any work or I don't do more than an hour or two, from home, usually just sneaking in an occasional look at email. This does mean that I probably work more hours during the week than most people but I'd rather do that and maintain a little bit of down time on the weekend.
- *Take at least one and preferably two, one- to two-week vacations per year where I completely unplug.* I was much better about this before we had kids (vacations aren't necessarily the most restful times anymore), though I am seeing promising signs that we will reverse course on this front as the kids get older. Even in the early years of the business—those years where I felt like I could and should work every spare moment—Mariquita and I did one major, international, two-week, fully unplugged vacation each year. No email. No calls. Sometimes

not even a cell phone. I gave my team my itinerary and told them how to find me in case the building burned down.

- *Take a weekend or two each year to hang out with friends.* Mariquita and I have a standing deal: each of us is entitled to a couple of weekends away with friends each year where the other one covers the home front. Although this has gotten harder to schedule over the years (and not everyone has a deal like this with his or her spouse!), the occasional golf or ski boys' weekend has been incredibly fun and refreshing.
- *Use most of my train commute time and some of my airplane time, for personal reading.* I can never quite manage to use all of it for myself but I use at least half—that's enough to keep me reading a couple dozen nonbusiness books per year and *The Economist* every week.
- Foster an outside interest or two. Kevin Ryan, a multiple time CEO in the New York tech industry, has a great saying: "You can do *anything* you want but you can't do *everything* you want." It's so true. You can and should make time to do a couple of things outside of work that are most important to you, from spending time with your kids coaching a team or leading a scout troop to playing an instrument or taking cooking lessons. I also think that, for most CEOs, there is an element of goal-setting that can come along with this—usually, strong leaders drive themselves by setting large goals in their personal as well as their professional lives. Many (myself included) have set goals to complete marathons or triathlons or even (myself definitely not included) Ironman races. The goal doesn't have to be a physical one, either.
- *Learn to say no once in a while.* Any time I think about the topic of staying fresh and my ability to stop working once in a while, I come back to the my friend Seth's French Fry Theory of being a CEO. The theory is simple: "You always have room for one more fry." It's pretty spot-on, if you think about it. Fries are so tasty and so relatively small (most of the time), that it's easy to just keep eating—and eating and eating—them, one at a time. You're never too full for one more fry. You might not order another plate of them but one more? No problem. Ever. I've always thought that the French Fry Theory can be applied to many things, including other food items. It definitely applies to being a CEO.

As a CEO, you can always do one more thing. Send one more email. Read one more document. Sometimes you just need to draw the line, go home and stop working! The world we operate in is so dynamic that it's nearly impossible to ever feel like you're completely on top of your job. There's always more to be done and the trick to doing it well is knowing when to say "no" and take time for yourself.

Management Moment

Be Vulnerable

Brad Feld has a great opening to a post on his blog with this same title:

We are told that leaders must be strong. They must be confident. They must be unflinching. They must hide their fear. They must never blink. They cannot be soft in any way.

Bullshit.

It's true that sometimes, some leaders need to be unflinching. If the president of the United States were to tell one of our enemies that he's scared of them, we would have a serious national security problem on our hands. Most of the time, CEOs gain much more by being vulnerable than they give up.

I talk in a few places in this book about the value of admitting mistakes, which is one form of vulnerability. Another form of vulnerability is simply saying, "I don't know" when posed with a tough question. Yet another is to let a colleague in on your emotions about a particularly tough decision you have to make or your reaction to something that adversely impacted your company. There are even more extreme examples as well: although I certainly didn't plan on it, I once actually started to tear up in a development session with my senior team when discussing a couple of aspects of my nonwork life.

What all these things have in common is the presentation of CEO as Human Being. They make it okay for everyone around you to also be human beings. They do as much to create an environment of trust as anything else you can do.

CHAPTER FORTY-FIVE

YOUR FAMILY

Someone told me once entrepreneurs are almost always either in their 20s or 50s because they're either "single and have nothing to lose," or "have already made a lot of money and put their kids through college and have nothing to lose." I'm not sure how true that statement is anymore—at least not in the U.S. tech scene, where I know lots of entrepreneurs in their 30s and 40s—but there's something to it.

There's a real incompatibility between the energy, time and long-range timing of financial return involved with a startup and having a family. You can't take your stock options to the store to buy diapers or cash them in for your monthly mortgage payment! Many people find themselves as both CEOs of startups and moms or dads at the same time, so it's worth writing a little bit about how the two coexist. I knew one particularly impressive female CEO of a company in our industry, Stephanie Healy, who started Vente with her husband as her COO, then promptly had four kids in six years, all while doing her job as CEO, then sold her company to a larger company in the industry. Wow!

Every person's family and family circumstances are different and it's hard to generalize suggestions in ways that make sense. I thought I'd focus on three topics that matter:

- Making room for home life
- Involving family in work
- Bringing work principles to home in smart ways

MAKING ROOM FOR HOME LIFE

I've already discussed the concept of "me time" in the previous chapter. It's critical if you want to maintain your sanity as a CEO. When you're a CEO who has a family, there is the related concept of "us time" or "family time" that you also have to maintain. You—and those around you—need to be comfortable that you have two critically important priorities in your life: your company and your family. Both could absorb 100 percent of your time and at any given moment the needs of one will have to outweigh the needs of the other. Perhaps most important, you will do your best to balance those needs out over the long haul but not necessarily within a given day, week, month, or even quarter or year.

One way of ensuring enough family time is to create a home Operating System just like your company or personal Operating System. This could be the subject of a whole book or chapter but the main point for the moment is that if you have some regular routines at home that you're expected to participate in (Friday night dinner at home, coaching a kid's sports team, etc.), you anchor your week or month or quarter around those as much as you use your board meetings or staff meetings as anchors to your calendar.

INVOLVING FAMILY IN WORK

I am fortunate enough to have a fellow businessperson as a spouse. More than that, Mariquita and I worked together at two different companies before we were married and have hugely overlapping personal and professional networks. Mariquita also happens to be incredibly smart and levelheaded. As a result, she has been my most helpful adviser on a number of tough situations at work.

I know a number of CEOs whose spouses aren't in the business world—and no one's young kids are in that world (yet!). The typical reaction is to completely separate work and home and not discuss work "after hours." This kind of separation might work well for some people but I don't think it could ever work for me. As time marches on, our personal lives and personal time increasingly bleed into our professional lives and professional time and vice versa.

My solution has always been to involve family in work, as much as is possible or practical. If I'm doing a little work at home and my kids ask me what I'm doing, I try not to just say "work" or "email." I try to pause and explain what I'm actually doing in ways that they can understand. If I have a tough day at work and we're talking about "what happened today" around the dinner table, I don't mind telling everyone why I had a tough day. I try to explain why Daddy has to take yet another business trip and what I'm going to do in Place X.

I'd like to think that if I had a spouse who was a teacher or doctor that I'd be able to do a modified version of the same with her as well. Again, *at best*, we spend half our waking hours at work and half with our family, so we might as well make sure that our family knows what we do—and is proud of it.

Mariquita Blumberg Presents a Field Guide for Significant Others

Mariquita and I got engaged about six weeks after I started Return Path, so she has been with me and the company every step of the way. With apologies to my co-founders, my board, my executive team and every member of the Return Path team, I have to concede that Mariquita has probably been my most valuable business partner in these years. These are her thoughts about being in a startup family.

When Matt first started his company, I didn't know what to expect and, quite frankly, I didn't think about it much. I loved him so I would support him in whatever he wanted to do. It turns out that supporting a startup CEO is different from supporting someone who's building his career in accounting. It is invigorating, frustrating, inspiring, and tiring all at once. It is both about you and not about you. It is about playing a role when you don't have a role. It is about being your CEO's number one fan!

Starting a company is effectively like having a child. Running a startup is a 24-hour-a-day labor of love, one that results in disturbed sleep, tests of patience and a roller coaster of emotions. As a significant other, you're along for the ride—for richer, for poorer, for better, for worse.

A couple of tips for dealing with the unexpected, unplanned and uncontrollable "child" that is a startup and for supporting your CEO in this exciting but daunting adventure:

- *Welcome the "child" into the family.* Don't make your CEO choose between you and the "child." It's not a fun conversation—and you may not like the outcome. Do make sure that your CEO knows that your relationship, your real children, your extended family, your house, and all the other aspects of life are still in need of his or her attention. Sometimes the "child" can become so demanding that the CEO can lose sight of the bigger picture. Paint it for them.
- *Be a co-parent.* Don't ask your CEO to leave his work at the office; it isn't possible. Listen, because often a CEO doesn't have anyone to speak to

openly about all that is going on and how they are feeling about their "child's" behavior. Learn about the business, because you want to be able to enjoy the highs. (You will inevitably hear about the lows.) Finally, contribute. Sometimes the best ideas come from having a good understanding of the business but an arm's-length view.

- *Be proud.* Don't share the company temper tantrums broadly; no one needs to know that this "child" isn't perfect. Instead, be a cheerleader and an advocate for the company and for your CEO. Talk about the great service that this company will provide to people, even if it has yet to be realized. Be proud of your CEO, be proud of the "child" you are helping them raise and be proud of yourself for being the understanding and supportive person that your CEO needs in their corner, unconditionally.

Just as with kids, the challenging times feel like they go on forever while you're going through them but, in retrospect, the years fly by. I can't believe that Return Path is almost 14 years old and I'm eager to see what the teenage years bring.

Mariquita Blumberg, Return Path's No. 1 Fan

BRINGING WORK PRINCIPLES HOME

As Mariquita and I wrote in our contribution to Brad Feld's book *Startup Life*, a marriage is the ultimate startup: building a shared environment with shared values and shared resources and working toward a shared goal. You and your spouse are co-founders in the most important type of organization—a family—and a constantly changing one at that, with kids arriving, growing up and having continuously new and different needs. A family needs to be led and run, consciously, thoughtfully and with a clear division of roles and responsibilities.

Mariquita and I work together to set goals for ourselves individually, our kids individually and our family as a whole—just like you would in any organization. We hold ourselves accountable to what we are trying to accomplish with regular check-ins. It isn't all work—the play part of the family is critical as well—but being intentional about what we are trying to build as a family takes time and has been an important commitment for us. The work principles of setting goals and budgets, creating an Operating System and following through on commitments, have helped us build our family life in really positive ways.

Similarly, I have been struck over the years by the realization that there are some real similarities between being a CEO and being a parent. To be clear, I don't think of my kids as employees (although there have been moments when I've wanted to put one or the other of them on some kind of formal performance plan). Just as important, I don't think of my employees as children! Skills required to be good at both jobs are very similar.

Here's why: *Success as a CEO or as a parent requires core interpersonal competencies.* For example:

- *Decisiveness.* Be wishy-washy at work and the team can get stuck in a holding pattern. Be wishy-washy with kids and they run their agenda, not yours.
- *Listening.* As my friend Anita says, you have two ears and one mouth for a reason. Listening to your team at work—and also listening for what's not being said—is the best way to understand what's going on in your organization. Kids need to be heard as well. The best way to teach good verbal communication skills is to ask questions and then listen actively and attentively to the responses.
- *Focus.* Basically, no one benefits from multitasking, even if it feels like a more efficient way of working. Anyone you're spending time with, whether professionally or at home, deserves your full attention. The reality is that the human brain is full of entropy anyway, so even a focused conversation, meeting or play time, is somehow compromised. Actually doing other activities at the same time destroys the human connection.
- *Patience.* For the most part, steering people to draw their own conclusions about things at work is key. Even if it takes longer than just telling them what to do, it produces better results. With kids, patience takes on a whole new meaning but giving them space to work through issues and scenarios on their own, while hard, clearly fosters independence.
- *Alignment.* If you and your senior staff disagree about something, cross-communication confuses the team. If you and your spouse aren't on the same page about something, just watch those kids play the two of you off each other. A united front at the top is key!

I assume that entrepreneurs who have families have gone through a lot of this chapter's experiences themselves, so I'll close with one very clear and unambiguous piece of advice. If you're a single entrepreneur, make sure you (1) make time for a social life so that someday you *can* have a partner and/or family and (2) before you commit to a permanent partnership—and certainly before you decide to have kids—make sure you think long and hard about whether you're ready for the changes that will invariably come and impact you and your business. If you're ready to move ahead, be intentional about changing your work life to make room for home.

Management Moment

Don't Just Speak—Be Heard

Often, a very clear conversation can end up with two very different understandings down the road. This is the problem I'd characterize as "what gets said isn't necessarily what gets heard."

Why does this happen? Sometimes, what gets said isn't 100 percent crystal clear. More often than not, this is around delivering bad news—delivering difficult news is hard and not for the squeamish. This problem can be fixed by brute force. If you are giving someone their last warning before firing him, don't mumble something about "not great performance" and "consequences." Look him in the eye and say, "If you do not do x, y and z in the next 30 days, you will be fired."

In other cases, the person on the receiving end of the conversation may *want* to hear something else. Solving this problem is more challenging. To get around this issue, try asking the person to whom you're speaking to "play back in your own words what you just heard." See if they get it right. Also send a very clear follow-up email after the conversation, recapping it and asking for confirmation of receipt.

Sometimes, things get lost in translation. Clarity of message, boldness of approach and forcing playback and written confirmation are a few ways to close the gap between what gets said and what gets heard.

CHAPTER FORTY-SIX

TRAVELING

For my 40th birthday a few years back, my team gave me a poster from FlightMemory.com that plotted all of my air travel for a full 12-month period on a world map: 34 airports, 90 flights, 157,000 miles. While it was entertaining to know that I circumnavigated the globe 6.3 times that year—and while I am not immune to the perks of getting upgraded for being a frequent flier—that was a very sobering moment!

Business travel is inevitable. I've done a ton of it throughout my career no matter what job I've had. The reality is that no matter how connected the world is, sometimes there's no substitute for showing up for something in person. As CEO, you need to do a lot of this. Even if your company is 100 percent in one location, you are your company's main ambassador, which means you need to be out of the office and meeting with customers, partners, suppliers, and speaking at industry events regularly. All of those are likely to involve some degree of travel, even in the most local of businesses.

SEALING THE DEAL WITH A HANDSHAKE

While you have to watch expenses, sometimes it's worth traveling 5,000 miles for a five-minute meeting. I relearned this lesson a few years back: We were negotiating a big deal with a company on the West Coast and we were at a tense and critical spot in the negotiations. I knew that the only way to move the deal forward to a handshake and a term sheet was to meet face-to-face with the decision makers on the other side of the table, in person. So, I got on a plane. It wasn't my first choice of activities: the trip was a long way to go for a really short meeting. It was 100 percent worthwhile, with a very specific mission accomplished.

It's important to be present *and* accounted for in business settings and with everyone's busy schedules and increasingly frenzied and multitasking office environments, it's harder than ever to really get someone's attention. There's just no substitute for looking someone in the eye and doing a real handshake, not a virtual one. Of course, you can't travel all the time, so learning how to say "no" to a potential trip, even if it's a client visit or speaking engagement, is important. There's no formula for this but when you start to know flight attendants on a first-name basis, that's a good sign that it's time to cut back.

MAKING THE MOST OF TRAVEL TIME

In addition to the mission you're traveling for, there are ancillary benefits to being on the road. There are four things I try to take advantage of while traveling:

1. *Time for project work*. If your day is anything like mine, it's pretty full of meetings and interruptions. Once in a while, you have some actual work that you have to do, whether it's writing a new investor presentation, mapping out your game plan for next year, thinking through a tough strategic question, reviewing massive amounts of material—or writing chapters of a book about being a startup CEO. Long-form travel time is a great opportunity for this kind of work.
2. *Time with a colleague*. One thing I've always appreciated in my career but have grown even more attached to of late, is traveling with colleagues. Any time I have an opportunity to do so, I jump on it. First, I find that I get solid work time in with a colleague in transit: it's a check-in meeting that isn't rushed with a hard stop, interrupted by the phone or visitors and in person. Second, I find that I get more creative work time in with a colleague on a flight, especially a long one. Some of the time that isn't in a structured meeting invariably turns to brainstorming or more idle work chatter. Some great ideas have come out of flights I've taken in the past 13 years! Finally, my colleague and I get more social time than usual on a plane. Social time is an incredibly important part of managing and developing personal connections with employees. Time spent next to each other in the air, in an airport security line or lounge or in a rental car always lends itself to learning more about what's

going on in someone's life. Don't get me wrong: even when I travel with someone from Return Path, we each have some quiet time to read, work, sleep and contemplate life. The work and work-related aspects of the experience are not to be ignored.

3. *Time for myself.* You can see that I value staying fresh, which I do by a combination of taking time for myself and pursuing hobbies outside of work. Depending on your Operating System, you can make business travel time a time for this. A few hours of relatively undisturbed time on a plane can be just enough time to watch the *Star Wars* trilogy on your iPad, read three Harlan Coben novels or catch up on sleep.
4. *Time to be out of touch.* This is the flip side of "time for myself," meaning that sometimes it's okay, even good, to be a bit out of touch. When you're out of sight, sometimes people at work bother you less. Particularly with international travel, people don't seem to want to call: you're a larger number of time zones off, so people just don't think to reach out. Even if I'm doing email once or twice a day when time permits, it's different than being on top of every little thing at the office. It's a good thing to be out of touch a bit when you're not officially unplugged for a vacation. Your company will be fine.

STAYING DISCIPLINED ON THE ROAD

When you travel as much as I do, you can't lean on the excuse that you're out of town and therefore off the hook when it comes to personal discipline. In terms of managing myself while I'm on the road, I also have a few simple rules that I try to stick to, no matter what.

- *I take care of myself.* I get good sleep. In the winter, I take Airborne when I'm flying, which I've found cuts down on getting colds from my fellow passengers. I stick to my exercise routine religiously. It helps reduce jetlag, plus I have more time to exercise when I'm on the road. I am not picky about hotels and try to stay at places that are inexpensive but I have one solid rule, which is that there has to be a good, and preferably 24-hour, hotel gym. Sometimes I try running outside, which can be a nice way to see another place but I hate running in the dark in a strange city, so that doesn't always work. I've also developed a couple of exercise routines that I can do even in a small hotel room: push-ups, sit-ups, Pilates. Bringing along Xertubes (www.spri.com) allows me to do a 15- to 30-minute strength workout in a hotel room at any time of day, often without needing to bring along much in the way of workout clothes or shoes.

- *I squeeze every minute out of each day*. Being home comes with lots of things to do: Commuting. Time with family. Down time in front of a screen. Those things can evaporate when you're on the road. On the road, you can work 15 hours per day, get in a good dinner, enough sleep and exercise. Some of my most productive and simultaneously most "me" times are on business trips as a result of squeezing every minute out of the day.
- *I find time to take some little bit of joy in wherever I am*. Dinners out, whether alone or (more likely) with colleagues or clients, are a minimum. For international travel, that's particularly tasty but unless you're doing a lot of travel to Peoria (sorry, Peoria), there's probably some great local cuisine to seek out. Especially with international travel, I also try to block out at least a couple of hours to see some local sights. That doesn't always work out but if I've never been to that city or country before, I make an extra effort. I once hired a taxi to give a colleague and me a rapid-fire tour of Istanbul, and another time a colleague and I who were in Copenhagen took a cab over the bridge to Malmo, Sweden, for a cup of coffee because neither of us had ever been to Sweden before. Hardly a substitute for a vacation, but it was better than nothing.

CHAPTER FORTY-SEVEN

TAKING STOCK

At the end of every year, I take a few minutes to refresh my Operating System for the coming year. I reflect on how the business is doing, on my goals and development plans, and on what I want to accomplish in the coming year. Although most of that work is focused on how to move the business forward, I also make sure to take stock of my own career.

CELEBRATING "YES"; ADDRESSING "NO"

Whenever I take stock of the past year, I always ask myself four questions:

- Am I having fun at work?
- Am I learning and growing as a professional?
- Is my work financially rewarding enough, either in the short term or in the long term?
- Am I having the impact I want to have on the world?

Of course, I always shoot for four "yes" responses. As long as I get at least two or three "yesses," I feel like I'm in good shape and I know which one or two things to work on in the coming year. That's one of the main inputs I have into setting my agenda for the coming year.

Any time the answer to one of those questions is "no," I ask "why?"

ARE YOU HAVING FUN?

Are the people around me not fun people? Then I am hiring poorly. Are they fun people who aren't having fun currently? Then either they're working too hard or they aren't seeing enough reward or recognition for their efforts they're frustrated because their efforts aren't going anywhere or they aren't well equipped to do the jobs they have to do for any number of reasons. Is everyone around me having fun, except me? Then the problem clearly rests with me.

If I'm not enjoying what I'm doing, then I either need to delegate it, learn to enjoy it or recognize that if I have to do it and I will never enjoy it. I either have to tolerate it or find another job!

ARE YOU LEARNING AND GROWING AS A PROFESSIONAL?

There are a lot of sources of learning and growth that you can and should have as a CEO. I've mentioned some of them in other parts of the book. If your business is changing at all—you're in a dynamic industry, your business is just growing or you're pivoting or changing directions, for example—then you have a tiger by the tail and are likely to get dragged into learning and growing by the natural momentum of the business. What if it's not? What if your startup is not adding people or changing product direction? What if it's going sideways? Then you need to push yourself to learn and grow on your own.

Dive into books or take a business class. Think about your business's largest problem and go meet with five other people in the world who have run across comparable problems and solved them. If nothing else, spend time writing down the problems you have and work through a root-cause analysis. Become even more of an expert in some aspect of your business. Any of these things will help you get smarter about what you're doing.

IS IT FINANCIALLY REWARDING?

You may work at a nonprofit or be highly altruistic about your work but my guess is that if you're reading this book, you care about putting your talents to work so that you can make money for yourself and your family to live nicely, both today and in the future. If you're feeling like the financial reward isn't there in your job, it can be extremely demotivating and cause you to check out.

If it's a short-term problem (e.g., your salary is too low or you missed this year's numbers and didn't get a bonus), then you can attack that directly by either looking closely at your compensation with your board's Compensation Committee and looking at external or by making sure you are realistic and fair when you structure next year's incentive compensation program. If you are concerned about long-term financial rewards, there could be a number of causes, each of which has its own solution. If it's because your business isn't building enough value fast enough, then you're faced with more existential problems of what business you're in or thorny issues about how well you're executing—and now you have your main agenda item for the upcoming year—and maybe that's around selling the company. If it's because you don't own enough equity in your company or if it's because your company's cap table has too much preferred stock sitting in front of your common stock and you're worried that you won't make much money even if your company does well, then you need to discuss that problem openly and honestly with your board or Compensation Committee, or at least with one trusted director.

Finally, if your needs have changed even though the circumstances of your business haven't, you need to think hard about whether you can change the circumstances of your business, whether it's appropriate for you to have one of the above kinds of conversations with your board or whether you should be in the job in the first place. It's one thing to be a hero in the first two years of your company and pay yourself $75,000 while you live in a studio apartment at age 25. It's another to do that when you're 35 with two kids and a mortgage.

ARE YOU MAKING AN IMPACT?

As I mentioned earlier, impact is a broad term and having impact on the world as a CEO doesn't mean that your company has to be developing a cure for a disease. Whether it's family, friends, colleagues, clients, or some slice of humanity, you should be able to have a real impact on others around you. In your role as CEO, the bare minimum impact you should have is on your colleagues. If your company is creating jobs or if you're helping create a great work environment for people, remember that those are both quite impactful on the world around you.

So if you answer "no" to this last "take stock" question, the problem could be as simple as you not thinking broadly about what impact means. If you truly feel like you and, by extension, your business, aren't having any impact on anyone—that's a sign that you might be in the wrong job!

Long-Time Startup CEO Bob Blumberg on Living an Integrated Entrepreneurial Life

My dad is my entrepreneurial hero. He started his company in 1981 and ran it with two massive pivots along the way until he sold it almost 30 years later. I've asked him to share some of his thoughts on how to manage yourself for the long haul. If anyone knows about that, it's him!

Entrepreneurs may start their companies at any age, from their 20s to their 60s. They can be single, married with or without kids, divorced with or without kids—and they could be in any of those family states at any point in their company's growth cycle. The key to making it all work is an unusual combination of self-discipline, flexibility and the ability to constantly reprioritize.

At any stage, there will usually be more demands on your time than you can meet. It would be great to have a 27-hour day, while limiting everyone else to 24! (Maybe there's an invention and a company-to-be in that idea!) You can't let your company founder or fall apart while you take care of personal or family matters but you can't allow your family or personal life to crumble while you tend to your business needs.

You will work best by anticipating needs and issues and dealing with them before they become crises. Once you fall into a reacting mode, it's difficult to climb back out.

One way to think about pending issues that require your attention is in a 2 × 2 matrix—is an issue serious or not-so-serious and is it time critical or not? This can help sort out the order of doing things while keeping a focus on the issues that really need your attention, even though they may not yet be crises. Obviously, each issue also has to be given the test of "can all or part of this be delegated?"

If your business succeeds but your marriage or children do not because you haven't put the time into your home life, you have not truly succeeded. If they succeed personally but your business fails, you have not succeeded in that case either. You must maintain the self-discipline to do at least the absolute minimum required for your own well-being, constantly reprioritize where you need to focus attention and, above all, be able to communicate clearly to those who need to know why you are making the choices that you do. You need to sell your wife and children on the importance of your work, sell your colleagues on how seriously you take your family responsibilities and convince yourself that you have to be in top mental and physical condition to accomplish all that is needed—let alone requested—of you.

Bob Blumberg, Founder & CEO Emeritus of SMS Technologies

A NOTE ON EXITS

When I started Return Path in the froth of the Internet boom in 1999, someone told me I should hire a writer to follow me around and record everything that happened in the formative weeks and months of the business. The person actually said to me, "You can publish a book about how quickly you built and sold the business—it will be called *Ready, Set, Exit*."

One of the most unfortunate stereotypes about startup CEOs is that we're only in it for the exit: the business equivalent of real estate investors who flip a dozen properties a year. That may describe some startup CEOs but it shouldn't describe you.

There is no such thing as an exit strategy for a great company. There are only growth strategies, customer development strategies and global expansion strategies. Great companies might be bought but they're rarely sold. Work hard to build a great company and you might get bought—at an amazing price. Work hard at selling your company and somebody might pick up the scraps.

Exits and Liquidity

Tim Miller is the chairman and CEO of Rally Software (which completed a successful initial public offering while I was writing this book) since 2003 and is singularly focused on making Rally Software a great company. Rally and Return Path are companies that have been leading parallel lives in the Boulder, Colorado, area for years and Tim and I frequently compare notes. Like all great entrepreneurs, Tim's focus has been on growth rather than exits—but that doesn't mean he hasn't given the latter considerable thought.

For a startup entrepreneur, a strategic sale represents a life-altering opportunity to build a personal balance sheet that provides a safety net for career and family. First-time entrepreneurs in this scenario often have little or no assets in the bank—other than equity in the company. As a result, many people simply pick a sale price that satisfies a financial goal then proceed to focus on reaching that valuation. This "number" is a useful goal to set and should be reevaluated annually as the business progresses. When the thrilling opportunity arises to be able to sell for the "number," it's hard to argue against selling the business, putting the money in the bank and using it to fund your next startup. Once you have got that level of safety and security, you can take another run at building something truly exceptional.

Determining the right number isn't always easy. My advice is to think about the company in terms of a balance sheet number versus an income statement number. Let's look at a very simple income statement example. A company generating 5 percent free cash flow per year from total revenue of $10 million annually at a steady state can generate $1.5 million in cash over a three-year period. However, analyzing the assets in a balance sheet approach shows that the $10 million run rate business could potentially be sold for $10 million, even at a modest 1x price/sales multiple. The question you have to ask is which would you prefer from a financial perspective—$500,000 per year with all the risk associated with running a going concern or $10 million in cash that you could put in the bank?

In the meantime, remain laser focused on growing the company; it will be compound in value as it grows. In the preceding example, the $10 million run rate business growing at 100 percent per year could generate $500,000 year one, $1 million in year two, $2 million in year three, and so on. In this compound growth example, the cash for shareholders would be $3.5 million after three years. If the company were sold for a 1x price/sales multiple in year three, the sale would be worth $40 million.

There are several factors to consider when contemplating a sale. First of all, there will almost always be a better price/sales multiple if the buyer initiates the conversation about acquisition. They will most likely have a more optimistic perspective on the company if they discover the business through a strategic focus on building their company, as opposed to reacting to a company that's looking to sell. Great outcomes are bought, not sold.

The question is how to position the company to be bought for a higher multiple. First and foremost, grow and invest in the business for the long term. There are no shortcuts to building a truly valuable business. Also, make sure to build relationships with strategic partners who might be potential buyers. If and when they come to talk about a potential sale, engage in the conversation so they know about your company but consider a sale only if they offer a significant premium to the true balance sheet value of the company. The premium for a 100 percent growth company would, of course, be much larger than the premium for a 10 percent growth company—so grow, grow, grow.

Of course, a sale isn't the only successful outcome for a startup. The other is to remain a long-term stand-alone company and eventually go public.

The downsides of being under public investor scrutiny are outweighed by the upsides of continuing to run a successful company. The only way to reach that potential is to scale and grow at a rate of at least 25 to 30 percent annually. When growth slips, so does the likelihood of an eventual initial public offering.

Given the active M&A market for emerging growth companies, it is extremely difficult to build long-term stand-alone company, especially in the tech sector. The best way to reduce the chances of an unwanted sale while maximizing shareholder value is to grow at the fastest rate possible. In that case, only a premium valuation would cause shareholders to opt for a strategic sale.

However, these two outcomes aren't mutually exclusive. It's always good practice to consider the possibility of an acquisition before or even *after* an IPO. Regardless of whether you eventually sell, go public or do both, the imperative for startup CEOs remains the same: grow!

Tim Miller, CEO, Rally Software

FIVE RULES OF THUMB FOR SUCCESSFULLY SELLING YOUR COMPANY

Return Path is the first company I've built and we haven't sold it. I don't have experience as a CEO in selling a company, though I did live through and work on the sale of MovieFone to AOL in 1999 and I've helped many CEOs work through acquisitions of their own companies. I try not thinking much about exits as they pertain to Return Path but I couldn't help formulating a few best practices in case it ever comes up:

- *Optimize the value of the transaction*. Always have multiple bidders (see my comments about a BATNA in Part Three). You can literally double or triple the deal price that way. If there is ever a time for financial engineering, it's now. I've seen deals with collars and no caps—brilliant.
- *Find the company a good home*. It's your baby. You do want to find a good home for it. This could be in conflict with optimizing the value of the transaction, so be prepared to factor that in—up to some level.

- *Balance authenticity and transparency with being smart about internal communications.* Deals fall through all the time. Don't overcommunicate too early or you risk sending the message that you're looking for an exit when all you were doing was exploring an option.
- *It ain't over till it's over.* Again, deals can fall through at any moment. Keep running your business, fully engaged, until the ink is dry.
- *Once it's over, it's over.* You're still the CEO but now you have a (new) boss. "Even though the deal was called a merger," I once heard Ted Leonsis tell the MovieFone founders, "please remember that you have been acquired." Figure out how to best set your team and products up for success in the new environment, regardless of how long or short you plan to stay at the new company.

Finally, remember that *going public is not an exit.* It's the next stage in your company's evolution and in fact it requires that you and your senior team double down on the business and your jobs for several years.

CONCLUSION

I would never claim that writing this book—or even running a company for more than a decade—has given me all the answers. The one thing I hope I can claim is that with these two experiences I've finally figured out what questions I should be asking. There are hundreds of them, on topics ranging from . . . you've made it this far, so you know how far ranging the topics are! As Return Path continues to grow and enter new phases in *its* story, a whole new set of questions will arise. (I hope that someone is planning a startup IPOs volume for this series.) I look forward to thinking through the new questions, reconsidering my answers to the old ones, and, above all, *practicing* the craft of being a startup CEO.

My hope is that this book will inspire other startup CEOs, current or aspiring, to do the same. I wouldn't want anybody to feel that reading this book was an end in itself, any more than reading *The South Beach Diet* or *The 4-Hour Body* would be an end in itself. Think of me as your personal trainer and *Startup CEO* as a workout manual: I can set some guidelines, issue a few warnings and offer words of encouragement and advice. Now it's up to you to get to the gym and practice, practice, practice! The payoff is phenomenal—and unlike the drudgery of treadmills and weight machines, facing the challenges of running a startup day-to-day is a thrilling and intellectually stimulating task that never feels repetitive.

I've already quoted Fred Wilson to the effect that being a startup CEO is "lonely," a "heavy duty," and a "thankless task." The number of topics I've covered in this book—and the number of times I've insisted that I'm just scratching the surface—might also suggest that being a startup CEO is one of the hardest, riskiest and most stressful jobs in the world, too. Well, it is! If you are motivated and creative, enjoy building things and enjoy being around people and creating a sense of purpose for a team, it's also the best job in the world.

WHAT DID I MISS?

This is a complex topic, and every time I asked another CEO to read it and provide feedback, I got an idea for a new chapter.

Join the dialog at www.startuprev.com/startupceo and let me know what topics I should cover online or in a future version of the book! 

BIBLIOGRAPHY

Allen, David. *Getting Things Done: The Art of Stress-Free Productivity* (Penguin, 2001).

Blanchard, Kenneth H., Spencer Johnson, and Constance Johnson. *The One Minute Manager* (New York: HarperCollins, 1982).

Blank, Steven Gary. *The Four Steps to the Epiphany: Successful Strategies for Products that Win* (Lulu Enterprises Incorporated, 2008).

Charan, Ram. *Profitable Growth Is Everyone's Business: 10 Tools You Can Use Monday Morning* (Random House Digital, 2004).

Christensen, Clay. *The Innovator's Dilemma: When New Technologies Cause Great Firms to Fail* (Harvard Business Review Press, 1997).

Christensen, Clay. *Seeing What's Next: Using Theories of Innovation to Predict Industry Change* (Harvard Business Review Press, 2004).

Christensen, Clay, and Michael Raynor. *The Innovator's Solution: Creating and Sustaining Successful Growth* (Harvard Business School Press, 2003).

Collins, Jim. *Good to Great: Why Some Companies Make the Leap . . . and Others Don't* (HarperCollins, 2001).

Collins, Jim, and Jerry I. Porras. *Built to Last: Successful Habits of Visionary Companies* (HarperCollins, 2011).

Cooper, Brant, and Patrick Vlaskovits. *The Entrepreneur's Guide to Customer Development: A Cheat Sheet to the Four Steps to the Epiphany* (CustDev, 2010).

Covey, Stephen. *The Eighth Habit: From Effectiveness to Greatness* (Free Press, 2011).

Covey, Stephen. *The 7 Habits of Highly Effective People: Powerful Lessons in Personal Change* (Simon & Schuster, 2004).

Dawkins, Richard. *Climbing Mount Improbable* (W. W. Norton & Company, 1997).

Feld, Brad. *Startup Communities: Building an Entrepreneurial Ecosystem in Your City* (John Wiley & Sons, 2012).

Feld, Brad. *Startup Metrics: Making Sense of the Numbers in Your Startup* (John Wiley & Sons, 2013).

Feld, Brad, and Amy Batchelor. *Startup Life: Surviving and Thriving in a Relationship with an Entrepreneur* (John Wiley & Sons, 2013).

Feld, Brad, and David Cohen. *Do More Faster: TechStars Lessons to Accelerate Your Startup* (John Wiley & Sons, 2010).

Feld, Brad, and Jason Mendelson. *Venture Deals: Be Smarter Than Your Lawyer and Venture Capitalist* (John Wiley & Sons, 2012).

Feld, Brad, and Mahendra Ramsinghani. *Startup Boards: Recreating the Board of Directors to Be Relevant to Entrepreneurial Companies* (John Wiley & Sons, 2013).

Gladwell, Malcolm. "The Tweaker: The Real Genius of Steve Jobs," *The New Yorker*, November 14, 2011.

Godin, Seth. *Purple Cow: Transform Your Business by Being Remarkable* (Penguin, 2003).

Godwin, Doris Kearns. *Team of Rivals: The Political Genius of Abraham Lincoln* (Simon & Schuster, 2005).

Goldratt, Eliyahu M. *The Goal: A Process of Ongoing Improvement* (Gower, 2004).

Goldratt, Eliyahu M. *It's Not Luck* (North River Press, 1994).

Grove, Andrew S. *High Output Management* (Vintage, 1995).

Kim, Chan, and Renee Mauborgne. *Blue Ocean Strategy: How to Create* (Harvard Business Press, 2004).

Isaacson, Walter. *Steve Jobs* (Simon & Schuster, 2011).

Kidder, David. *The Startup Playbook: Secrets of the Fastest-Growing Startups from Their Founding Entrepreneurs* (Chronicle Books, 2013).

Lencioni, Patrick. *The Advantage: Why Organizational Health Trumps Everything Else in Business* (Hoboken, NJ: John Wiley & Sons, 2012).

Lencioni, Patrick. *Death by Meeting: A Leadership Fable . . . about Solving the Most Painful Problem in Business* (Hoboken, NJ: John Wiley & Sons, 2010).

Lencioni, Patrick. *The Five Temptations of a CEO: A Leadership Fable* (New York: John Wiley & Sons, 2000).

Lencioni, Patrick. *The Four Obsessions of an Extraordinary Executive: A Leadership Fable* (Hoboken, NJ: John Wiley & Sons, 2010).

Lencioni, Patrick. *The Three Signs of a Miserable Job: A Fable for Managers (And Their Employees)* (Hoboken, NJ: John Wiley & Sons, 2010).

Maurya, Ash. *Running Lean: Iterate from Plan A to a Plan that Works* (O'Reilly Media, Inc., 2012).

Moore, Geoffrey. *Inside the Tornado* (Capstone, 1995).

Moore, Geoffrey. Crossing the Chasm: Marketing and Selling Technology Projects (HarperCollins, 2009).

Moore, Geoffrey. *Escape Velocity: Free Your Company's Future from the Pull of the Past* (HarperCollins, 2011).

Morey, David, and Scott Miller. *The Underdog Advantage: Using the Power of Insurgent Strategy to Put Your Business on Top* (McGraw-Hill Professional, 2004).

Nalbantian, Haig R., and Richard A. Guzzo, "Making Mobility Matter" (*Harvard Business Review*, March 2009).

Nazar, Jason and Rochelle Bailis. *How to Start a Business* (Docstoc Inc., 2012).

Porter, Michael. *Competitive Strategy: Techniques for Analyzing Industries and Competitors* (Simon & Schuster, 2008).

Porter, Michael. *Competitive Advantage: Creating and Sustaining Superior Performance* (Simon & Schuster, 2008).

Ries, Al, and Jack Trout, *Positioning: The Battle for Your Mind* (McGraw-Hill Education, 2003).

Ries, Eric. *The Lean Startup: How Today's Entrepreneurs Use Continuous Innovation to Create Radically Successful Businesses* (Random House, 2011).

Smart, Brad. *Topgrading: The Proven Hiring and Promoting Method that Turbocharges Company Performance* (Penguin, 2012).

Stalk, George, and Rob Lachenauer. *Hardball: Are You Playing to Play or Playing to Win?* (Harvard Business Press, 2004).

Stalk, George. "Curveball: Strategies to Fool the Competition," *Harvard Business Review*, September 2006.

ABOUT THE COMPANION WEB SITE

Startup CEO is part of the Startup Revolution series. On the Startup Revolution website (http://startuprev.com/startupceo) you will find a variety of resources, including the spreadsheets and templates mentioned in this book. (Whenever you see the icon in the margin, you can find the resource I'm discussing on the Startup Revolution site.) You'll also find our blog, discussion forums, video interviews with contributors to this book—and a large community of current and aspiring startup CEOs.

INDEX

Excerpt from *Startup Boards*

INTRODUCTION

The word *boardroom* conjures up images of important people, puffing on cigars or sipping scotch, while sitting in leather chairs in wood-paneled rooms. These important people are talking about important things that determine the future of your company. Formality and seriousness hangs in the air. Big decisions are being made.

Startup boards are not that fancy and not as complex. First time CEOs and founders often have an elevated view of the boardroom. While this type of board may exist in some cases, a startup board is typically a small group of people trying to help build your company.

Over the years, we've served on hundreds of boards. A few were great, many were good, and some were terrible. When things in the company were going smoothly, the board was congratulatory and supportive. When there were challenges, some boards helped and some boards hurt. The tempo and interactions of these boards varied dramatically. In some cases reality prevailed; in others it was denied.

In 2010, Brad realized that the default structure of a startup board was an artifact of the past 40 years, dating back to the way early venture-backed company boards operated. Things had changed and evolved some, but the dramatic shift in communication patterns and technology over the past decade hadn't been incorporated into the way most boards worked. As a result, Brad ran a two-year experiment where he tried lots of different things, some successful, some not. As with every experiment, he did more of what worked, modified and killed what didn't, tried new things, and measured a lot of stuff.

The idea for this book emerged during this experiment. We decided that in addition to describing the new startup board approach that resulted from Brad's experiment, it was important to lay the groundwork and explain clearly how startup boards historically worked, and how they could be most effective, and what the challenges were. Brad's new board approach built on the traditional board of directors, so rather than throw it out, we use a highly-functioning one as the basis for a new, evolved, and much more effective approach.

While the topic may feel dry, we've tried, as Brad and Jason Mendelson (Foundry Group, Managing Director) did in *Venture Deals: Be Smarter Than Your Lawyer and Venture Capitalist*, to take a serious topic, cover it rigorously, but do it in English with our own brand of humor. Our goal is to demystify how a board of directors works, discuss historical best and worst practices, and give you a clear set of tools for creating and managing and awesome board.